D0360226

PORTUGUESE PHRASEBOOK

WITHDRAWN

Compiled by
LEXUS

www.roughguides.com

Credits

Portuguese Phrasebook	Rough Guides Reference
Compiled by: Lexus with Norma de Oliveira Tait	Director: Andrew Lockett
Lexus series editor: Sally Davies	Editors: Kate Berens, Tom Cabot, Tracy Hopkins, Matthew Milton, Joe Staines
Layout: Sachin Tanwar	
Picture research: Scott Stickland	

Publishing information

First edition published in 1996.
This updated edition published October 2011 by
Rough Guides Ltd, 80 Strand, London, WC2R 0RL
Email: mail@roughguides.com

Distributed by the Penguin Group:
Penguin Books Ltd, 80 Strand, London, WC2R 0RL
Penguin Group (USA), 375 Hudson Street, NY 10014, USA
Penguin Group (Australia), 250 Camberwell Road, Camberwell,
Victoria 3124, Australia
Penguin Group (New Zealand), Cnr Rosedale and Airborne Roads,
Albany, Auckland, New Zealand

Rough Guides is represented in Canada by Tourmaline Editions Inc.,
662 King Street West, Suite 304, Toronto, Ontario, M5V 1M7

Printed in Singapore by Toppan Security Printing Pte. Ltd.

264 pages

A catalogue record for this book is available from the British Library.

978-1-84836-743-2

1 3 5 7 9 8 6 4 2

CONTENTS

How to use this book

The **Rough Guide Portuguese Phrasebook** is a highly practical introduction to the contemporary language. It gets straight to the point in every situation you might encounter: in bars and shops, on trains and buses, in hotels and banks, on holiday or on business. Laid out in clear A–Z style with easy-to-find, colour-coded sections, it uses key words to take you directly to the phrase you need – so if you want some help booking a room, just look up "room" in the dictionary section.

The phrasebook starts off with **Basics**, where we list some essential phrases, including words for numbers, dates and telling the time, and give guidance on pronunciation, along with a short section on the different regional accents you might come across. Then, to get you started in two-way communication, the Scenarios section offers dialogues in key situations such as renting a car, asking directions or booking a taxi, and includes words and phrases for when something goes wrong, from getting a flat tyre or asking to move apartments to more serious emergencies. You can listen to these and download them for free from www.roughguides.com/phrasebooks for use on your computer, MP3 player or smartphone.

Forming the main part of the guide is a double dictionary, first English–Portuguese, which gives you the essential words you'll need plus easy-to-use phonetic transliterations wherever pronunciation might be a problem. Then, in the Portuguese–English dictionary, we've given not just the phrases you'll be likely to hear (starting with a selection of slang and colloquialisms) but also many of the signs, labels

and instructions you'll come across in print or in public places. Scattered throughout the sections are travel tips direct from the authors of the Rough Guides guidebook series.

Finally, there's an extensive **Menu reader**. Consisting of separate food and drink sections, each starting with a list of essential terms, it's indispensable whether you're eating out, stopping for a quick drink or looking around a local food market.

Boa viagem!
Have a good trip!

BASICS

Pronunciation

In this phrasebook, the Portuguese has been written in a system of imitated pronunciation so that it can be read as though it were English, bearing in mind the notes on pronunciation given below:

a	as in hat	J	as in the 's' sound in pleasure
ay	as in may		
eh	as in get	o	as in not
g	as in goat	oh	as in slow
i	as in it	oo	as in boot
ī	as in might	ow	as in now

In words such as não nowng and bem bayng, the final 'g' in the pronunciation signifies a nasal sound and should barely be sounded. Letters given in bold type indicate the part of the word to be stressed.

Abbreviations

adj	adjective	mpl	masculine plural
f	feminine	pl	plural
fam	familiar	pol	polite
fpl	feminine plural	sing	singular
m	masculine		

Notes

There are two verbs that translate **'to be'** – ser and estar – depending on whether the verb is describing a permanent or temporary state. For example, sou inglês **I am English**; estou cansado **I am tired**.

Where two words are given as a translation, as in **our** nosso/nossa, the first is used with masculine nouns, the second with feminine nouns.

The word **the** before a masculine noun is o; before a feminine noun it is a. In the case of plurals it is os and as respectively. For example, o livro **the book**; os livros **the books**; a garrafa **the bottle**; as garrafas **the bottles**.

Basic phrases

yes sim seeng

no não nowng

OK está bem shta bayng

hello/hi olá

good morning bom dia
bong dee-a

good evening/good night
boa noite boh-a noh-it

see you! até logo! ateh logoo

goodbye adeus aday-oosh

please se faz favor, por favor
si fash favohr, poor favohr

yes please sim, por favor seeng

thanks, thank you (said by man/
woman) obrigado/obrigada
obrigadoo

no thanks, no thank you não
obrigado/obrigada nowng

thank you very much muito
obrigado/obrigada mweengtoo

don't mention it não tem de quê
nowng tayng di kay

not at all de nada di nada

how do you do? muito prazer
mweengtoo prazayr

how are you? como está?
kohmoo shta

fine, thanks (said by man/woman)
bem, obrigado/obrigada
bayng obrigadoo

pleased to meet you
(said to man/woman)
muito prazer em conhecê-lo/
conhecê-la mweengtoo prazayr
ayng kon-yisayloo

excuse me (to get past)
com licença kong lisaynsa
(to get attention) se faz favor
si fash favohr
(to say sorry) desculpe dishkoolp

(I'm) sorry tenho muita pena
tayn-yoo mweengta payna

sorry?/pardon (me)? (didn't
understand) como? kohmoo

what did you say? o que disse?
oo ki dees

I see/I understand percebo
pirsayboo

I don't understand não percebo
nowng

do you speak English?
fala inglês? inglaysh

I don't speak Portuguese
não falo português
nowng faloo poortoogaysh

can you speak more slowly?
pode falar mais devagar?
pod falar mīj divagar

could you repeat that?
podia repetir? poodee-a ripiteer

can you write it down?
pode escrever isso?
pod shkrivayr eesoo

I'd like... queria... kiree-a

can I have...? pode dar-me...?
pod darmi

do you have...? tem...? tayng

how much is it? quanto é?
kwantweh

cheers! saúde! sa-ood

it is... é...; está... eh; shta

where is...? onde é...?; onde
está...? ohndeh; ohnd shta

is it far? é longe? eh lohnJ

Dates

Use the numbers on page 11 to express the date.

the first of September oong di sit**ay**mbroo um de Setembro

the second of December d**oh**-iJ di diz**ay**mbroo dois de Dezembro

the twenty first of January v**ee**nti-oong di Jan**ay**roo vinte-e-um de Janeiro

Days

Monday segunda-feira sig**oo**nda f**ay**ra

Tuesday terça-feira t**ay**rsa f**ay**ra

Wednesday quarta-feira kw**a**rta f**ay**ra

Thursday quinta-feira k**ee**nta f**ay**ra

Friday sexta-feira s**ay**shta f**ay**ra

Saturday sábado s**a**badoo

Sunday domingo doom**ee**ngoo

Months

January Janeiro Jan**ay**roo

February Fevereiro fivr**ay**roo

March Março m**a**rsoo

April Abril abr**ee**l

May Maio mī-oo

June Junho J**oo**n-yoo

July Julho J**oo**l-yoo

August Agosto ag**oh**shtoo

September Setembro sit**ay**mbroo

October Outubro oht**oo**broo

November Novembro noov**ay**mbroo

December Dezembro diz**ay**mbroo

Time

what time is it? que horas são? k-y**o**rash sowng

one o'clock uma hora **oo**ma **o**ra

two o'clock duas horas d**oo**-az **o**rash

it's one o'clock é uma hora eh **oo**ma **o**ra

it's two o'clock são duas horas sowng doo-az**o**rash

it's three o'clock são três horas trayz**o**rash

five past one uma e cinco **oo**mi s**ee**nkoo

ten past two duas e dez d**oo**-azi dehsh

quarter past one uma e um quarto **oo**mi-oong kw**a**rtoo

quarter past two duas e um quarto d**oo**-azi-oong

half past ten dez e meia dehz ee m**ay**-a

twenty to ten dez menos vinte dehJ m**ay**nooJ veent

quarter to ten dez menos um quarto dehJ m**ay**nooz oong kw**a**rtoo

at eight o'clock às oito horas az**oh**-itoo **o**rash

at half past four às quatro e meia ash kw**a**troo ee m**ay**-a

2 a.m. duas da manhã d**oo**-aJ da man-yang

2 p.m. duas da tarde tard
6 a.m. seis da manhã
  saysh da man-y**a**ng
6 p.m. seis da tarde tard
noon meio-dia m**a**y-oo d**ee**-a
midnight meia-noite m**a**y-a n**o**h-it
an hour uma hora **oo**ma **o**ra
a minute um minuto
  oong min**oo**too
two minutes dois minutos
  d**oh**-iJ min**oo**toosh
a second um segundo
  oong sig**oo**ndoo
a quarter of an hour um quarto
  de hora kw**a**rtoo d**o**ra
half an hour meia hora
  m**a**y-a **o**ra
three quarters of an hour
  três quartos de hora
  traysh kw**a**rtoosh d**o**ra

Numbers

0 zero z**eh**roo
1 um oong
2 dois d**oh**-ish
3 três traysh
4 quatro kw**a**troo
5 cinco s**ee**nkoo
6 seis saysh
7 sete seht
8 oito **oh**-itoo
9 nove nov
10 dez dehsh
11 onze ohnz
12 doze dohz
13 treze trayz

14 catorze kat**oh**rz
15 quinze keenz
16 dezasseis dizas**ay**sh
17 dezassete dizas**eh**t
18 dezoito diz**oh**-itoo
19 dezanove dizan**o**v
20 vinte veent
21 vinte e um v**ee**nti-oong
22 vinte e dois v**ee**nti
  d**oh**-ish
23 vinte e três v**ee**nti traysh
30 trinta tr**ee**nta
31 trinta e um tr**ee**nti-oong
32 trinta e dois tr**ee**nti d**oh**-ish
40 quarenta kwar**ay**nta
50 cinquenta sinkw**ay**nta
60 sessenta ses**ay**nta
70 setenta set**ay**nta
80 oitenta oh-it**ay**nta
90 noventa noov**ay**nta
100 cem sayng
101 cento e um s**ay**ntwee oong
120 cento e vinte veent
200 duzentos dooz**ay**ntoosh,
  duzentas dooz**ay**ntash
300 trezentos triz**ay**ntoosh,
  trezentas triz**ay**ntash
400 quatrocentos kwatros**ay**ntoosh,
  quatrocentas kwatros**ay**ntash
500 quinhentos keen-y**ay**ntoosh,
  quinhentas keen-y**ay**ntash
600 seiscentos sayshs**ay**ntoosh,
  seiscentas sayshs**ay**ntash
700 setecentos setes**ay**ntoosh,
  setecentas setes**ay**ntash
800 oitocentos oh-itoos**ay**ntoosh,
  oitocentas oh-itoos**ay**ntash

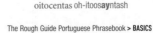

900 novecentos nove**sayn**toosh, novecentas nove**sayn**tash
1,000 mil meel
2,000 dois mil d**oh**-ish
5,000 cinco mil s**ee**nkoo
10,000 dez mil dehsh
1,000,000 um milhão mil-y**ow**ng

um is used with masculine nouns, uma with feminine nouns:

um carro oong k**a**rroo **one car**
uma bicicleta **oo**ma bisikl**eh**ta **one bike**

With multiples of a hundred, the -os ending is used with masculine nouns, the -as ending with feminine nouns:

trezentos homens triz**ayn**tooz **oh**mayngsh **300 men**
quinhentas mulheres keen-y**ayn**ta mool-y**eh**rish **500 women**

Ordinals

1st primeiro prim**ay**roo
2nd segundo sig**oo**ndoo
3rd terceiro tirs**ay**roo
4th quarto kw**a**rtoo
5th quinto k**ee**ntoo
6th sexto s**a**yshtoo
7th sétimo s**eh**timoo
8th oitavo oh-it**a**voo
9th nono n**oh**noo
10th décimo d**eh**simoo

Regional accents

Portuguese derives from the language of the common Roman soldier and, over the centuries, was influenced, particularly in the south of the country, by the Arabic-speaking Moors. Modern Standard Portuguese is the urban cultured Portuguese of Lisbon and surround-

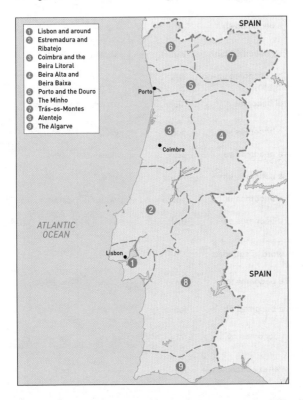

1 Lisbon and around
2 Estremadura and Ribatejo
3 Coimbra and the Beira Litoral
4 Beira Alta and Beira Baixa
5 Porto and the Douro
6 The Minho
7 Trás-os-Montes
8 Alentejo
9 The Algarve

SPAIN

Porto

ATLANTIC OCEAN

Coimbra

Lisbon

SPAIN

ing areas, and this is the pronunciation that is given in this book and which will stand you in good stead wherever you travel in Portugal.

	Portuguese word	Lisbon & Ribatejo	Central-West (Coimbra)
v becomes b	volta	volta	volta
s becomes sh	saia	sī-ya	sī-ya
sh becomes tsh	chouriço	shooreesoo	shooreesoo
ou becomes oh-oo	dou	doh	doh
ei becomes e	dinheiro	deen-yehroo	deen-yehroo
o becomes wo	porto	pohrtoo	pohrtoo
e becomes ye	peso	payzoo	payzoo
a becomes eh	fumar	foomehr	foomar
o becomes ur	pouco	pohkoo	pohkoo
u becomes ew	multa	moolta	moolta
o at the end of a word is sounded	copo	kop	kopoo
u becomes aw	lua	loo-a	loo-a
a becomes eh	fumar	foomahr	foomahr
i becomes ay	filha	feel-ya	feel-ya
l after i becomes lh	fila	feela	feela

The Rough Guide Portuguese Phrasebook > **BASICS**

The following chart gives examples of some of the accent differ-
ences. There are, of course, quite a number of regional overlaps.

Northwest & Northeast	Central-East	South & Algarve	Azores & Madeira
bo**l**ta	v**o**lta	v**o**lta	v**o**lta
s**ī**-ya (NW) shī-ya (NE)	sh**ī**-ya	s**ī**-ya	s**ī**-ya
tshoor**ee**soo	shoor**ee**soo	shoor**ee**soo	shoor**ee**soo
d**oh**-oo	doh	doh	doh
deen-y**ay**roo	deen-y**eh**roo	deen-y**eh**roo	deen-y**eh**roo (Az) deen-y**ay**roo (Mad)
pw**oh**rtoo	p**oh**rtoo	p**oh**rtoo	p**oh**rtoo
p-**yay**zoo	p**ay**zoo	p**ay**zoo	p**ay**zoo
foom**ar**	foom**eh**r	foom**ar**	foom**eh**r
p**oh**koo	p**ur**koo	p**oh**koo	p**ur**koo
m**oo**lta	m**ew**lta	m**oo**lta	m**ew**lta
k**o**poo	kop	kop	kop
l**oo**-a	l**oo**-a	l**oo**-a	l**oo**-a (Az) l**aw**-a (Mad)
foom**ah**r	foom**eh**r	foom**ah**r	foom**eh**r
f**ee**l-ya	f**ee**l-ya	f**ee**l-ya	f**ee**l-ya (Az) f**ay**l-ya (Mad)
f**ee**la	f**ee**la	f**ee**la	f**ee**la (Az) f**ay**l-ya (Mad)

SCENARIOS

Download these scenarios as MP3s from
www.roughguides.com/phrasebooks

1. Accommodation

▶ Is there an inexpensive hotel you can recommend?
Pode recomendar-me um hotel não muito caro?
pod rikoomayndarmi oong ohtel nowng mweengtoo karoo

▶▶ I'm sorry, they all seem to be fully booked.
Sinto muito, todos parecem estar totalmente cheios.
seentoo mweengtoo tohdoosh paresayng shtar tootalmaynt shay-oosh

▶ Can you give me the name of a good middle-range hotel?
Pode dar-me o nome de um bom hotel de preço médio?
pod darmi oo nohm doong bong ohtel di praysoo mehd-yoo

▶▶ Let me have a look; do you want to be in the centre?
Deixe-me ver; deseja ficar no centro?
dayshmi vayr disayJa fikar noo sayntroo

▶ If possible.
Se possível.
si pooseevil

▶▶ Do you mind being a little way out of town?
Importa-se de ficar um pouco fora da cidade?
importasi di fikar oong pohkoo fora da sidad

▶ As long as it's not too far out.
Desde que não seja demasiado longe.
dayJdi ki nowng sayJa dimaz-yadoo lohnJ

▶ Where is it on the map?
Onde está no mapa?
ohnd shta noo mapa

▶ Can you write the name and address down?
Pode escrever o nome e a morada para mim?
pod shkrivayr o nohm ee a moorada para meeng

▶ I'm looking for a room in a private house.
Procuro um quarto numa casa particular.
prookooroo oong kwartoo nooma kaza partikoolar

2. Banks

bank account	a conta bancária	kohnta bankar-ya
to change money	trocar dinheiro	trookar deen-yayroo
cheque	o cheque	shehk
to deposit	depositar	dipoozitar
euro	o euro	ay-ooroo
pin number	PIN	peen
pound	a libra	leebra
to withdraw	levantar	livantar

▶ Can you change this into euros?
Pode trocar isto por euros?
pod trookar eeshtoo poor ay-ooroosh

    ▶▶ How would you like the money?
    Como quer o dinheiro?
    kohmoo kehr oo deen-yayroo

▶ Small notes.   ▶ Big notes.
Notas pequenas.   Notas grandes.
notash pikaynash   notash grandsh

▶ Do you have information in English about opening an account?
Tem informação em inglês sobre como abrir uma conta?
tayng infoormasowng ayng inglaysh sohbr kohmoo abreer ooma kohnta

    ▶▶ Yes, what sort of account do you want?
    Sim, que tipo de conta deseja abrir?
    seeng ki teepoo di kohnta disayJa abreer

▶ I'd like a current account.
Gostaria de abrir uma conta corrente.
gooshtaree-a dabreer ooma kohnta koorraynt

    ▶▶ Your passport, please.
    O seu passaporte, por favor.
    oo say-oo pasaport poor favohr

▶ Can I use this card to draw some cash?
Posso utilizar este cartão para levantar dinheiro?
posoo ootilizar aysht kartowng para livantar deen-yayroo

    ▶▶ You have to go to the cashier's desk.
    Precisa ir ao caixa.
    priseeza eer ow kīsha

▶ I want to transfer this to my account at Banco Totta & Açores.
Desejo transferir isto para a minha conta no Banco Totta & Açores.
dizay**J**oo transhfir**ee**r **ee**shtoo para m**ee**n-ya k**oh**nta noo bankoo t**o**ta-yas**oh**rish

▶▶ OK, but we'll have to charge you for the phonecall.
Está bem, mas vamos ter de cobrar a chamada telefónica.
shta bayng ma**J** v**a**moosh tayr di k**oo**brar a sham**a**da telef**oh**nika

3. Booking a room

shower	o duche	doosh
telephone in	o telefone no	telef**oh**n noo
the room	quarto	kw**a**rtoo
payphone in	o telefone público	telef**oh**n p**oo**blikoo noo
the lobby	no hall	hall

▶ Do you have any rooms?
Tem quartos vagos?
tayng kw**a**rtoosh v**a**goosh

▶▶ For how many people?
Para quantas pessoas?
para kw**a**ntash pis**oh**-ash

▶ For one/for two.
Para uma pessoa/para duas pessoas.
para **oo**ma pis**oh**-a/para d**oo**-ash pis**oh**-ash

▶▶ Yes, we have rooms free.
Sim, temos.
seeng t**ay**moosh

▶▶ For how many nights?
Para quantas noites?
para kw**a**ntash n**oh**-itsh

▶ Just for one night.
Só uma noite.
saw **oo**ma n**oh**-it

▶ How much is it?
Qual é o preço?
kwal eh oo pr**ay**soo

▶▶ 90 euros with bathroom and 70 euros without bathroom.
90 euros com casa de banho e 70 euros sem casa de banho.
noovaynta **ay**-ooroosh kong k**a**za di b**a**n-yoo ee set**ay**nta **ay**-ooroosh
sayng k**a**za di b**a**n-yoo

▶ Does that include breakfast?
O pequeno almoço está incluído?
oo pik**ay**noo alm**oh**soo shta inklw**ee**doo

▶ Can I see a room with bathroom?
Posso ver um quarto com casa de banho?
p**o**soo vayr oong kw**a**rtoo kong k**a**za di b**a**n-yoo

▶ OK, I'll take it.
Sim, fico com este.
seeng f**ee**koo kong aysht

▶ When do I have to check out?
Quando tenho de fazer o check out?
kw**a**ndoo t**ay**n-yoo di faz**ay**r oo check out

▶ Is there anywhere I can leave luggage?
Há algum lugar onde posso deixar a bagagem?
a alg**oo**ng loog**a**r ohnd p**o**soo daysh**a**r a baga**j**ayng

4. Car hire

automatic	automático	owtoomatikoo
full tank	depósito cheio	dipozitoo shay-oo
manual	manual	manwal
rented car	o carro de aluguer	karroo daloogehr

▶ I'd like to rent a car.
Queria alugar um carro.
kiree-a aloogar oong karroo

>> ▶▶ For how long?
Por quanto tempo?
poor kwantoo taympoo

▶ Two days.
Dois dias.
doh-iJ dee-ash

▶ I'll take the...
Fico com o...
feekoo kong oo...

▶ Is that with unlimited mileage?
E com quilometragem ilimitada?
eh kong kilomitrajayng ilimitada

>> ▶▶ It is.
Sim.
seeng

>> ▶▶ Can I see your driving licence please?
Posso ver a sua carta de condução, por favor?
posoo vayr a soo-a karta di kondoosowng poor favohr

>> ▶▶ And your passport.
E o seu passaporte.
yoo say-oo pasaport

▶ Is insurance included?
O seguro está incluído?
oo sigooroo shta inklweedoo

>> ▶▶ Yes, but you have to pay the first 100 euros.
Sim, mas tem que pagar os primeiros 100 euros.
seeng mash tayng ki pagar oosh primayroosh sayng ay-ooroosh

>> ▶▶ Can you leave a deposit of 100 euros?
Pode deixar um depósito de 100 euros?
pod dayshar oong dipozitoo di sayng ay-ooroosh

▶ And if this office is closed, where do I leave the keys?
E se o escritório estiver fechado, onde posso deixar as chaves?
ee s-yoo shkritor-yoo shtivehr fishadoo ohnd posoo dayshar ash shavsh

▶▶ You drop them in that box.
Pode depositá-las naquela caixa.
pod dipoozitalash nakehla kīsha

5. Car problems

brakes	os travões	travoyngsh
to break down	avariar	avariar
clutch	a embraiagem	aymbrī-aJayng
diesel	o gasóleo	gazol-yoo
flat battery	a bateria em baixo	batiree-a ayng bīshoo
flat tyre	o pneu furado	pnay-oo fooradoo
petrol	a gasolina	gazooleena

▶ Excuse me, where is the nearest petrol station?
Por favor, onde fica a bomba de gasolina mais próxima?
poor favohr ohnd feeka bohmba di gazooleena mīsh prosima

▶▶ In the next town, about 5km away.
Na próxima cidade, a cerca de cinco quilómetros.
na prosima seedad a sayrka di seenkoo kilomitroosh

▶ The car has broken down.
O carro avariou-se.
oo karroo avari-oh-si

▶▶ Can you tell me what happened?
Pode explicar o que aconteceu?
pod shplikar oo k-yakoontesay-oo

▶ I've got a flat tyre.
Tenho um pneu furado.
tayn-yoo oong pnay-oo fooradoo

▶ I think the battery is flat.
Acho que a bateria está em baixo.
ashoo ky-a batiree-a shtah ayng bīshoo

▶▶ Can you tell me exactly where you are?
Pode explicar exactamente onde está?
pod shplikar ezatamaynt ohndshta

▶ I'm about 2km outside of Beja on the Neves Road.
Estou a cerca de dois quilómetros de Beja na estrada das Neves.
stoh a sayrka di doh-ish kilomitroosh di behJa na shtrada dash nehvish

▶▶ What type of car? What colour?
Que tipo de carro é? De que cor?
ki teepoo di karroo eh, di ki kohr

▶ Can you send a tow truck?
Pode enviar um reboque?
pod ayngvee-ar oong rebok

6. Children

baby	o bebé	bebeh
boy	o rapaz	rapash
child	a criança	kree-ansa
children	as crianças	kree-ansash
cot	a cama de bebé	kama di bebeh
formula	o leite em pó para bebés	layt ayng paw para bebehsh
girl	a rapariga	rapareega
highchair	a cadeira de bebé	kadayra di bebeh
nappies (diapers)	as fraldas	fraldash

▶ We need a babysitter for tomorrow evening.
Precisamos de uma babysitter para amanhã à noite.
priseezamoosh dooma babysitter paraman-yang a noh-it

▶▶ For what time?
Para que horas?
par k-yorash

▶ From 7.30 to 11.00.
Das sete e meia às onze.
dash seht ee may-a ash ohnz

▶▶ How many children? How old are they?
Quantas crianças são? Que idade têm?
kwantash kree-ansash sowng, ki eedad tay-ayng

▶ Two children, aged four and eighteen months.
Duas crianças, de quatro anos e oito meses.
doo-ash kree-ansash di kwatroo anoosh ee oh-itoo mayzish

▶ Where can I change the baby?
Onde posso mudar a fralda do bebé?
ohnd po**soo** moodar a fralda doo beb**eh**

▶ Could you please warm this bottle for me?
Pode-me aquecer este biberão, faz favor?
p**od**-mi akes**ay**r aysht bibir**ow**ng fash fav**oh**r

▶ Can you give us a child's portion?
Pode dar-nos meia dose?
pod d**a**r-noosh m**ay**-a doz

▶ We need two child seats.
Precisamos de duas cadeiras de carro para crianças.
priseez**a**moosh di d**oo**-ash kad**ay**rash di karroo para kree-**a**nsash

▶ Is there a discount for children?
Dão desconto para crianças?
downg dishk**oh**ntoo para kree-**a**nsash

7. Communications: Internet

@	arroba	arr**oh**ba
at sign	a arroba	arr**oh**ba
computer	o computador	kompootad**ohr**
email	o mail	mail
Internet	a Internet	**i**nterneht
keyboard	o teclado	tik**la**doo
mouse	o rato	r**a**too

▶ Is there somewhere I can check my emails?
Há aqui algum sítio onde eu possa ver os meus mails?
a ak**ee** alg**oo**m s**ee**t-yoo ohnd**ay**-oo p**o**sa vayr oosh m**ay**-oosh mailsh

▶ Do you have Wi-Fi?
Têm Wi-fi?
t**ay**-ayng w**ee**-fee

▶ Is there an Internet café around here?
Há um café Internet aqui perto?
a oong kaf**eh i**nterneht ak**ee** p**eh**rtoo

▶▶ Yes, there's one in the shopping centre.
Sim, há um no centro comercial.
seeng a oong noo s**ay**ntroo komayrs-y**al**

▶▶ Do you want fifteen minutes, thirty minutes or one hour?
Deseja um período de quinze minutos, meia hora ou uma hora?
dizay Ja oong piree-oodoo di keenz minootoosh may-a ora oh ooma ora

▶ Thirty minutes please. Can you help me log on?
Meia hora, faz favor. Pode ajudar-me a iniciar a sessão?
may-a ora fash favohr, pod aJoodarmi a inis-yar a sisowng

- -

▶▶ OK, here's your password.
Sim, aqui está a sua senha.
eeng akee shta a soo-a sayn-ya

▶ Can you change this to an English keyboard?
Pode mudar para o teclado britânico?
pod moodar paroo tikladoo britanikoo

▶ I'll take another quarter of an hour.
Queria mais um quarto de hora.
kiree-a mīz oong kwartoo dora

▶ Is there a printer I can use?
Têm uma impressora que possa usar?
tay-ayng oomimprisohra ki posoosar

8. Communications: phones

mobile phone (cell phone)	um telemóvel	telemovil
payphone	um telefone público	telefohn pooblikoo
phone call	um telefonema	telefoonayma
phone card	um cartão de telefone	kartowng di telefohn
phone charger	o carregador de telemóvel	karrigadohr di telemovil
SIM card	um cartão SIM	kartowng seeng

▶ Can I call abroad from here?
Posso telefonar daqui para o estrangeiro?
posoo telefonar dakee paroo shtranJayroo

▶ How do I get an outside line?
Como posso obter uma linha externa?
kohmoo posoo oobtayr ooma leen-ya shtehrna

▶ What's the code to call the UK/US from here?

Qual é o código para ligar para o Reino Unido/para os Estados Unidos daqui?

kwal**eh** oo k**o**digoo para lee**gar** par**oo** raynoon**ee**edoo/par**oo**sh shtad**oo**z oonee**doo**sh dak**ee**

zero	zero	ze**hr**oo
one	um	oong
two	dois	d**oh**-ish
three	três	traysh
four	quatro	kw**a**troo
five	cinco	s**ee**nkoo
six	seis	saysh
seven	sete	seht
eight	oito	**oh**-ítoo
nine	nove	nov

▶ Hello, can I speak to Rita?

Está, posso falar com a Rita?

shta p**o**sso falar kong a r**ee**ta

> ▶▶ Yes, that's me.
> Sim, sou eu.
> seeng soh **ay**-oo

▶ Do you have a charger for this?

Tem um carregador para este?

tayng oong karrigad**oh**r para aysht

▶ Can I buy a SIM card for this phone?

Posso comprar um cartão SIM para este telemóvel?

p**o**soo komprar oong kart**ow**ng seeng para aysht telem**o**vil

9. Directions

on the right	à direita	a-dir**ay**ta
on the left	à esquerda	a-shk**ay**rda
over there	ali adiante	al**ee** ad-yant
past the...	depois do...	dip**oh**-ish doo...
opposite	em frente	ayng fraynt
in front of	em frente de	ayng fraynt di
just after	logo a seguir a	l**o**goo a sig**ee**r a
further	mais longe	mi.J lohnJ
near	perto	p**eh**rtoo
next	próximo	pr**o**simoo
street	rua	r**oo**-a
turn off	saída	sa-**ee**da
back	voltar	voltar
straight ahead	sempre em frente	s**ay**mprayng fraynt

▶ Hi, I'm looking for Avenida do Brasil.

Olá, estou à procura da Avenida do Brasil.

o**o**la shtoh a prook**oo**ra da avin**ee**da doo braz**ee**l

▶▶ Sorry, never heard of it.
Desculpe, nunca ouvi falar desta avenida.
dishkoolp noonka ohvee falar dehshta avineeda

▶ Hi, can you tell me where Avenida do Brasil is?
olá, pode dizer-me onde fica a Avenida do Brasil?
oola pod dizayrmi ohnd feeka avineeda doo brazeel

▶▶ I'm a stranger here too.
Também sou um visitante aqui.
tambayng soh oong vizitant akee

▶ Hi, Avenida do Brasil, do you know where it is?
Olá, Avenida do Brasil, sabe onde fica?
oola avineeda doo brazeel sab ohnd feeka

▶ Where?
Onde?
ohnd

▶ Which direction?
Em que direcção?
ayng ki direhsowng

▶▶ Around the corner.
Fica ao virar a esquina.
feeka ow veerar ashkeena

▶▶ Left at the second traffic lights.
À esquerda no segundo semáforo.
a-shk**ay**rda noo sig**oo**ndoo sim**a**fooroo

▶▶ Then it's the first street on the right.
Depois é a primeira rua à direita.
dip**oh**-ish eh a prim**ay**ra r**oo**-a-dir**ay**ta

10. Emergencies

accident	o acidente	asid**ay**nt
ambulance	a ambulância	amb**oo**lans-ya
consul	o cônsul	k**oh**nsool
embassy	a embaixada	aymb**i**shada
fire brigade	os bombeiros	bomb**ay**roosh
police	a polícia	pool**ee**s-ya

▶ Help!
Socorro!
sook**oh**rroo

▶ Can you help me?
Pode ajudar-me?
pod aJood**a**rmi

▶ Please come with me! It's really very urgent.
Por favor, venha comigo! É realmente muito urgente.
poor fav**oh**r v**ay**n-ya koom**ee**goo eh r-yalm**ay**nt mw**ee**ngtoo oorJ**ay**nt

▶ I've lost my keys.
Perdi as minhas chaves.
pird**ee** aJ m**ee**n-yash sh**a**vsh

▶ My car is not working.
O meu carro não está a funcionar.
oo m**ay**-oo k**a**rroo nowng shta a foons-yoon**a**r

▶ My purse has been stolen.
A minha carteira foi roubada.
a m**ee**n-ya kart**ay**ra f**oh**-i rohb**a**da

▶ I've been mugged.
Fui assaltada.
fwee asalt**a**da

▶▶ What's your name?
Como se chama?
ko**h**moo si sha**ma**

▶▶ I need to see your passport.
Preciso de ver o seu passaporte.
pris**ee**zoo di vayr oo s**ay**-oo pasap**or**t

▶ I'm sorry, all my papers have been stolen.
Desculpe, roubaram-me todos os documentos.
dishk**oo**lp rohba-rowngmi t**oh**dooz ooJ dookooma**yn**toosh

11. Friends

▶ Hi, how're you doing?
Olá, como estás?
oo**la** ko**h**moo shtash

▶▶ OK, and you?
Bem e tu?
bayng ee too

▶ Yeah, fine.   ▶ Not bad.
Estou bem.   Menos mal.
shtoh bayng   m**ay**nooJ mal

▶ Do you know Mark?
Conheces o Mark?
kon-y**eh**siz oo mark

▶ And this is Anna.
E esta é a Anna.
ee e**h**sht eh a **a**na

▶▶ Yeah, we know each other.
Sim, conhecemo-nos.
seeng kon-yis**ay**moonoosh

▶ Where do you know each other from?
De onde se conhecem?
dohnd si kon-y**eh**sayng

▶▶ We met at Manoel's place.
Conhecemo-nos na casa do Manoel.
kon-yis**ay**moonooJ na k**a**za doo manoo-**eh**l

▶ That was some party, eh?
Foi uma festa de arromba, não foi?
f**oh**-i **oo**ma fe**h**shta darr**oh**mba nowng f**oh**-i

▶▶ The best.
Não podia ser melhor.
nowng pood**ee**-a sayr mil-y**or**

▶ Are you guys coming for a beer?
Querem beber uma cerveja?
ke**h**rayng bib**ay**r **oo**ma sirv**ay**Ja

▶▶ Cool, let's go.
Óptimo, vamos lá.
otimoo v**a**mooJ la

▶▶ No, I'm meeting Maria.
Não, vou-me encontrar com a Maria.
nowng v**oh**mi aynkohntr**a**r kong a mar**ee**-a

▶ See you at Manoel's place tonight.
Até mais logo em casa do Manoel hoje à noite
at**eh** mîJ l**o**goo na k**a**za doo manoo-**eh**l ohJ a-n**oh**-it

▶▶ See you.
Até logo.
at**eh** l**o**goo

12. Health

antibiotics	os antibióticos	antib-y**o**tikoosh
antiseptic ointment	uma pomada anti-séptica	poom**a**da antis**eh**ptik
cystitis	cistite	sisht**ee**t
dentist	o dentista	dent**ee**shta
diarrhoea	a diarreia	d-yarr**ay**-a
doctor	o médico	m**eh**dikoo
hospital	o hospital	oshpit**al**
ill	doente	dwaynt
medicine	o remédio	rim**eh**d-yoo
painkillers	os analgésicos	analj**eh**zikoosh
pharmacy	a farmácia	farmas-ya
to prescribe	receitar	risayt**ar**
thrush	cândida	k**a**ndida

▶ I'm not feeling very well.
Não me sinto muito bem.
nowng mi s**ee**ntoo mw**ee**engtoo bayng

▶ Can you get a doctor?
Pode chamar um médico?
pod shamar oong mehdikoo

▶▶ Where does it hurt?
Onde dói?
ohnd doy

▶ It hurts here.
Dói aqui.
doy akee

▶▶ Is the pain constant?
É uma dor constante?
eh ooma dohr konshtant

▶ It's not a constant pain.
Não é uma dor constante.
nowng eh ooma dohr konshtant

▶ Can I make an appointment?
Posso marcar uma consulta?
posoo markar ooma konsoolta

▶ Can you give me something for...?
Pode dar-me qualquer coisa para...?
pod darmi kwalkehr koh-iza para…

▶ Yes, I have insurance.
Sim, tenho seguro.
seeng tayn-yoo sigooroo

13. Hotels

maid	a camareira	kamaraya
manager	o gerente	Jeraynt
room service	o serviço de	sirveesoo di
	quartos	kwartoosh

▶ Hello, we've booked a double room in the name of Cameron.
Olá, reservámos um quarto de casal no nome de Cameron.
oola rizirvamoosh oong kwartoo di kazal noo nohm di cameron

▶▶ That was for four nights, wasn't it?
É para quatro noites, não é?
eh para kwatro noh-itsh nowng eh

▶ Yes, we're leaving on Saturday.
Sim, partimos no sábado.
seeng parteemoosh noo sabadoo

▶▶ Can I see your passport please?
Posso ver o seu passaporte, faz favor.
posoo vayr oo say-oo pasaport fash favohr

▶▶ There you are, room 321 on the third floor.
Aqui tem, quarto trezentos e vinte e um no terceiro andar.
akee tayng kwartoo trizayntoosh ee veenti-oong noo tirsayroo andar

▶ I can't get this keycard to work.
Esta chave electrónica não funciona.
ehshta shav eletroneeka nowng foons-yona

▶▶ Sorry, I need to reactivate it.
Desculpe, preciso de a reactivar.
dishkoolp priseezoo di a r-yateevar

▶ What time is breakfast?
A que horas é o pequeno almoço?
a k-yorash eh oo pikaynoo almohsoo

▶ There aren't any towels in my room.
Não há toalhas no meu quarto.
nowng a twal-yash noo may-oo kwartoo

▶ My flight isn't until this evening, can I keep the room a bit longer?
O meu voo é à noite, posso ficar no quarto até mais tarde?
oo may-oo voh-oo eh a noh-it posoo fikar noo kwartoo ateh mīsh tard

▶ Can I settle up? Is this card OK?
Posso pagar a conta? Aceitam este cartão?
posoo pagar a kohnta, asaytowng aysht kartowng

14. Language difficulties

a few words	poucas palavras	pohkash palavrash
interpreter	o intérprete	intehrprit
to translate	traduzir	tradoozeer

►► Your credit card has been refused.
O seu cartão de crédito foi recusado.
oo say-oo kartowng di krehditoo foh-i rikoozadoo

► What, I don't understand. Do you speak English?
O quê, não percebe. Fala inglês?
oo kay nowng pirsayboo, fala inglaysh

►► This card isn't valid.
Este cartão não é válido.
aysht kartowng nowng eh validoo

► Could you say that again?
Pode repetir, por favor?
pod ripiteer poor favohr

► Slowly.
Devagar.
divagar

► I understand very little Portuguese.
Percebo muito pouco português.
pirsayboo mweengtoo pohkoo poortoogaysh

► I speak Portuguese very badly.
Falo muito mal o português.
faloo mweengtoo mal oo poortoogaysh

►► You can't use this card to pay.
Não pode utilizar este cartão para pagar.
nowng pod ootilizar aysht kartowng para pagar

►► Do you understand?
Compreende?
kompr-yaynd

► Sorry, no.
Desculpe, não compreendo.
dishkoolp nowng kompr-yayndoo

► Is there someone who speaks English?
Há alguém que fale inglês?
a algayng ki fal inglaysh

► Oh, now I understand.
Ah, agora percebo.
ah agora pirsayboo

► Is that OK now?
Está tudo bem agora?
shta toodoo bayng agora

15. Meeting people

▶ Hello.
Olá.
oola

▶▶ Hello, my name's Joana.
Olá, o meu nome é Joana.
oola oo may-oo nohm eh Joo-ana

▶ Graham, from England, Thirsk.
Chamo-me Graham; moro em Thirsk na Inglaterra.
shamoomi graham moroo ayng thirsk na inglatehrra

▶▶ Don't know that, where is it?
Não conheço, onde fica?
nowng kon-yaysoo ohnd feeka

▶ Not far from York, in the North; and you?
Perto de York, no Norte, e você?
pehrtoo di york noo nort ee vosay

▶▶ I'm from Coimbra; here by yourself?
Sou de Coimbra, está sozinho aqui?
soh di kweembra, shta sozeen-yoo akee

▶ No, I'm with my wife and two kids.
Não, estou com a minha mulher e dois filhos.
nowng shtoh kong a meen-ya mool-yehr ee doh-ish feel-yoosh

▶ What do you do?
Qual é o seu emprego?
kwal eh oo say-oo aympraygoo

▶▶ I'm in computers.
Trabalho com computadores.
trabal-yoo kong kompootadohrish

▶ Me too.
Eu também.
ay-oo tambayng

▶ Here's my wife now.
Aqui está a minha mulher.
akee shta a meen-ya mool-yehr

▶▶ Nice to meet you.
Muito prazer.
mweengtoo prazayr

16. Nightlife

dancing	dançar	dansar
electro	electro	electro
folk	folk	folk
heavy metal	heavy metal	heavy metal
hip-hop	hip-hop	hip-hop
jazz	jazz	Jazz
rock	rock	rock

▶ What's a good club for...?
Há um bom nightclub de...?
a oong bong nightclub di...

> ▶▶ There's going to be a great gig at the Pavilhão Atlântico tomorrow night.
> Vai haver um concerto fantástico no Pavilhão Atlântico amanhã à noite.
> vi avayr oong konsayrtoo fantashtikoo noo paveel-yowng atlantikoo aman-yang a noh-it

▶ Where can I hear some local music?
Onde posso ouvir música local?
ohnd posoo ohveer moozika lookal

▶ Can you write down the names of the best bars around here?
Pode escrever os nomes dos melhores bares aqui perto?
pod shkrivayr oosh nohmish doosh mil-yorish barish akee pehrtoo

>> That depends what you're looking for.
Depende da sua preferência.
dipaynd da soo-a prifirayns-ya

▶ The place where the locals go.
O lugar que as pessoas daqui frequentam.
oo loogar ky-ash pisoh-ash dakee frikwayntowng

▶ A place for a quiet drink.
Um lugar sossegado para tomar uma bebida.
oong loogar soosegadoo para toomar ooma bibeeda

>> The casino in Vila Moura is very good.
O casino de Vila Moura é muito bom.
oo kazeenoo di veela mohra eh mweengtoo bong

▶ What type of clothes should I wear?
Que tipo de roupa devo usar?
ki teepoo di rohpa dayvoo oozar

>> You can wear what you like.
Pode vestir-se como preferir.
pod visteersi kohmoo prifireer

▶ What time does it close?
A que horas fecha?
a k-yorash fehsha

17. Post offices

airmail	correio aéreo	koorray-oo a-ehr-yoo
post card	o postal	pooshtal
post office	os correios	koorray-oosh
stamp	o selo	sayloo

▶ What time does the post office close?
A que horas fecham os correios?
a k-yorash fayshowng oosh koorray-oosh

▶▶ Five o'clock weekdays.
Às cinco horas nos dias de semana.
ash seenkoo orash nooJ dee-aJ di simana

▶ Is the post office open on Saturdays?
Os correios abrem aos sábados?
oosh koorray-oosh abrayng owsh sabadoosh

▶▶ Until midday.
Até ao meio-dia.
ateh ow may-oo dee-a

| CARTAS | letters |
| ENCOMENDAS | parcels |

▶ I'd like to send this registered to England.
Queria enviar isto registado para Inglaterra.
kiree-a aynv-yar eeshtoo riJishtadoo para inglatehrra

▶▶ Certainly, that will cost 10 euros.
Com certeza, são 10 euros.
kong sirtayza sowng dehz ay-ooroosh

▶ And also two stamps for England, please.
E mais dois selos para Inglaterra, por favor.
ee mïJ doh-ish sayloosh para inglatehrra poor favohr

▶ Do you have some airmail stickers?
Tem autocolantes para via aérea?
tayng owtookoolantsh para vee-a a-ehr-ya

▶ Do you have any mail for me?
Há algum correio para mim?
a algoom koorray-oo para meeng

18. Restaurants

bill	a conta	kohnta
menu	a ementa	emaynta
table	a mesa	mayza

▶ Can we have a non-smoking table?
Queremos uma mesa para não fumadores.
kiraymooz ooma mayza para nowng foomadohrish

▶ There are two of us.
É para duas pessoas.
eh para doo-ash pisoh-ash

▶ There are four of us.
É para quatro pessoas.
eh para kwatroo pisoh-ash

▶ What's this?
O que é isto?
oo k-yeh **ee**shtoo

>> It's a type of fish.
É um tipo de peixe.
eh oong **tee**poo di paysh

>> It's a local speciality.
É uma especialidade local.
eh **oo**ma shpis-yalid**a**d look**a**l

>> Come inside and I'll show you.
Venha cá que eu mostro-lhe.
v**ay**n-ya ka ki **ay**-oo m**o**shtrool-yi

▶ We would like two of these, one of these, and one of those.
Queremos dois destes, um destes e um desses.
kir**ay**mooJ d**oh**-ish d**ay**shtish oong d**ay**stish ee oong d**ay**sish

>> And to drink?
E para beber?
ee para bib**ay**r

▶ Red wine.
Vinho tinto.
v**ee**n-yoo t**ee**ntoo

▶ White wine.
Vinho branco.
v**ee**n-yoo br**a**nkoo

▶ A beer and two orange juices.
Uma cerveja e dois sumos de laranja
ooma sirvay**J**a ee d**oh**-ish s**oo**moo**J** di laran**J**a

▶ Some more bread please.
Mais pão, por favor.
mïsh powng poor fav**oh**r

> ▶▶ How was your meal?
> Estava tudo bem?
> sht**a**va **too**doo bayng

▶ Excellent, very nice!
Excelente, muito bom!
ish-sel**ay**nt mw**ee**ngtoo bong

> ▶▶ Anything else?
> Mais alguma coisa?
> míz alg**oo**ma k**oh**-iza

▶ Just the bill thanks.
Apenas a conta, por favor.
ap**ay**naz a k**oh**nta poor fav**oh**r

19. Self-catering accommodation

air-conditioning	o ar condicionado	ar kondees-yoon**a**doo
apartment	o apartamento	apartam**ay**ntoo
cooker	o fogão	foog**ow**ng
fridge	o frigorífico	frigoor**ee**fikoo
heating	o aquecimento	akesim**ay**ntoo
hot water	a água quente	**a**gwa kaynt
lightbulb	a lâmpada	l**a**mpada
toilet	a casa de banho	k**a**za di ban-yoo

▶ The toilet's broken, can you get someone to fix it?
A sanita está avariada, pode arranjar alguém para a reparar?
a san**ee**ta shta avari-**a**da pod arran**J**ar alg**ay**ng para a repar**a**r

▶ There's no hot water.
Não há água quente.
nowng a **a**gwa kaynt

▶ Can you show me how the air-conditioning works?
Pode mostrar-me como funciona o ar condicionado?
pod mooshtr**a**rmi k**oh**moo foons-y**o**na oo ar kondees-yoon**a**doo

▶▶ OK, what apartment are you in?
OK, em que apartamento está?
OK ayng ki apartamayntoo shta

▶ We're in number five.
Estamos no número cinco.
shtamoosh noo noomiroo seenkoo

▶ Can you move us to a quieter apartment?
Pode mudar-nos para um apartamento mais silencioso?
pod moodarnoosh par oong apartamayntoo mīsh silayns-yohzoo

▶ Is there a supermarket nearby?
Há um supermercado aqui perto?
a oong soopermirkadoo akee pehrtoo

▶▶ Have you enjoyed your stay?
Gostou da sua estadia?
goostoh da soo-a shtadee-a

▶ Brilliant holiday, thanks!
Férias fantásticas, obrigado!
fehr-yash fantashtikash ohbrigadoo

20. Shopping

▶▶ Can I help you?
Posso ajudá-la?
posoo aJoodala

▶ Can I just have a look around?
Posso só dar uma olhada?
posoo saw dar ooma ol-yada

▶ Yes, I'm looking for…
Sim, queria…
seeng kiree-a…

▶ How much is this?
Quanto custa isto?
kwantoo kooshta eeshtoo

ABERTO	open
CAIXA	cash desk
FECHADO	closed
SALDOS	sale
TROCAR	to exchange

▶▶ Thirty-two euros.
Trinta e dois euros.
treenti doh-iz ay-ooroosh

▶ OK, I think I'll have to leave it; it's a little too expensive for me.
Tudo bem, acho que vou ter de desistir, é caro demais para mim.
toodoo bayng ashoo ki voh tayr di dizishteer eh karoo dimīsh para meeng

▶▶ How about this?
E que tal este?
ee ki tal aysht

▶ Can I pay by credit card?
Posso pagar com cartão de crédito?
posoo pagar kong kartowng di krehditoo

▶ It's too big.
É demasiado grande.
eh dimaz-yadoo grand

▶ It's too small.
É demasiado pequeno.
eh dimaz-yadoo pikaynoo

▶ It's for my son – he's about this high.
É para o meu filho – ele é mais ou menos deste tamanho.
eh paroo may-oo feel-yoo ayl eh mïz oh maynoosh daysht taman-yoo

▶▶ Will there be anything else?
Mais alguma coisa?
mïz algooma koh-iza

▶ That's all thanks.
Isso é tudo obrigada.
eesoo eh toodoo obrigada

▶ Make it twenty euros and I'll take it.
Reduza para vinte euros e eu compro.
ridooza para veent ay-ooroosh ee ay-oo kohmproo

▶ Fine, I'll take it.
Está bem, fico com ele.
shta bayng feekoo kong ayl

21. Shopping for clothes

to alter	alterar	altirar
bigger	maior	mï-or
just right	mesmo bem	mayshmoo bayng
smaller	menor	minor
to try on	provar	proovar

▶ Can I help you?
Posso ajudá-la?
posoo aJoodala

▶▶ No thanks, I'm just looking.
Não obrigada, estou só a ver.
nowng ohbrigada shtoh saw a vayr

▶ Do you want to try that on?
Deseja provar esse?
dis**ay**Ja proo**var** ays

> ▶▶ Yes, and I'll try this one too.
> Sim, e vou provar este também.
> seeng ee voh proo**var** aysht tamb**ay**ng

> ▶▶ Do you have it in a bigger size?
> Tem este num tamanho maior?
> tayng aysht noong tam**a**n-yoo m**ī**-**o**r

> ▶▶ Do you have it in a different colour?
> Tem este numa cor diferente?
> tayng aysht n**oo**ma kohr difi**ray**nt

▶ That looks good on you.
Fica-lhe bem.
f**ee**kal-yi bayng

> ▶▶ Can you shorten this?
> Pode pôr isto mais curto?
> pod pohr **ee**shtoo mīsh k**oo**rtoo

▶ Sure, it'll be ready on Friday, after 12.00.
Com certeza, ficará pronto na sexta-feira, depois do meio-dia.
kong sirt**ay**za fikar**a** pr**oh**ntoo na s**ay**shta-f**ay**ra dip**oh**-ish doo m**ay**-oo d**ee**-a

22. Sightseeing

art gallery	a galeria de arte	gali**ree**-a dart
bus tour	uma excursão	shkoors**ow**ng di
	de autocarro	owt**oo**k**a**rroo
city centre	o centro da cidade	s**ay**ntroo da sid**a**d
closed	fechado	fish**a**doo
guide	o guia	g**ee**-a
museum	o museu	mooz**ay**-oo
open	aberto	ab**eh**rtoo

▶ I'm interested in seeing the old town.
Estou interessado em conhecer a cidade antiga.
shtoh intris**a**doo ayng kon-yis**ay**r a sid**a**d ant**ee**ga

▶ Are there guided tours?
Há excursões com guia?
a shkoors**ow**ngsh kong g**ee**-a

▶▶ I'm sorry, it's fully booked.
Lamento, mas acabaram-se os lugares.
lamayntoo maz akabarowngsi ooz loogarish

▶ How much would you charge to drive us around for four hours?
Quanto cobraria para nos levar a passear por quatro horas?
kwantoo koobraree-a para nooJ livar a pas-yar poor kwatroo orash

▶ Can we book tickets for the concert here?
Podemos reservar bilhetes para o concerto aqui?
poodaymoosh rizirvar bil-yaytsh paroo konsayrtoo akee

>> Yes, in what name?
Sim, em que nome?
seeng ayng ki nohm

>> Which credit card?
Qual é o cartão de crédito?
kwaleh oo kartowng di krehditoo

▶ Where do we get the tickets?
Onde levantamos os bilhetes?
ohnd livantamooz ooJ bil-yaytsh

>> Just pick them up at the entrance.
Levante-os na entrada.
livant-yoosh na ayntrada

▶ Is it open on Sundays?
Abrem aos domingos?
abrayng owJ doomeengoosh

▶ How much is it to get in?
Quanto é a entrada?
kwantweh a ayntrada

▶ Are there reductions for groups of six?
Dão desconto para grupos de seis pessoas?
downg dishkohntoo para groopooJ di saysh pisoh-ash

▶ That was really impressive!
Foi sensacional!
foh-i saynsas-yoonal

23. Taxis

▶ Can you get us a taxi?
Pode chamar-nos um táxi?
pod shamarnoosh oong taxi

>> For now? Where are you going?
Para agora? Para onde vão?
paragora, parohnd vowng

▶ To the town centre.
Para o centro da cidade.
paroo **say**ntroo da see**dad**

▶ I'd like to book a taxi to the airport for tomorrow.
Gostaria de reservar um táxi para o aeroporto para amanhã.
gooshta**ree**-a di rizir**var** oong taxi pa**roo**-ayroo**poh**rtoo paraman-**yang**

>> Sure, at what time? How many people?
Claro, para que horas? Quantas pessoas?
kl**aroo** para k-**yo**rash, kw**antash** pis**oh**-ash

▶ How much is it to Monte Gordo?
Quanto é daqui a Monte Gordo?
kwant**weh** dak**ee** a m**oh**nt g**oh**rdoo

▶ Right here is fine, thanks.
Aqui está bem, obrigado.
ak**ee** shta bayng ohbrig**ad**oo

▶ Can you wait here and take us back?
Pode esperar aqui e levar-nos de volta?
pod shpir**ar** ak**ee** ee lev**ar**noosh di **vo**lta

>> How long are you going to be?
Quanto tempo vão demorar?
kw**antoo ta**ympoo vowng dimoo**rar**

24. Trains

to change trains	mudar de comboio	moo**dar** di komb**oy**-oo
platform	a plataforma	plata**for**ma
return	um bilhete de ida e volta	bil-**yay**t deedī **vo**lta
single	um bilhete de ida	bil-**yay**t **dee**da
station	a estação	shtas**ow**ng
stop	a paragem	para.**la**yng
ticket	o bilhete	bil-**yay**t

▶ How much is...?
Quanto é...?
kwantw**eh**...

▶ A single, second class to...
Um bilhete de ida, segunda classe para...
oong bil-**yay**t **dee**da sig**oo**nda klass p**ara**...

▶ Two returns, second class to...
Dois bilhetes de ida e volta, segunda classe para...
doh-ish bil-yaytsh deedī volta sigoonda klass para...

▶ For today.
Para hoje.
para ohJ

▶ For tomorrow.
Para amanhã.
para aman-yang

▶ For next Tuesday
Para a próxima terça-feira.
para prosima tayrsa fayra

▶▶ There's a supplement for the Intercity.
Há um suplemento para o Intercidades.
a oong sooplimayntoo paroo intersidadsh

▶▶ Do you want to make a seat reservation?
Deseja reservar o seu assento?
disayJa rizirvar oo say-oo asayntoo

▶▶ You have to change at Entroncamento.
Tem de mudar de comboio em Entroncamento.
tayng di moodar di komboy-oo ayng ayntronkamayntoo

▶ Is this seat free?
Este lugar está livre?
aysht loogar shta leevr

▶ Excuse me, which station are we at?
Se faz favor, que estação é esta?
si fash favohr ki shtasowng eh ehshta

▶ Is this where I change for Oporto?
É aqui que faço a mudança para o Porto?
eh akee ki faswa moodansa paroo pohrtoo

ENGLISH
→ PORTUGUESE

A

a, an um, *f* uma oong, **oo**ma

about: about 20 mais ou menos
vinte miz oh **may**noosh veent

it's about 5 o'clock por volta
das cinco poor – **seen**koo

a film about Portugal um
filme sobre Portugal oong feelm
sohbr poortoogal

above acima as**ee**ma

abroad no estrangeiro noo
shtranJayroo

absolutely! (I agree) com certeza!
kong sirt**ay**za

absorbent cotton o algodão em
rama algood**ow**ng ayng

accelerator o acelerador
asilirad**oh**r

accept aceitar asay**tar**

accident o acidente aseed**aynt**

there's been an accident
houve um acidente ohv oong

accommodation o alojamento
alooJam**ay**ntoo

accurate exacto ez**a**too

ache a dor dohr

my back aches tenho dor
nas costas **tayn**-yoo – nash
k**osh**tash

across: across the road
do outro lado da rua
doo **oh**troo ladoo da **roo**-a

adapter o adaptador adaptad**oh**r

address a morada moor**a**da

what's your address? qual é
a sua morada? kwal eh a s**oo**-a

address book o livro de
moradas l**ee**vroo di moor**a**dash,
o livro de endereços
ayndir**ay**soosh

admission charge a entrada
aynt**ra**da

adult (*male/female*) o adulto
ad**oo**ltoo, a adulta

advance: in advance adiantado
ad-yant**a**doo

aeroplane o avião av-y**ow**ng

Africa a África

African (*adj*) africano afrik**a**noo

after depois dip**oh**-ish

after you você primeiro
vos**ay** prim**ay**roo

after lunch depois do almoço
dwalm**oh**soo

afternoon a tarde tard

in the afternoon à tarde

this afternoon esta tarde
ehshta

aftershave o aftershave

aftersun cream a loção para
depois do sol
loos**ow**ng – dip**oh**-ish doo

afterwards depois

again outra vez **oh**tra vaysh

against contra

age a idade eed**a**d

ago: a week ago há uma
semana a **oo**ma simana

an hour ago há uma hora **o**ra

agree: I agree concordo
konk**o**rdoo

AIDS a SIDA s**ee**da

air o ar

by air de avião dav-y**ow**ng

air-conditioning o ar condicionado kondis-yoon**a**doo

airmail: by airmail por via aérea poor v**ee**-a-**ehr**-ya

airmail envelope o envelope de avião aynvil**o**p dav-y**ow**ng

airport o aeroporto a-ayroop**oh**rtoo

to the airport, please para o aeroporto, se faz favor paroo – si fash fav**oh**r

airport bus o autocarro do aeroporto owtook**a**rroo doo

aisle seat o lugar de corredor loog**a**r di koorrid**oh**r

alarm clock o despertador dishpirtad**oh**r

alcohol o álcool **a**lko-ol

alcoholic alcoólico alko-**o**likoo

all: all the boys todos os meninos t**oh**dooz ooJ min**ee**noosh

all the girls todas as meninas t**oh**daz aJ min**ee**nash

all of it todo t**oh**doo

all of them todos t**oh**doosh

that's all, thanks (said by man/woman) é tudo, obrigado/obrig**a**da eh t**oo**doo obrig**a**doo

allergic: I'm allergic to... (said by man/woman) sou alérgico/al**é**rgica a... soh al**ehr**Jikoo

allowed: is it allowed? é permitido? eh pirmit**ee**do

all right está bem shta bayng

I'm all right estou bem sht**oh**

are you all right? (fam) estás bem? sht**a**sh

(pol) está bem? sht**a**

almond a amêndoa am**ay**ndoo-a

almost quase kwaz

alone só saw

alphabet o alfabeto alfab**e**too

a a	**j** J**o**ta	**s** ehs
b bay	**k** k**a**pa	**t** tay
c say	**l** el	**u** oo
d day	**m** em	**v** vay
e eh	**n** en	**w** vay d**oo**ploo
f ehf	**o** o	**x** sheesh
g Jay	**p** pay	**y** **ee**psilon
h aga	**q** kay	**z** zay
i ee	**r** err	

already já Ja

also também tamb**ay**ng

although embora aymb**o**ra

altogether totalmente tootalm**ay**nt

always sempre s**ay**mpr

am: I am sou soh; estou sht**oh** (see note on p.8)

a.m.: at seven a.m. às s**e**te da manhã ash – man-y**a**ng

amazing (surprising) espantoso shpant**oh**zoo

(very good) estupendo shtoop**ay**ndoo

ambulance a ambulância amboolans-ya

call an ambulance! chame uma ambulância! sham **oo**ma

America a América

American americano amirik**a**noo

I'm American (male/female) sou americano/americ**a**na

among entre ayngtr

amount a quantia kwant**ee**-ya

amp: a 13-amp fuse um fusível de tr**e**ze amperes oong foozeevel di – amp**eh**rish

and e ee

angry zang**a**do

animal o anim**a**l

ankle o tornozelo toornooz**a**yloo

anniversary (wedding) o aniversário (de casamento) anivirs**a**r-yoo (di kazam**a**yntoo)

annoy: this man's annoying me este homem está a aborrecer-me aysht **oh**mayng shta aboorris**a**yrmi

annoying aborrecido aboorris**ee**doo, importuno import**oo**noo

another outro **oh**troo

can we have another room? pode dar-nos outro quarto? pod d**a**r-nooz – kw**a**rtoo

another beer, please **ou**tra cerveja, por favor sirv**a**yJa poor fav**oh**r

antibiotics os antibióticos antib-y**o**tikoosh

antifreeze o anticongelante –konJil**a**nt

antihistamines os anti-histamínicos –isht**a**meenikoosh

antique: is it an antique? é uma antiguidade? eh **oo**ma antigweed**a**d

antique shop a casa de antiguidades k**a**za dantigweed**a**dsh

antiseptic o anti-séptico

any: have you got any bread/tomatoes? tem pão/tom**a**tes? tayng

do you have any? tem?

sorry, I don't have any desculpe, não tenho dishk**oo**lp nowng t**a**yn-yoo

anybody alguém alg**a**yng

does anybody speak English? alguém fala inglês? ingl**a**ysh

there wasn't anybody there não estava lá ninguém nowng sht**a**va la ning**a**yng

anything qualquer coisa kwalk**eh**r k**oh**-iza

anything else? mais alguma coisa? mīz alg**oo**ma k**oh**-iza

nothing else, thanks (said by man/woman) mais n**a**da, obrigado/obrig**a**da obrig**a**doo

would you like anything to drink? gostaria de beber alguma coisa? gooshtar**ee**-a di bib**a**yr

I don't want anything, thanks (said by man/woman) não quero nada, obrigado/obrigada nowng k**eh**roo

apart from além de al**a**yng di

apartment o apartamento apartam**a**yntoo

apartment block o bloco de apartamentos bl**o**koo dapartam**a**yntoosh

aperitif o aperitivo apirit**ee**voo

apology as desculpas
disk**oo**lpash

appendicitis a apendicite
apendi-s**ee**t

appetizer a entrada ayntr**a**da

apple a maçã mas**a**ng

appointment a marcação
markas**ow**ng

**good morning, how can
I help you?** bom dia, que
deseja? bong d**ee**-a ki dis**ay**Ja

**I'd like to make an
appointment** queria fazer
uma marcação kir**ee**-a faz**ay**r

what time would you like?
que hora prefere?
k-y**o**ra pref**eh**ri

three o'clock três horas
trayz **o**rash

**I'm afraid that's not
possible, is four o'clock
all right?** infelizmente, não
é possível, quatro horas está
bem? infili૩**may**ngt nowng eh
poos**ee**vil kw**a**troo **o**rash
shta bayng

yes, that will be fine sim,
está bem seeng

the name was…? o nome
é…? oo n**oh**m

apricot o damasco dam**a**shkoo

April Abril abr**ee**l

Arab (*adj*) árabe **a**rabi

are: we are somos s**oh**moosh;
estamos sht**a**moosh

you are (você) é (vos**ay**-)eh;
(você) está shta

they are são sowng; estão
sht**ow**ng (*see note on p.8*)

area a região riJ-y**ow**ng

area code o código

arm o braço br**a**soo

**arrange: will you arrange it
for us?** pode organizar isto
para nós? p**o**di – **ee**shtoo – nosh

arrival a chegada shig**a**da

arrive cheg**a**r

when do we arrive? a que
horas chegamos?
k-y**o**rash shig**a**moosh

has my fax arrived yet? meu
fax já chegou?
may-oo – Ja shig**oh**

we arrived today chegámos
hoje shig**a**moosh ohJ

art a arte art

art gallery a galeria de arte
galir**ee**-a d**a**rt

artist (*male/female*) o/a artista
art**ee**shta

as: as big as tão grande quanto
towng gr**a**nd kw**a**ntoo

as soon as possible
logo que possível l**o**goo ki
poos**ee**vil

ashtray o cinzeiro sinz**ay**roo

ask perguntar pirgoont**a**r, pedir
pid**ee**r

I didn't ask for this não pedi
isto nowng pid**ee ee**shtoo

could you ask him to…?
importa-se de lhe pedir que…?
import**a**si di l-yi – ki

asleep: she's asleep ela está a dormir **eh**la shta a doormeer

aspirin a aspirina ashpir**ee**na

asthma a asma **a**Jma

astonishing espantoso shpant**oh**zoo

at: at the hotel no hot**e**l noo

at the station na estação nashtas**ow**ng

at six o'clock às seis horas ash sayz **o**rash

at América's na casa do América dwam**eh**rikoo

athletics o atletismo atlet**ee**Jmoo

Atlantic Ocean o Oceano Atlântico ohs-yanoo atl**a**ntikoo

ATM o caixa automático k**ī**sha owtoom**a**tikoo

at sign o sinal de arroba seen**a**l darr**oh**ba

attractive atraente atra-**ay**nt

aubergine a beringela bireenJe**h**la

August Agosto ag**oh**shtoo

aunt a tia t**ee**-a

Australia a Austrália owshtr**a**l-ya

Australian (*adj*) australiano owshtr**a**l-yanoo

I'm Australian (*male/female*) sou australiano/australi**a**na soh

automatic automático owtoom**a**tikoo

automatic teller o caixa automático k**ī**sha owtoom**a**tikoo

autumn o Outono oht**oh**noo

in the autumn no Outono noo

avenue a avenida avin**ee**da

average (not good) mais ou menos m**ī**z oh m**ay**noosh

on average em média ayng m**eh**d-ya

awake: is he awake? ele já acordou? ayl Ja akoord**oh**

away: go away! vá-se embora! vasi aymb**o**ra

is it far away? fica longe? f**ee**ka lohnJ

awful horrível ohrr**ee**vil

axle o eixo **ay**shoo

B

baby o bebé beb**eh**

baby food a comida de bebé koom**ee**da di

> **Travel tip** Changing facilities for babies in restaurants and public toilets are largely non-existent, but nappies (diapers) are widely available in supermarkets and pharmacies, as are formula milk and jars of baby food – though don't expect the range of choices you might be used to at home.

baby's bottle o biberão bibir**ow**ng

baby-sitter a baby-sitter

back (of body) as costas k**o**shtash

(back part) a parte posterior part pooshteri**oh**r

at the back atrás atr**a**sh

can I have my money

54 The Rough Guide Portuguese Phrasebook > ENGLISH➔PORTUGUESE

back? posso reaver o meu dinheiro? p**o**soo r-yav**ay**r oo m**ay**-oo deen-y**ay**roo

to come/go back volt**a**r

backache a dor nas costas d**o**hr nash k**o**shtash

bacon o bac**o**n

bad mau mow, *f* má

a bad headache uma dor de cabeça forte **oo**ma dohr di kab**ay**sa fort

badly mal

bag o saco s**a**koo

(handbag) a mala de mão di m**o**wng

(suitcase) a mala

baggage a bagagem bag**a**Jayng

baggage check o depósito de bagagem dip**o**zitoo di bag**a**-Jayng

baggage claim a reclamação de bagagens riklamas**o**wng di bag**a**-Jayngsh

bakery a padaria padar**ee**-a

balcony a var**a**nda

a room with a balcony um quarto com varanda oong kw**a**rtoo kong

bald careca kar**eh**ka

ball a b**o**la

(small) a bolinha bol**ee**n-ya

ballet o ballet

ballpoint pen a caneta esferográfica shfir**oo**-gr**a**fika

banana a ban**a**na

band (musical) a b**a**nda

bandage a ligadura ligad**oo**ra

Bandaid o adesivo adez**ee**voo

bank (money) o banco b**a**nkoo

bank account a conta bancária bank**a**r-ya

bar o bar

a bar of chocolate uma tablete de chocolate tabl**eh**t di shookool**a**t

barber's o barbeiro barb**ay**roo

basket o cesto s**ay**shtoo

(in shop) o cesto de compras di k**o**hmprash

bath o banho b**a**n-yoo

can I have a bath? posso tomar banho? p**o**soo toom**a**r

bathroom a casa de banho k**a**za di

with a private bathroom com casa de banho kong

bath towel a toalha de banho tw**a**l-ya

bathtub a banheira ban-y**ay**ra

battery a pilha p**ee**l-ya

(for car) a bateria batir**ee**-a

bay a baía ba-**ee**-a

be ser sayr; estar shtar (*see note on p.8*)

beach a praia pr**ī**-a

on the beach na praia

beach mat o colchão de praia kolsh**o**wng di pr**ī**-a

beach umbrella o chapéu de sol shap**eh**-oo

beans os feijões faiJ**oy**ngsh

French beans os feijões-verdes –v**ay**rdsh

broad beans as favas f**a**vash

beard a barba b**a**rba

beautiful bonito boon**ee**too
because porque poork**ay**
  because of... por causa do...
  poor k**ow**za doo
bed a c**a**ma
  I'm going to bed now vou
  p**a**ra a cama ag**o**ra voh
bed and breakfast alojamento e
  pequeno almoço aloo**J**am**ay**ntwee
  pik**ay**noo alm**oh**soo
bedroom o quarto kw**a**rtoo
beef a carne de v**a**ca karn di
beer a cerveja sirv**ay**Ja
  two beers, please duas
  cervejas, por favor d**oo**-ash
  sirv**ay**Jash poor fav**oh**r
before antes antsh
begin começar koomes**a**r
  when does it begin? quando
  é que começa? kw**a**ndoo
  eh ki koom**eh**sa

beginner (*male/female*) o/a
  principiante prinsip-y**a**nt
beginning: at the beginning
  no início noo in**ee**s-yoo
behind atrás atr**a**sh
  behind me atrás de mim
  di meeng
beige bege
Belgian (*adj*) belga
Belgium a Bélgica beh**l**Jika
believe acredit**a**r
below abaixo ab**ī**shoo
belt o cinto s**ee**ntoo
bend (in road) a curva k**oo**rva
berth (on ship) o beliche bil**ee**sh
beside: beside the... junto
  da... J**oo**ntoo
best o melhor mil-y**o**r
better melhor
  are you feeling better? está
  melhor? shta

between entre ayntr

beyond para além de paralayng di

bicycle a bicicleta bisiklehta

big grande grand

too big grande demais dimīsh

it's not big enough não é suficientemente grande nowng eh soofis-yayntimaynt

bike a bicicleta bisiklehta

(motorbike) a motocicleta mootoosiklehta

bikini o bikíni

bill a conta

(US) a nota

could I have the bill, please? pode-me dar a conta, por favor? pod-mi – poor favohr

bin o caixote de lixo kishot di leeshoo

bin liners os sacos de lixo sakoosh

bird o pássaro pasaroo

birthday o dia de anos dee-a danoosh

happy birthday! feliz aniversário! fileez anivirsar-yoo

biscuit a bolacha boolasha

bit: a little bit um pouco oong pohkoo

a big bit um pedaço grande pidasoo grand

a bit of... um pedaço de...

a bit expensive um pouco caro pohkoo karoo

bite (by insect) a picada pikada

(by dog) a mordedura moordedoora

bitter (taste etc) amargo amargoo

black preto praytoo

blanket o cobertor koobirtohr

bleach (for toilet) a lixívia lisheev-ya

bless you! santinho! santeen-yoo

blind cego sehgoo

blinds as persianas pirs-yanash

blister a bolha bol-ya

blocked (road) cortado koortadoo

(pipe, sink) entupido ayntoopeedoo

blond (adj) louro lohroo

blood o sangue sang

high blood pressure a tensão arterial alta taynsowng artir-yal

blouse a blusa blooza

blow-dry secar com secador kong sikadohr

I'd like a cut and blow-dry queria cortar e fazer brushing kiree-a – ee fazayr

blue azul azool

blue eyes os olhos azuis ol-yoosh azoo-ish

blusher o blusher

boarding house a pensão paynsowng

boarding pass o cartão de embarque kartowng daymbark

boat o barco barkoo

(for passengers) o ferry-boat

body o corpo kohrpoo

boiled egg o ovo cozido ohvoo koozeedoo

boiler a caldeira kaldayra

bone o osso ohsoo

(in fish) a espinha shp**ee**n-ya

bonnet (of car) o capot kap**oh**

book o livro l**ee**vroo

(verb) reservar rizirv**ar**

can I book a seat? posso
reservar um lugar? p**o**soo –
oong loog**ar**

DIALOGUE

I'd like to book a table for
two queria reservar uma
mesa para dois kir**ee**-a –
ooma m**ay**za para d**oh**-ish

what time would you like
it booked for? para que
horas? k-y**o**rash

half past seven sete e meia
seh-tee-m**ay**-a

that's fine está bem shta
b**ay**ng

and your name? e o seu
nome? yoo s**ay**-oo nohm

bookshop, bookstore a livraria
livrar**ee**-a

boot (footwear) a b**o**ta

(of car) o porta-bagagens
p**o**rta-bagaJ**ay**ngsh

border (of country) a fronteira
front**ay**ra

bored: I'm bored (said by
man/woman) estou chateado/
chate**a**da shtoh shat-y**a**doo

boring maçador masad**oh**r

**born: I was born in
Manchester** nasci em
Manchester nash-s**ee** ayng

I was born in 1960 nasci em
mil novec**e**ntos e sess**e**nta

borrow pedir emprestado
pid**ee**r aymprisht**a**doo

may I borrow...? posso
pedir... emprestado? p**o**soo

both ambos **a**mboosh

bother: sorry to bother you
desculpe incomodá-lo
dishk**oo**lp eenkoo-mood**a**loo

bottle a garr**a**fa

a bottle of house red uma
garrafa de vinho da casa tinto
ooma – di v**ee**n-yoo da k**a**za
t**ee**ntoo

bottle-opener o abre-garrafas
abrigarr**a**fash

bottom (of person) o traseiro
traz**ay**roo

at the bottom of... (hill) no
sopé do... noo soop**eh** doo

box a caixa k**ī**sha

box office a bilheteira bil-yit**ay**ra

boy o rapaz rap**a**sh

boyfriend o namorado
namoor**a**doo

bra o soutien soot-y**a**ng

bracelet a pulseira pools**ay**ra

brake o travão trav**ow**ng

brandy o brandy

Brazil Brasil braz**ee**l

Brazilian (adj) brasileiro
brazil**ay**roo

bread o pão p**ow**ng

white bread o pão branco
br**a**nkoo

brown bread o pão escuro
shk**oo**roo

wholemeal bread o pão
integral eentigr**a**l

break partir

  I've broken the... quebrei o/a... kibray oo

  I think I've broken my wrist acho que parti o pulso ashoo ki – oo poolsoo

break down avariar

  I've broken down meu carro avariou may-oo karroo avari-oh

breakdown (mechanical) a avaria avaree-a

breakdown service o pronto-socorro prohntoo sookohrroo

breakfast o pequeno almoço pikaynoo almohsoo

break-in: I've had a break-in minha casa foi roubada meen-ya kaza foh-i rohbada

breast o peito paytoo

breathe respirar rishpirar

breeze a brisa breeza

bridge (over river) a ponte pohnt

brief breve brehv

briefcase a pasta pashta

bright (light etc) brilhante bril-yant

  bright red vermelho vivo veevoo

brilliant (idea, person) brilhante bril-yant

bring trazer trazayr

  I'll bring it back later trago isto de volta mais tarde tragoo eeshtoo di – mīsh tard

Britain a Grã-Bretanha grang britan-ya

British britânico britanikoo

brochure o folheto fool-yaytoo

broken partido parteedoo

bronchitis bronquite bronkeet

brooch o alfinete alfinayt

broom a vassoura vasohra

brother o irmão eermowng

brother-in-law o cunhado koon-yadoo

brown castanho kashtan-yoo

bruise a contusão kontoozowng

brush (for hair, cleaning) a escova shkova

  (artist's) o pincel peensehl

bucket o balde bowld

buffet car a carruagem restaurante karrwa-Jayng rishtowrant

buggy (for child) a cadeirinha de bebé kadayreen-ya di bebeh

building o edifício idifees-yoo

bulb (light bulb) a lâmpada

bullfight a tourada tohrada

bullfighter o toureiro tohrayroo

bullring a praça de touros prasa di tohroosh

bull-running as garraiadas garrī-adash

bumper o pára-choques para-shoksh

bunk o beliche bileesh

bureau de change o câmbio kamb-yoo

burglary o roubo rohboo

burn a queimadura kaymadoora

  (verb) queimar

burnt: this is burnt isto está queimado eeshtoo shta kaymadoo

burst: a burst pipe um cano rebentado oong kanoo ribayntadoo

bus o autocarro owtookarroo

what number bus is it to…? qual é o número do autocarro para…? kwal-**eh** oo n**oo**miroo doo

when is the next bus to…? a que horas é o próximo autocarro para…? k-y**o**raz eh oo pr**o**simoo

what time is the last bus? a que horas é o último autocarro? **oo**ltimoo

DIALOGUE

does this bus go to…? este autocarro vai para…? aysht – vī

no, you need a number… não, tem que apanhar o número… nowng tayng k-yapang-yar oo n**oo**miroo

business o negócios nig**o**s-yoosh

bus station a estação dos autocarros shtas**ow**ng dooz owtook**a**rroosh

bus stop a paragem do autocarro par**a**Jayng doo owtook**a**rroo

bust o peito p**a**ytoo·

busy (restaurant etc) frequentado frikwaynt**a**doo

I'm busy tomorrow (said by man/woman) estou ocupado/ ocupada amanhã sht**o**h okoop**a**doo – aman-y**a**ng

but mas mash

butcher's o talho tal-yoo

butter a manteiga mant**a**yga

button o botão boot**ow**ng

buy compr**a**r

where can I buy…? onde posso comprar…? ohnd p**o**soo

by: by bus de autocarro dowtook**a**rroo

by car de carro di k**a**rroo

written by… escrito por… shkr**ee**too poor

by the window à janela

by the sea à beira-mar

by Thursday na quinta-feira

bye adeus ad**a**y-oosh

C

cabbage a couve kohv

cabin (on ship) o camarote kamar**o**t

cable car o teleférico telef**eh**rikoo

café o café kaf**eh**

cagoule o impermeável de nylon impirmia-vil di

cake o bolo b**oh**loo

cake shop a pastelaria pashtila-r**ee**-a

call chamar sham**a**r

(to phone) telefonar telefoon**a**r

what's it called? como se chama isto? k**oh**moo si sh**a**ma **ee**shtoo

he/she is called… ele/ela chama-se… ayl/**eh**la sham**a**si

please call the doctor

por favor, chame o médico
poor fav**oh**r sham-yoo m**eh**dikoo

**please give me a call at...
a.m. tomorrow** chame-me,
por favor, às... horas amanhã
sh**a**mi-mi – ash... **o**rash
aman-y**a**ng

please ask him to call me
por favor, peça a ele que me
telefone p**e**sa-a ayl ki-mi telef**oh**n

call back: I'll call back later
volto mais tarde v**o**ltoo
m**i**sh tard

(phone back) volto a telefonar
mais tarde v**o**ltwa telefoon**a**r

**call round: I'll call round
tomorrow** vou aí amanhã
voh a-**ee** aman-y**a**ng

camcorder a câmara de vídeo
di v**ee**d-yoo

camera a máquina fotográfica
m**a**kina footoogr**a**fika

camera shop a loja de artigos
fotográficos l**o**ja dart**ee**goosh
footoogr**a**fikoosh

camp acamp**a**r

can we camp here?
podemos acampar aqui?
pood**ay**moosh – ak**ee**

camping gas o gás para
campismo gash p**a**ra
kamp**ee**Jmoo

campsite o parque de campismo
park di kamp**ee**Jmoo

can a l**a**ta

a can of beer uma lata
de cerveja di sirv**ay**Ja

can: can you...? você pode...?
vos**ay** pod

can I have...? posso ter...?
p**o**soo tayr

I can't... não posso... nowng

Canada o Canadá

Canadian canadiano kanad-
y**a**noo

I'm Canadian (male/female)
sou canadiano/canadi**a**na soh

canal o canal

cancel cancelar kansil**a**r

candle a vela

candies os rebuçados
riboos**a**doosh

canoe a canoa kan**oh**-a

canoeing a canoagem
kanw**a**-J**a**yng

can-opener o abre-latas
abril**a**tash

cap (hat) o boné boon**eh**

(of bottle) a tampa

car o carro k**a**rroo

by car de carro

caravan a roulotte rool**o**t

caravan site o parque de
campismo park di kamp**ee**Jmoo

carburettor o carburador
karboorad**oh**r

card (birthday etc) o cartão
kart**ow**ng

here's my (business) card
aqui está o meu cartão (de
visitas) ak**ee** sht**a** oo m**a**y-oo
kart**ow**ng (di viz**ee**tash)

cardigan o casaco de malha
kaz**a**koo di m**a**l-ya

cardphone o telefone de cartão
telef**oh**n di kart**ow**ng

careful cuidadoso kwidad**oh**zoo

be careful! cuidado! kwid**a**doo

caretaker (*male/female*) o/a guarda gw**a**rda

car ferry o ferry-boat

car hire o aluguer de automóveis aloog**eh**r dowtoom**o**vaysh

carnival o carnaval

car park o parque de estacionamento park di shtas-yonam**ay**ntoo

carpet a carpete karp**eh**t

carriage (of train) a carruagem karrwa-Jayng

carrier bag o saco plástico sakoo plashtikoo

carrot a cenoura sin**oh**ra

carry levar livar

carry-cot o porta-bebés porta-beb**eh**sh

carton o pacote pak**o**t

carwash a lavagem automática lavaJayng owtoom**a**tika

case (suitcase) a mala

cash o dinheiro deen-y**ay**roo

(*verb*) descontar dishkongtar

will you cash this for me? pode descontar isto para mim? pod – **ee**shtoo – meeng

cash desk a caixa k**i**sha

cash dispenser o caixa automático owtoom**a**tikoo

cassette a cass**e**te

cassette recorder o gravador de cassetes gravad**oh**r di

castle o castelo kasht**eh**loo

casualty department o serviço de urgências sirv**ee**soo doorJ**a**yns-yash

cat o gato g**a**too

catch pegar, apanhar apan-yar

where do we catch the bus to…? onde podemos apanhar o autocarro para…? ohnd pood**ay**mooz apan-yar oo owtookarroo

cathedral a catedral katidral

Catholic (*adj*) católico kat**o**likoo

cauliflower a couve-flor k**oh**v-flor

cave a caverna kav**e**rna

ceiling o tecto t**eh**too

celery o alho francês al-yoo frans**ay**sh

cellar (for wine) a cave kav

cellular phone o telefone celular telef**oh**n siloolar

cemetery o cemitério simit**eh**r-yoo

centigrade centígrado sent**ee**gradoo

centimetre o centímetro sent**ee**mitroo

central central sen-tral

central heating o aquecimento central akesim**ay**ntoo

centre o centro s**ay**ntroo

how do we get to the city centre? como é que vamos para o centro da cidade? k**oh**moo eh ki vamoosh – oo s**ay**ntroo da sidad

cereal os cereais siri-**ī**sh

certainly certamente sirtam**ay**nt

certainly not certamente que não ki nowng

chair a cadeira kad**ay**ra

champagne o champanhe shamp**a**n-yi

change (money) o troco tr**oh**koo

(*verb*: money) trocar tro**okar**

can I change this for…? posso trocar isto por…? p**o**soo – **ee**shtoo

I don't have any change não tenho troco nowng t**ay**n-yoo

can you give me change for a 20 euro note? pode trocar-me uma n**o**ta de vinte euros? pod trook**a**rmi **oo**ma – di veent **ay**-ooroosh

do we have to change (trains)? temos de mudar? tay**moosh** di mood**a**r

yes, change at Coimbra/ no, it's a direct train sim, troque em Coimbra/não, é um comboio directo seeng tro-**kee**ng kw**eem**bra/nowng eh oong komb**oh**-yo dir**eh**too

changed: to get changed mudar de roupa mood**a**r di r**oh**pa

chapel a capela kap**eh**la

charge o preço pr**ay**soo

(*verb*) custar koosht**a**r

charge card o cartão de débito kart**ow**ng di d**eh**beetoo

cheap barato bar**a**too

do you have anything cheaper? tem alguma coisa mais barata? tayng alg**oo**ma k**oh**-iza mish

check (US) o cheque shehk

(US: bill) a c**o**nta

see **bill**

check verific**a**r

could you check the…, please? pode verificar o …, se faz favor? pod – oo… si fash fav**oh**r

checkbook o livro de cheques l**ee**vroo di sh**eh**ksh

check card o cartão de garantia kart**ow**ng di garant**ee**-a

check-in o ch**e**ck-in

check in fazer o check-in faz**ay**r oo

where do we have to check in? onde temos que fazer o check-in? **oh**nd tay**moosh**k

cheek (on face) a bochecha boosh**ay**sha

cheerio! adeuzinho! aday-oo**zee**n-yoo

cheers! (toast) saúde! sa-**oo**d

cheese o queijo k**ay**ʃoo

chemist's a farmácia farm**a**s-ya

cheque o cheque shehk

do you take cheques? aceitam cheques? as**ay**towng sh**eh**ksh

cheque book o livro de cheques l**ee**vroo di sh**eh**ksh

cheque card o cartão de garantia kart**ow**ng di garant**ee**-a

cherry a cereja sir**ay**ʃa

chess o xadrez shadr**ay**sh

chest o peito p**ay**too

chewing gum a pastilha elástica pashteel-ya ilashtika

chicken o frango frangoo

chickenpox a varicela varisehla

child a criança kry-ansa

   children as crianças kry-ansash

child minder a ama

children's pool a piscina infantil pish-seena infanteel

children's portion a dose para crianças doz – kry-ansash

chin o queixo kayshoo

china a porcelana poorsilana

Chinese (*adj*) chinês shinaysh

chips as batatas fritas batatash freetash

chocolate o chocolate shookoolat

   milk chocolate o chocolate com leite kong layt

   plain chocolate o chocolate puro pooroo

   a hot chocolate um chocolate quente oong – kaynt

choose escolher shkool-yayr

Christian name o nome próprio nohm propr-yoo

Christmas o Natal

   Christmas Eve a Véspera de Natal vehshpira di

   merry Christmas! feliz Natal! fileeɹ

church a igreja igrayɹa

cider a cidra seedra

cigar o charuto sharootoo

cigarette o cigarro sigarroo

cigarette lighter o isqueiro ishkayroo

cinema o cinema sinayma

circle o círculo seerkooloo

   (in theatre) a plateia platay-a

Travel tip To the delight of English-speaking visitors, cinemas almost always show films with the original sound-track and Portuguese subtitles. Listings can be found in local newspapers and prices are usually reduced at matinées and on Mondays.

---

city a cidade sidad

city centre o centro da cidade sayntroo

clean (*adj*) limpo leempoo

   can you clean this for me? pode limpar isto para mim? pod leempar eeshtoo – meeng

cleaning solution (for contact lenses) a solução de limpeza sooloosowng di leempayza

cleansing lotion o creme de limpeza kraym di

clear claro klaroo

clever inteligente intiliɹaynt

cliff o rochedo rooshaydoo

climb escalar shkalar

cling film a película aderente pileekoola adiraynt

clinic a clínica kleenika

cloakroom o vestiário visht-yar-yoo

clock o relógio riloɹ-yoo

close (*verb*) fechar fishar

what time do you close?
a que horas fecham?
k-**yo**rash **fay**showng

we close at 8 p.m. on weekdays and 6 p.m. on Saturdays fechamos às oito da noite durante a semana e às seis da tarde aos sábados fisha-mooz az-**oh**-itoo da **noh**-it dooranta simana yash **say**sh da tard owsh sabadoosh

do you close for lunch?
fecham para almoço?
al**moh**soo

yes, between 1 and 3.30 p.m. sim, entre a uma e as três e meia da tarde seeng **ayn**tri-a-**oo**ma ee ash traysh ee **may**-a da tard

closed fechado fish**a**doo

cloth (fabric) o tecido tis**ee**doo

(for cleaning etc) o pano p**a**noo

clothes a roupa r**oh**pa

clothes line o estendal sht**e**nd**a**l

clothes peg a mola de roupa di r**oh**pa

cloud a nuvem n**oo**vayng

cloudy enevoado inivw**a**doo

clutch a embraiagem aymbrī-a**j**ayng

coach (bus) o autocarro owtook**a**rroo

(on train) a carruagem karrw**a**-**j**ayng

coach station a estação dos autocarros sht**a**s**ow**ng dooz owtook**a**rroosh

coach trip a excursão shkoors**ow**ng

coast a costa k**o**shta

on the coast na costa

coat (long coat) o sobretudo soobrit**oo**doo

(jacket) o casaco kaz**a**koo

coathanger a cruzeta krooz**ay**ta

cockroach a barata bar**a**ta

cocoa o cacau kak**ow**

coconut o coco k**oh**koo

cod o bacalhau fresco bakal-**yow** fr**ay**shkoo

dried cod o bacalhau

code (for phoning) o indicativo indikat**ee**voo

what's the (dialling) code for Oporto? qual é o indicativo do Porto? kwal eh oo – doo **poh**rtoo

coffee o café kaf**eh**

two coffees, please dois cafés, por favor d**oh**-ish kaf**eh**sh poor fav**oh**r

coin a moeda mw**eh**da

Coke a coca-cola

cold frio fr**ee**-oo

I'm cold tenho frio t**ay**n-yoo

I have a cold estou constipado sht**oh** konshtip**a**doo

collapse: he's collapsed ele desmaiou ayl diji**mī**-**oh**

collar o colarinho koolar**een**-yoo

collect buscar boosh**k**ar

I've come to collect... vim buscar... veeng boosh**k**ar

collect call a chamada paga no destinatário sham**a**da p**a**ga noo dishtinat**a**r-yoo

college o colégio kool**ehj**-yoo

colour a cor kohr

do you have this in other colours? tem isto de outras cores? tayng **ee**shto-di **oh**trash k**oh**rish

colour film o filme colorido feelm koolooreedoo

comb o pente paynt

come vir veer

where do you come from? donde é? dohnd**eh**

I come from Edinburgh sou de Edimburgo soh dedeen**boo**rgoo

come back voltar

I'll come back tomorrow volto amanhã v**o**ltoo aman-y**a**ng

come in entrar ayntr**a**r

comfortable confortável konfoort**a**vil

compact disc o CD say day

company (business) a companhia kompan-y**ee**-a

compartment (on train) o compartimento kompartim**ay**ntoo

compass a bússola b**oo**soola

complain reclamar riklam**a**r

complaint a reclamação riklamas**ow**ng

I have a complaint tenho uma reclamação t**ay**n-yoo

completely completamente komplitam**ay**nt

computer o computador kompootad**oh**r

concert o concerto kons**ay**rtoo

concussion o traumatismo trowmat**ee**Jmoo

conditioner (for hair) o creme amaciador kraym amas-yad**oh**r

condom o preservativo prizirvat**ee**voo

conference a conferência konfir**ay**ns-ya

confirm confirmar konfirm**a**r

congratulations! parabéns! parab**ay**ngsh

connecting flight o voo de ligação v**oh**-oo di ligas**ow**ng

connection a ligação

conscious consciente konsh-sy**ay**nt

constipation a prisão de ventre priz**ow**ng di v**a**yntr

consulate o consulado
konsooladoo

contact contactar

contact lenses as lentes de
contacto layntsh di kontatoo

contraceptive o contraceptivo
kontrasipteevoo

convenient conveniente
konvin-yaynt

  that's not convenient não é
conveniente nowng eh

cook cozinhar kozeen-yar

  not cooked mal cozido
koozeedoo

cooker o fogão foogowng

cookie a bolacha boolasha

cooking utensils os utensílios
de cozinha ootaynseel-yoosh
di koozeen-ya

cool fresco frayshkoo

cork a rolha rohl-ya

  (material) a cortiça koorteesa

corkscrew o saca-rolhas saka-
rohl-yash

corner o canto kantoo

  in the corner no canto noo

cornflakes os cornflakes

correct (right) certo sehrtoo

corridor o corredor koorridohr

cosmetics os cosméticos
kooJmehtikoosh

cost custar kooshtar

  how much does it cost?
quanto custa? kwantoo kooshta

cot a cama de bebé kama di bebeh

cotton o algodão algoodowng

cotton wool o algodão em rama
ayng

couch (sofa) o sofá soofa

couchette o beliche bileesh

cough a tosse tos

cough medicine o xarope
sharop

could: could you…? podia…?
poodee-a

  could I have…? queria…?
kiree-a

  I couldn't… (wasn't able to) não
pude… nowng pood

country (nation) o país pa-eesh

  (countryside) o campo kampoo

countryside o campo

couple (two people) o casal kazal

  a couple of… um par de…
oong par di

courgette a courgette

courier (male/female) o/a guia
gee-a

course (main course etc) o prato
pratoo

  of course é claro eh klaroo

  of course not claro que não
ki nowng

cousin (male/female) o primo
preemoo, a prima

cow a vaca

crab o caranguejo karang-gayJoo

cracker a bolacha de água e sal
boolasha dagwa ee

craft shop a loja de artesanato
loJa dartizanatoo

crash a colisão kolisowng

  I've had a crash tive uma
colisão teev ooma

crazy doido doh-idoo

cream as natas na**tash**

  (lotion) o creme kraym

  (colour) creme

creche a creche

credit card o cartão de crédito
kar**tow**ng di kr**eh**deetoo

  do you take credit cards?
aceitam cartões de crédito?
a**say**towng kart**oy**ngsh

  can I pay by credit card?
posso pagar com cartão de
crédito? **po**soo – kong

  **which card do you want
to use?** que cartão deseja
utilizar? ki kar**tow**ng dis**ay**Ja
ootili**zar**

  Access/Visa

  yes, sir sim, senhor
s**een**g sin-y**or**

  what's the number? qual é
o número? kwal**eh**
oo n**oo**miroo

  and the expiry date? e a
data de validade? ya d**a**ta
de vali**dad**

credit crunch a crise do crédito
kreez doo kr**eh**deetoo

crisps as batatas fritas bat**a**tash
fr**ee**tash

crockery a loiça l**oh**-isa

crossing (by sea) a travessia
trav**ee**-a

crossroads o cruzamento
kroozam**ay**ntoo

crowd a multidão mooltid**ow**ng

crowded apinhado apeen-y**a**doo

crown (on tooth) a ponte pohnt

cruise o cruzeiro krooz**ay**roo

crutches as muletas mool**ay**tash

cry chorar shoo**rar**

cucumber o pepino pip**ee**noo

cup a chávena sh**a**vena

  a cup of…, please uma
chávena de…, se faz favor
si fash fav**ohr**

cupboard o armário arm**ar**-yoo

cure curar koo**rar**

curly encaracolado
ayn-karak**oo**ladoo

current a corrente koorr**aynt**

curtains as cortinas koort**ee**nash

cushion a almofada almoof**a**da

custom o hábito **a**beetoo

customs a alfândega alf**a**ndiga

cut o corte kort

  (verb) cortar

  I've cut myself cortei-me
koort**ay**mi

cutlery os talheres tal-y**eh**rish

cycling o ciclismo sikl**ee**Jmoo

cyclist (male/female) o/a ciclista
sikl**ee**shta

D

dad o papá

daily diariamente d-yar-yam**ay**nt

  (adj) diário d-y**ar**-yo

damage avariar avari-**ar**

  damaged avariado avari-**a**do

  **I'm sorry, I've damaged
this** desculpe, avariei isto

dishk**oo**lp avari-**ay ee**shtoo

damn! raios me partam!
ra-yoosh mi p**a**rtowng

damp (*adj*) húmido **oo**meedoo

dance a dança d**a**nsa

(*verb*) dan**ç**ar

would you like to dance?
queres dançar? k**e**hrish

dangerous perigoso pirig**oh**zoo

Danish (*adj*, language)
dinamarquês dinamark**ay**sh

dark (*adj*) escuro shk**oo**roo

it's getting dark está a
escurecer shta-a-shk**oo**res**ay**r

date: what's the date today?
qual é a d**a**ta hoje? kwal eh – **o**hJ

**let's make a date for next
Monday** vamos marc**a**r
p**a**ra a pr**ó**xima segunda-feira
v**a**moosh – pr**o**sima sig**oo**nda
f**ay**ra

dates (fruit) as tâmaras t**a**marash

daughter a filha f**ee**l-ya

daughter-in-law a n**o**ra

dawn a madrugada madro**o**g**a**da

at dawn de madrug**a**da di

day o dia d**ee**-a

the day after o dia seguinte
sig**ee**nt

the day after tomorrow
depois de amanhã
dip**oh**-ish daman-yang

the day before o dia anterior
antir-y**o**hr

the day before yesterday
anteontem ant-y**oh**ntayng

every day todos os dias
t**oh**dooz-ooJ d**ee**-ash

all day o dia todo t**oh**doo

in two days' time dentro de
dois dias d**ay**ntroo di d**oh**-iJ

have a nice day bom dia
bong

day trip a excursão de um
dia shkoors**ow**ng doong d**ee**-a

dead morto m**oh**rtoo

deaf surdo s**oo**rdoo

deal (business) o negócio nig**o**s-yoo

it's a deal é negócio fechado
eh – fish**a**doo

death a morte mort

decaffeinated coffee o café
descafeinado kaf**eh** dishkafay-
een**a**doo

December Dezembro
dez**ay**mbroo

decide decidir disid**ee**r

we haven't decided yet
ainda não decidimos
a-**ee**nda nowng disid**ee**-moosh

decision a decisão disiz**ow**ng

deck (on ship) o convés konv**eh**sh

deckchair a cadeira de lona
kad**ay**ra di l**oh**na

deep fundo f**oo**ndoo

definitely de certeza di sirt**ay**za

definitely not de certeza que
não ki nowng

degree (qualification) a
licenciatura lisayns-yat**oo**ra

delay o atraso atr**a**zoo

deliberately de propósito
di proop**o**zitoo

delicatessen a charcutaria
sharkootar**ee**-a

delicious delicioso
dilis-**yoh**zo

deliver entregar ayntrig**a**r

delivery (of mail) a distribuição
dishtribwees**ow**ng

Denmark a Dinamarca dinam**a**rka

dental floss o fio dentário
fee-oo dent**a**r-yoo

dentist (*male/female*) o/a dentista
dent**ee**shta

dentures a dentadura postiça
dentad**oo**ra poosht**ee**sa

deodorant o desodorizante
dizoodoor**i**zant

department o departamento
dipartam**ay**ntoo

department store os grandes
armazéns grandz armaz**a**yngsh

departure a saída sa-**ee**da

departure lounge a sala de
embarque daymb**a**rk

depend: it depends depende
dip**ay**nd

it depends on... depende
de... di

deposit (payment) o depósito
dip**o**zitoo

description a descrição
dishkri-**sow**ng

dessert a sobremesa sobrim**ay**za

destination o destino disht**ee**noo

develop desenvolver
disaynvolv**ay**r

diabetic (*male/female*)
o diabético d-yab**eh**tikoo, a
diab**é**tica

diabetic foods os alimentos
para diabéticos alim**ay**ntoosh
d-yab**eh**tikoosh

dial marc**a**r

dialling code o indicativo
indikat**ee**voo

diamond o diamante d-yam**a**nt

diaper a fralda

diarrhoea a diarreia dy-arr**a**y-a

**do you have something
for diarrhoea?** tem algum
antilaxante? tayng alg**oo**ng
anti-lash**a**nt

diary (for business) a agenda
a_J_**a**ynda

(for personal experiences) o diário
oo diar-yoo

dictionary o dicionário
dis-yoon**a**r-yoo

didn't *see* **not**

die morrer moorr**a**yr

diesel o gasóleo gaz**o**l-yoo

diet a dieta d-y**eh**ta

I'm on a diet estou de dieta
shtoh di

**I have to follow a special
diet** tenho que seguir uma
dieta especial t**a**yn-yoo ki sig**ee**r
ooma – shpis-y**a**l

difference a diferença difir**a**ynsa

what's the difference?
qual é a diferença? kwal eh

different diferente difir**ay**nt

this one is different
este é diferente aysht eh

a different table outra mesa
ohtra m**ay**za

difficult difícil dif**ee**sil

difficulty a dificuldade difik**oo**ldad

dinghy o bote de borracha
bot di boor**ra**sha

dining room a sala de jantar
di **J**antar

dinner (evening meal) o jantar

to have dinner jantar

direct (*adj*) directo dir**eh**too

is there a direct train? há
um comboio directo? a oong
komb**oh**-yo

direction a direcção direhs**ow**ng

which direction is it? em que
direcção fica? ayng ki – f**ee**ka

is it in this direction? fica
nesta direcção? n**eh**shta

directory enquiries as
informações infoormas**oy**ngsh

dirt a sujidade soo**J**idad

dirty sujo s**oo**Joo

disabled deficiente difis-y**ay**nt

**is there access for the
disabled?** há acesso para
deficientes? a as**eh**soo –
difis-y**ay**ntsh

disappear desaparecer
dizaparis**ay**r

it's disappeared desapareceu
dizaparis**ay**-oo

disappointed decepcionado
disips-yoon**a**doo

disappointing decepcionante
disips-yon**a**nt

disaster a tragédia tra**J**eh**d-ya

disco o disco d**ee**shkoo

discount o desconto dishk**oh**ntoo

is there a discount? pode
fazer-me um desconto?
pod faz**ay**rm-oong

disease a doença dw**ay**nsa

disgusting nojento noo**J**ay**ntoo

dish (meal) o prato pr**a**too
(bowl) a tigela ti**J**e**h**la

dishcloth o pano de loiça
p**a**noo di l**oh**-isa

disinfectant o desinfectante
dizinfit**a**nt

disk (for computer) a disquete
dishk**eh**t

disposable diapers/nappies
as fraldas descartáveis
frald**a**J dishkart**a**vaysh

distance a distância disht**a**ns-ya

in the distance ao longe
ow lohn**J**

distilled water a água destilada
agwa disht**i**lada

district o bairro b**ī**rroo

disturb perturbar pirtoob**a**r

diversion (detour) o desvio
di**J**v**ee**-oo

diving board a prancha de saltos
pr**a**nsha di s**a**ltoosh

divorced divorciado
divoors-y**a**doo

dizzy: I feel dizzy sinto tonturas
s**ee**ntoo tont**oo**rash

do fazer faz**ay**r

what shall we do?
que vamos fazer? ki-va**moosh**

how do you do it?
como se faz? k**oh**moo si fash

will you do it for me?
importa-se de mo fazer?
imp**or**tasi di moo

how do you do? muito
prazer mw**ee**ngtoo praz**ay**r

nice to meet you muito
prazer

what do you do? (work) o
que é que faz? oo ki **eh**-ki faJ

I'm a teacher, and you?
(said by man/woman) sou
profess**or**/profess**or**a, e
você? soh – ee vos**ay**

I'm a student sou estud**a**nte

**what are you doing this
evening?** que vai fazer
hoje à noite?
ki v**ī** – **oh**J-ya n**oh**-it

**we're going out for a
drink, do you want to
join us?** vamos tomar uma
bebida, quer vir conosco?
v**a**moosh toomar **oo**ma
bib**ee**da kehr veer kon**oh**shkoo

do you want cream?
quer natas? **na**tash

I do, but she doesn't
quero, mas ela não
k**eh**roo maz-**eh**la nowng

doctor (*male/female*) o médico
m**eh**dikoo, a médica

we need a doctor
precisamos de um médico
prisiz**a**moosh doong

please call a doctor por
favor, chame um médico
poor fav**oh**r sham oong

where does it hurt?
onde dói? ohnd doy

right here bem aqui
bayng ak**ee**

does that hurt now?
dói ag**o**ra?

yes sim seeng

take this to the pharmacy
leve isto à farmácia
lehv **ee**sht-wa farm**a**s-ya

document o documento
dookoom**ay**ntoo

dog o cão kowng

doll a boneca boon**eh**ka

domestic flight voo doméstico
v**oh**oo doom**eh**shtikoo

donkey o burro b**oo**rroo

don't! não! nowng

don't do that! não faça isto!
f**a**sa **ee**shtoo

door a p**o**rta

doorman o porteiro poort**ay**roo

double duplo d**oo**ploo

double bed a cama de casal
di kaz**a**l

double room o quarto de casal
kw**a**rtoo

doughnut a fartura fart**oo**ra

down embaixo aymb**ī**shoo

down here aqui embaixo ak**ee**

put it down over there
deite-o lá d**ay**t-yoo la

it's down there on the right
é lá embaixo, à direita
eh – a dir**ay**ta

it's further down the road
é nesta rua mais abaixo
n**e**shta r**oo**-a miz ab**ee**shoo

download (*verb*) descarregar
dishkarrig**a**r

downmarket (restaurant etc)
barato bar**a**too

downstairs embaixo aymb**ee**shoo

dozen a dúzia d**oo**z-ya

  half a dozen a meia dúzia
m**ay**-a

drain (in sink, in road) o cano de
esgoto k**a**noo diJg**oh**too

draught beer imperial eempir-y**a**l

draughty: it's draughty faz
corrente de ar fash koorr**ay**nt dar

drawer a gaveta gav**ay**ta

drawing o desenho dis**ay**n-yoo

dreadful horrível ohrr**ee**vil

dream o sonho s**oh**n-yoo

dress o vestido visht**ee**doo

dressed: to get dressed
vestir-se visht**ee**rsi

dressing (for cut) o penso p**ay**nsoo

  salad dressing o tempero
taymp**ay**roo

dressing gown o roupão
rohp**ow**ng

drink a bebida bib**ee**da
(*verb*) beber bib**ay**r

  a cold drink uma bebida
fresca **oo**ma – fr**ay**shka

fancy a quick drink? vamos
tomar uma bebida? v**a**moosh
toomar **oo**ma bib**ee**da

can I get you a drink? o que
bebe? oo ki behb

**what would you like (to
drink)?** o que gostaria de
beber? gooshtar**ee**-ya di

I don't drink não bebo
nowng b**ay**boo

**I'll just have a drink of
water** só um copo de água
saw oong k**o**poo d**a**gwa

drinking water a água potável
agwa poot**a**vil

is this drinking water? esta
água é potável? shta – eh

drive conduzir kondooz**ee**r

we drove here viemos de
carro v-y**ay**moosh di k**a**rroo

I'll drive you home levo-o a
casa de carro l**eh**voo a k**a**za
di k**a**rroo

driver (of car: man/woman) o
condutor kondoot**oh**r
a condut**o**ra
(of bus: man/woman) o/a
motorista mootoor**ee**shta

driving licence a carta de
condução di kondoos**ow**ng

drop: just a drop, please (of
drink) só um pouco, se faz favor
saw oong p**oh**koo si fash fav**oh**r

drug o medicamento
medikam**ay**ntoo

drugs (narcotics) a droga dr**o**ga

drunk (*adj*) bêbado
b**ay**badoo

drunken driving a condução enquanto embriagado kondoos**ow**ng aynkwantoo aymbr-yag**a**doo

dry (*adj*) seco s**ay**koo

dry-cleaner a tinturaria teentoorar**ee**-a

duck o pato p**a**too

due: he was due to arrive yesterday ele devia chegar ontem ayl div**ee**-a shig**a**r **oh**ntayng

when is the train due? a que horas é o comboio? k-y**o**raz eh oo komb**oh**-yo

dull (pain) moinho moo-**een**-yoo

dummy (baby's) a chupeta shoop**ay**ta

during durante door**a**nt

dust o pó paw

dustbin o caixote de lixo k**ish**ot di l**ee**shoo

dusty empoeirado aympoo-ayr**a**doo

Dutch holandês oland**aysh**

duty-free (goods) duty-free

duty-free shop a free-shop

duvet o edredão idrid**ow**ng

DVD o DVD day-vay-day

E

each (every) c**a**da

how much are they each? quanto é cada um? kwantw**eh** – oong

ear a orelha or**ay**l-ya

earache: I have earache tenho dor de ouvidos t**ay**n-yoo dohr dohv**ee**doosh

early cedo s**ay**doo

early in the morning de manhã cedo di man-y**a**ng

I called by earlier passei aqui mais cedo pas**ay** akee m**ish**

earrings os brincos br**ee**nkoosh

east o leste lehsht

in the east no leste

Easter Páscoa p**a**shkwa

Travel tip Easter Week is celebrated with religious processions throughout the country, but most majestically in Braga, where it is full of ceremonial pomp, and at São Brás de Alportel in the Algarve, where there is a floral procession to the church.

Easter Week Semana Santa sim**a**na

easy fácil f**a**sil

eat comer koom**ay**r

we've already eaten, thanks (said by man/woman) já comemos, obrigado/ obrigada Ja koom**ay**moosh obrig**a**doo

eau de toilette a eau de toilette

EC CE say eh

economy class classe económica klas-ekoon**oh**mika

Edinburgh Edimburgo edeenb**oo**rgoo

eels as enguias ing**ee**-ash

egg o ovo **oh**voo

eggplant a beringela bireenJ**eh**la

either: either... or... ou...
ou... oh

either of them qualquer um
deles kwalkayr**oo**m d**ay**lish

elastic o elástico il**a**shtikoo

elastic band o elástico

elbow o cotovelo kootoov**ay**loo

electric eléctrico el**eh**trikoo

electrical appliances os
aparelhos eléctricos
apar**ay**l-yoosh

electric fire o aquecedor
eléctrico akesid**ohr**

electrician o electricista
eletris**ee**shta

electricity a electricidade
eletrisid**a**d

elevator (in building) o elevador
elevad**ohr**

else: something else outra
coisa **oh**tra k**oh**-iza

somewhere else noutro sítio
n**oh**troo s**ee**t-yoo

DIALOGUE

**would you like anything
else?** deseja mais alguma
coisa? dis**ay**Ja miz alg**oo**ma
k**oh**-iza

no, nothing else, thanks
(said by man/woman) não,
mais n**a**da, obrigado/
obrig**a**da nowng mish –
obrig**a**doo

email el email
(verb: person) enviar um email a
ayngvee-**ar** oong

(verb: text, file) enviar por email

embassy a embaixada aymbish**a**da

emergency a emergência
emirJ**ay**ns-ya

this is an emergency! isto é
uma emergência! **ee**shtoo
eh **oo**ma

emergency exit a saída
de emergência sa-**ee**da di
emayrJ**ay**ns-ya

empty vazio vaz**ee**-oo

end o fim feeng

at the end of the street no
fim da rua noo feeng da r**oo**-a

when does it end? quando
ac**a**ba? kw**a**ndoo

engaged (toilet, telephone)
ocupado okoop**a**doo

(to be married) noivo n**oh**-ivoo

engine (car) o motor
moot**ohr**

England a Inglaterra inglat**eh**rra

English (adj, language) inglês
ingl**ay**sh

I'm English (male/female) sou
inglês/ingl**e**sa soh

do you speak English? fala
inglês?

enjoy: to enjoy oneself
divertir-se divirt**ee**rsi

DIALOGUE

how did you like the film?
gostou do filme?
goost**oh** doo feelm

**I enjoyed it very much;
did you enjoy it?** gostei
imenso, você gostou?
goosht**ay** im**ay**nsoo vos**ay**
goosht**oh**

---

enjoyable divertido divirt**ee**doo

enlargement (of photo) a ampliação ampl-yas**ow**ng

enormous enorme en**o**rm

enough suficiente soofis-y**ay**nt

there's not enough… não há suficiente… nowng a

it's not big enough não é suficientemente grande eh soofis-yayntim**ay**nt

that's enough, thanks (said by man/woman) está bem, obrigado/obrigada shta bayng obrig**a**doo

entrance a entrada ayntr**a**da

envelope o envelope aynvil**o**p

epileptic (*male/female*) o epiléptico epil**eh**ptikoo, a epil**é**ptica

equipment o equipamento ekipam**ay**ntoo

error un erro **ay**rroo

especially especialmente shpis-yalm**ay**nt

essential essencial esayns-yal

it is essential that… é essencial que… eh – ki

EU UE oo eh

euro o euro **ay**-ooroo

Eurocheque o Eurocheque ay-ooroosh**eh**k

Eurocheque card o cartão Eurocheque kart**ow**ng

Europe a Europa ay-oor**o**pa

European (*adj*) europeu ay-ooroop**ay**-oo, *f* europeia ay-ooroop**ay**-a

even: **even the British** até os britânicos at**eh**-oosh brit**a**nikoosh

even men até mesmo os homens at**eh** may Jmo osh **oh**mayngsh

even if… mesmo se… si

evening a noite n**oh**-it

this evening esta noite **eh**shta

in the evening à noite

evening meal o jantar oo Jant**a**r

eventually no fim noo feeng

ever já Ja

every c**a**da

every day todos os dias t**oh**dooz-ooz d**ee**-ash

everyone toda a gente t**oh**da a Jaynt

everything tudo t**oo**doo

everywhere em toda a parte ayng t**oh**da part

exactly! exactamente! ezatam**ay**nt

exam o exame ez**a**m

example o exemplo ez**ay**mploo

for example por exemplo poor

excellent excelente ish-sil**ay**nt

excellent! excelente!

except excepto ish-s**eh**too

excess baggage o excesso
  de bagagem ish-**seh**soo di
  baga**J**ayng

exchange rate a cotação
  cambial kootas**ow**ng kamby**al**

exciting emocionante
  emoos-yoon**a**nt

excuse me (to get past) com
  licença kong lis**ay**nsa
  (to get attention) se faz favor
  si fash fav**ohr**
  (to say sorry) desculpe dishk**oo**lp

exhaust (pipe) o tubo de escape
  t**oo**boo dishk**a**p

exhausted (tired) exausto
  ez**ow**shtoo

exhibition a exposição
  shpoozis**ow**ng

exit a saída sa-**ee**da
  where's the nearest exit?
  onde é a saída mais próxima?
  ohnd**eh** – mish pr**o**sima

expect esperar shpir**ar**

expensive caro k**a**roo

experienced experiente
  shpir-**yay**nt

explain explicar shplik**ar**
  can you explain that? pode
  explicar-me isso?
  pod shplik**ar**m **ee**soo

express (mail) o correio expresso
  koorr**ay**-oo shpr**eh**soo
  (train) o Rápido r**a**pidoo

extension (telephone) a extensão
  shtens**ow**ng
  extension 221, please
  extensão duzentos e vinte e
  um, por favor dooza**yn**tooz ee
  v**ee**nti-oong poor fav**ohr**

extension lead a extensão
  shtens**ow**ng

**extra: can we have an extra
  one?** pode dar-nos mais um/
  uma? pod dar-noosh mish oong/
  ooma

do you charge extra for that? paga-se extra por isto? pagasi ayshtra poor eeshtoo

extraordinary extraordinário shtra-ohrdinar-yoo

extremely extremamente shtremamaynt

eye o olho ohl-yoo

will you keep an eye on my suitcase for me? pode dar uma olhada na minha mala, por favor? pod dar-oomool-yada na meen-ya mala poor avohr

eyebrow pencil o lápis para as sobrancelhas lapsh parash sobransayl-yash

eye drops as gotas para os olhos gohtash parooz ol-yoosh

eyeglasses (US) os óculos okooloosh

eyeliner o lápis para os olhos lapsh parooz ol-yoosh

eye make-up remover o desmaquilhador de olhos dishmakil-yadohr dol-yoosh

eye shadow a sombra para os olhos

F

face a cara

factory a fábrica fabrika

Fahrenheit Fahrenheit

faint (verb) desmaiar diJmī-ar

she's fainted ela desmaiou ehla diJmī-oh

I feel faint sinto que vou desmaiar seentoo ki voh

fair (funfair, tradefair) a feira fayra

(adj) justo Jooshtoo

fairly bastante bashtant

fake falso falsoo

fall cair ka-eer

she's had a fall ela deu uma queda ehla day-oo ooma kehda

fall (US) o Outono ohtohnoo

in the fall no Outono noo

false falso falsoo

family a família fameel-ya

famous famoso famohzoo

fan (electrical) a ventoinha vayntween-ya

(handheld) o leque lehk

(sports: man/woman) o adepto adehptoo, a adepta

fan belt a correia da ventoinha koorray-a da vayntween-ya

fantastic fantástico fantashtikoo

far longe lohnJ

is it far from here? é longe daqui? eh – dakee

no, not very far não, não é muito longe nowng – mweengtoo

well how far? bem, qual é a distância? bayng kwal eh a dishtans-ya

it's about 20 kilometres são mais ou menos vinte quilómetros sowng mīz oh maynoosh veengt kilomitroosh

fare o bilhete bil-yayt

farm a quinta keenta

fashionable na moda

fast rápido ra**pi**doo

fat (person) gordo **goh**rdoo

  (on meat) a gordura goord**oo**ra

father o pai pī

father-in-law o sogro **soh**groo

faucet a torneira toorn**ay**ra

fault o defeito di**fay**too

  sorry, it was my fault
  desculpe, foi culpa minha
  f**oh**-i k**oo**lpa m**ee**n-ya

  it's not my fault a culpa não é
  minha nowng eh m**ee**n-ya

faulty avariado avari**a**doo

favourite favorito favoor**ee**too

fax o fax

  to send a fax mandar um fax

February Fevereiro fivr**ay**roo

feel sentir saynt**ee**r

  I feel hot estou com calor
  shtoh kong kal**oh**r

  I feel unwell não me sinto
  bem nowng mi s**ee**ntoo bayng

  I feel like going for a walk
  estou com vontade de dar um
  passeio shtoh kong vontad di dar
  oong pas**ay**-oo

  how are you feeling? como
  se sente? k**oh**moo si saynt

  I'm feeling better sinto-me
  melhor s**ee**ntoomi mil-y**o**r

felt-tip (pen) a caneta de feltro
kan**ay**ta di f**ay**ltroo

fence a vedação vidas**ow**ng

fender o pára-choques parash**o**ksh

ferry o ferry-boat

festival o festival fisht**i**val

fetch buscar boosh**ka**r

  I'll fetch him vou buscá-lo
  voh booshka-loo

  **will you come and fetch
me later?** pode vir buscar-me
mais tarde? pod veer boosh**ka**rmi
mīsh tard

feverish febril febr**ee**l

few: a few alguns alg**oo**nsh

  I'll give you a few dou-lhe
  alguns d**oh**l-yalg**oo**nsh

  a few days poucos dias
  p**oh**koosh d**ee**-ash

fiancé o noivo n**oh**-ivoo

fiancée a noiva n**oh**iva

field o campo k**a**mpoo

fight a briga br**ee**ga

figs os figos f**ee**goosh

file o ficheiro fish**ay**roo

fill in preencher pri-aynsh**ay**r

  do I have to fill this in?
  tenho de preencher isto?
  t**ay**n-yoo di – **ee**shtoo

fill up encher aynsh**ay**r

  fill it up, please encha o
  depósito, por favor **ay**nsha oo
  dep**o**zitoo poor fav**oh**r

filling (in cake, sandwich) recheio
rish**ay**-oo

  (in tooth) o chumbo sh**oo**mboo

film o filme feelm

filter coffee o café de filtro
kaf**eh** di f**ee**ltroo

filter papers os filtros de café
feeltr**oo**sh

filthy nojento noo**ʃ**ayntoo

find encontrar aynkontr**a**r

I can't find it não consigo encontrar nowng konseegoo

I've found it encontrei-o aynkongtray-oo

find out descobrir dishkoobreer

could you find out for me? pode descobrir para mim? pod — meeng

fine (weather) bom bong

(punishment) a multa moolta

how are you? como está? kohmoo shta

I'm fine, thanks (said by man/ woman) bem, obrigado/ obrigada bayng obrigadoo

is that OK? assim está bem? aseeng shta bayng

that's fine, thanks está bem, obrigado/obrigada shta

finger o dedo daydoo

finish terminar

I haven't finished yet ainda não terminei a-eenda nowng terminay

when does it finish? quando é que termina? kwandoo eh ki termeena

fire o fogo fohgoo

(blaze) o incêndio insaynd-yoo

fire! fogo!

can we light a fire here? podemos fazer uma fogueira aqui? poodaymoosh fazayr ooma foogayra akee

it's on fire está a arder shta a ardayr

fire alarm o alarme de incêndios alarm dinsaynd-yoosh

fire brigade os bombeiros bombayroosh

fire escape a saída de emergência sa-eeda demirjayns-ya

fire extinguisher o extintor shtintohr

first primeiro primayroo

I was first (said by man/woman) eu era o primeiro/a primeira ay-oo ehra

at first ao princípio ow prinseep-yoo

the first time a primeira vez vaysh

first on the left primeira à esquerda a-shkayrda

first aid os primeiros socorros primayroosh sookorroosh

first aid kit a caixa de primeiros socorros kisha di

first class (travel etc) primeira classe klas

first floor o primeiro andar
(US) o rés de chão rehj doo

first name o nome próprio nohm propr-yoo

fish o peixe paysh
(verb) pescar pishkar

fishing village a aldeia de pescadores alday-a di pishkadohrish

fishmonger's a peixaria paysharee-a

fit (attack) ataque atak

fit: it doesn't fit me não me serve nowng mi sehrv

fitting room a cabina de provas
kabeena di provash

fix (repair) reparar

  can you fix this? (repair) pode
  reparar isto? pod – eeshtoo

fizzy gasoso gazohzoo

flag a bandeira bandayra

flannel a toalha de cara twal-ya di

flash (for camera) o flash

flat (apartment) o apartamento
apartamayntoo

  (adj) plano planoo

  I've got a flat tyre tenho
  um pneu furado tayn-yoo oong
  pnay-oo fooradoo

flavour o sabor sabohr

flea a pulga poolga

flight o voo voh-oo

flight number o número de voo
noomiroo di

flippers as barbatanas
barbata-nash

flood a inundação inoondasowng

floor (of room) o chão showng

  (storey) o andar

  on the floor no chão

florist a florista flooreeshta

flour a farinha fareen-ya

flower a flor flohr

flu a gripe greep

**fluent: he speaks fluent
Portuguese** ele fala português
fluentemente el – poortoogaysh
flwentimaynt

fly a mosca mohshka

  (verb: person) ir de avião eer
  dav-yowng

fog o nevoeiro nivwayroo

foggy: it's foggy está enevoado
shta inivwadoo

folk dancing a dança folclórica
dansa foolklorika

folk music a música folclórica
moozika

follow seguir sigeer

  follow me siga-me seegami

food a comida koomeeda

food poisoning a intoxicação
alimentar intoksikasowng

food shop/store a mercearia
mirs-yaree-a

foot (of person, measurement)
o pé peh

  on foot a pé

football (game) o futebol footbol

  (ball) a bola de futebol

football match o desafio de
futebol dizafee-oo di

**for: do you have something
for...?** (headache/diarrhoea etc)
tem alguma coisa para...?
tayng algooma koh-iza

autocarro para o Castelo de São Jorge? ohnd **po**soo apan-**yar** oo owtooka**rr**oo paroo kasht**eh**loo di sowng Jor**J**

the bus for o Castelo de São Jorge leaves from Praça do Comércio o autocarro para o Castelo de São Jorge sai da Praça do Comércio sĩ da pr**a**sa doo koom**eh**rsyo

how long have you been here for? há quanto tempo está aqui? a k**wan**too t**ay**mpoo shta ak**ee**

I've been here for two days, how about you? estou aqui há dois dias, e você? shtoh ak**ee** a d**oh**-i**J** dee-ash ee vos**ay**

I've been here for a week estou aqui há uma semana shtoh ak**ee** a **oo**ma sim**a**na

forehead a testa t**eh**shta

foreign estrangeiro shtranJ**ay**roo

foreigner (*male/female*) o estrangeiro shtranJ**ay**roo, a estrang**ei**ra

forest a floresta floor**eh**shta

forget esquecer shkis**ay**r

I forget, I've forgotten esqueci-me shkis**ee**mi

fork o garfo g**ar**foo

(in road) a bifurcação bifoorkas**owng**

form (document) o impresso impr**eh**soo

formal (dress) de cerimónia di sirim**on**-ya

fortnight a quinzena keenz**ay**na

fortunately felizmente filiJ**maynt**

forward: could you forward my mail? pode passar a enviar-me o correio? pod – aynv-**yar**mi oo koor**ray**-oo

forwarding address a nova morada moor**a**da

foundation cream o creme de base kraym di baz

fountain a fonte fohnt

foyer (of hotel, theatre) o foyer fwi-**ay**

fracture a fractura frat**oo**ra

France a França fr**a**nsa

free livre l**ee**vr

(no charge) gratuito grat**oo**-eetoo

is it free (of charge)? é gratuito? eh

freeway a autoestrada owtooshtr**a**da

freezer o congelador konJilad**oh**r

French (*adj*, language) francês frans**aysh**

French fries as batatas fritas bat**a**tash fr**ee**tash

frequent frequente frik**waynt**

how frequent is the bus to Évora? com que frequência há autocarros para Évora? kong ki frik**way**nsya a owtooka**rroosh** – **eh**voora

fresh fresco fr**ay**shkoo

fresh orange o sumo natural

de laranja s**oo**moo nat**oo**ra**l** di
lara**nj**a

Friday sexta-feira s**ay**shta f**ay**ra

fridge o frigorífico frig**oo**-re**e**fik**oo**

fried frito fre**e**t**oo**

fried egg o ovo estrelado
ohv**oo** shtril**a**d**oo**

friend (*male/female*) o amigo
am**ee**g**oo**, a am**ee**ga

friendly simpático sim**pa**tik**oo**

from de di

when does the next train
from Braga arrive? quando
chega o próximo comboio
de Braga? kw**a**nd**oo** sh**ay**g-**oo**
pr**o**sim**oo** komb**oh**-yo di

from Monday to Friday de
segunda a sexta-feira
di sig**oo**nda-a s**ay**shta f**ay**ra

from next Thursday a partir
da próxima quinta-feira
a part**ee**r da pr**o**sima k**ee**nta f**ay**ra

where are you from? de
onde é? d**ohn**d-**eh**
I'm from Slough sou de
Slough soh di

front a frente fr**ay**nt

in front em frente **ay**ng

in front of the hotel em
frente ao hotel ow

at the front na frente na

frost a geada J-**ya**da

frozen gelado Jil**a**d**oo**

frozen food a comida congelada
koom**ee**da ko**nj**il**a**da

fruit a fruta fr**oo**ta

fruit juice o sumo de fruta
s**oo**moo di fr**oo**ta

fry fritar

frying pan a frigideira fri**j**id**ay**ra

full cheio sh**ay**-oo

it's full of... está cheio de...
shta – di

I'm full (said by man/woman)
estou satisfeito/satisf**ei**ta shtoh
satisf**ay**too

full board a pensão completa
paynso**w**ng kompl**eh**ta

fun: it was fun foi divertido
f**oh**-i divirte**e**doo

funeral o funeral foon**e**ra**l**

funny (strange) estranho shtr**a**n-yoo
(amusing) engraçado
ayngras**a**doo

furniture a mobília
moob**ee**l-ya

further mais longe mī**J** lo**hnj**

it's further down the road
é mais abaixo na rua
ab**ī**shoo na r**oo**-a

how much further is it
to Santarém? quantos
quilómetros faltam para
Santarém? kw**a**ntoosh
kil**o**mitroosh f**a**ltowng –
santar**ay**ng
about 5 kilometres mais ou
menos cinco quilómetros
m**ī**z oh m**ay**noosh s**ee**nkoo

fuse o fusível fooz**ee**vi**l**

the lights have fused as
luzes fundiram-se a**J** l**oo**zish
foond**ee**rowngsi

fuse box a caixa de fusíveis kīsha di foozeevaysh

fuse wire o fio de fusível fee-oo di foozeevil

future o futuro footooroo

    in future no futuro noo

G

gallon o galão galowng

game (cards, match etc) o jogo Johgoo

    (meat) a caça kasa

garage (for fuel) a bomba de gasolina di gazooleena

    (for repairs, parking) a garagem garaJayng

garden o jardim Jardeeng

garlic o alho al-yoo

gas o gás gash

gas cylinder (camping gas) a bilha de gás beel-ya di gash

gasoline (US) a gasolina gazooleena

gas permeable lenses as lentes semi-rígidas layntsh simi-reeJidash

gas station a bomba de gasolina bohmba di gazooleena

gate o portão poortowng

    (at airport) o portão de embarque daymbark

gay o homossexual ohmoosekswal

gay bar o gay bar

gearbox a caixa de velocidades kīsha di viloosidadsh

gear lever a avalanca das mudanças dash moodansash

gears a mudança moodansa

general (adj) geral Jeral

gents (toilet) a casa de banho dos homens kaza di ban-yoo dooz ohmayngsh

genuine (antique etc) genuíno Jinweenoo

German (adj, language) alemão alimowng

German measles a rubéola roobeh-ola

Germany a Alemanha aliman-ya

get (fetch) ir buscar eer

    will you get me another one, please? pode trazer-me outro, por favor? pod trazayrmohtroo poor favohr

    how do I get to...? como vou para...? kohmoo voh

    do you know where I can get this? sabe onde posso comprar isto? sabohnd posoo – eeshtoo

get back (return) voltar

get in (arrive) chegar shigar

get off sair sa-**eer**

where do I get off? onde é
que saio? ohnd**eh** ki s**ī**-yoo

get on (to train etc) apanhar
apan-**yar**

get out (of car etc) sair sa-**eer**

get up (in the morning) levantar-se
livant**ar**si

gift a lembrança laymbr**a**nsa

gift shop a loja de
lembranças l**o**Ja di laymbr**a**nsash

gin o gin Jeeng

a gin and tonic, please um
gin-t**ó**nico por fav**o**r oong Jeeng
tonikoo poor fav**ohr**

girl a rapariga rapar**ee**ga

girlfriend a namor**a**da

give dar

**can you give me some
change?** pode dar-me troco?
pod darmi tr**oh**koo

I gave it to him dei-lhe d**a**yl-yi

will you give this to…? pode
dar isto a…? **ee**shtoo

**how much do you want
for this?** quanto quer
por isto? k**wa**ntoo kehr poor
eeshtoo

20 euros vinte euros
veent ay-**oo**roosh

I'll give you 15 euros dou-
lhe quinze euros d**oh**l-yi
keenz

give back devolver divolv**a**yr

glad contente kont**a**ynt

glass (material) o vidro v**ee**droo

(for drinking) o copo k**o**poo

a glass of wine um copo de
vinho oong – di **vee**n-yoo

glasses os óculos **o**kooloosh

gloves as luvas l**oo**vash

glue a cola k**o**la

go ir eer

**we'd like to go to the
Museu de Arte Antiga**
queremos ir ao Museu de
Arte Antiga kir**a**ymoosh eer ow
moos**ay**-oo dartant**ee**ga

where are you going? onde
vai? ohnd vi

where does this bus go?
p**a**ra onde vai este autocarro?
aysht owtook**a**rroo

let's go! vamos! v**a**moosh

she's gone (left) ele foi-se
embora ayl f**oh**-isaymb**o**ra

where has he gone? onde
ele foi? **oh**ndayl f**oh**-i

I went there last week fui lá
na semana pass**a**da fwee la
na sim**a**na

hamburger to go o
hamburger p**a**ra lev**a**r

go away ir embora eer aymb**o**ra

go away! vá-se embora!
v**a**s-aymb**o**ra

go back (return) volt**a**r

go down (the stairs etc) descer
dish**a**yr

go in entrar aynt**ra**r

go out (in the evening) sair sa-**eer**

**do you want to go out
tonight?** quer sair esta noite?
kehr – **eh**shta n**oh**-it

go through atravessar

go up (the stairs etc) subir soo**beer**

goat a ca**bra**

goat's cheese o queijo de cabra
kay**J**oo di

God Deus **day**-oosh

goggles os óculos protectores
o**koo**loosh proote**toh**rish

gold o ouro **oh**roo

golf o golfe golf

golf course o campo de golfe
kampoo di

good bom bong

good! bem! bayng

it's no good não presta nowng
prehshta

goodbye adeus a**day**-oosh

good evening boa noite b**oh**-a
n**oh**-it

Good Friday Sexta-Feira Santa
sayshta **fay**ra

good morning bom dia bong
dee-a

good night boa noite b**oh**-a
n**oh**-it

goose o ganso **gan**soo

got: we've got to leave temos
que ir **tay**moosh ki-**eer**

have you got any...? tem...?
tayng

government o governo
goo**vayr**noo

gradually gradualmente
gradwal**maynt**

grammar a gramática

gram(me) o grama

granddaughter a neta **neh**ta

grandfather o avô av**oh**

grandmother a avó a**vaw**

grandson o neto **neh**too

grapefruit a toranja too**ran**Ja

grapefruit juice o sumo de
toranja **soo**moo di too**ran**Ja

grapes as uvas **oo**vash

grass a relva **reh**lva

grateful agradecido agradi**see**doo

gravy o molho m**oh**l-yo

great (excellent) óptimo **o**timoo

that's great! isso é optimo!
eesoo eh

a great success um grande
sucesso oong grand soo**seh**soo

Great Britain a Grã-Bretanha
gran bri**tan**-ya

Greece a Grécia gr**ehs**-ya

greedy (for food) glutão gloo**towng**

Greek (adj, language) grego
graygoo

green verde **vayrd**

green card (car insurance) a carta
verde

greengrocer's o lugar loo**gar**

grey cinzento sin**zayn**too

grill o grelhador gril-ya**dohr**

grilled grelhado gril-ya**doo**

grocer's o merceeiro mirs-**yay**roo

ground o chão sh**owng**

on the ground no chão noo

ground floor o rés de chão
rehJ doo

group o grupo gr**oo**poo

guarantee a garantia garan**tee**-a

is it guaranteed? tem
garantia? tayng

guest (*male/female*) o convidado konvida**doo**, a convida**da**

guesthouse a pensão payns**ow**ng

guide (person) a guia g**ee**-a

guidebook o livro-guia l**ee**vroo–

guided tour a excursão com guia shkoors**ow**ng kong

guitar a vi**o**la

gum (in mouth) a gengiva Jen**J**e**e**va

gun a pistola pisht**o**la

gym o ginásio Jin**a**z-yoo

H

hair o cabelo kab**ay**loo

hairbrush a escova de cabelo shk**oh**va di

haircut o corte de cabelo kort

hairdresser's (unisex, women's) o cabeleireiro kabilayr**ay**roo

(men's) o barbeiro barb**ay**roo

hairdryer o secador de cabelo sikad**oh**r di kab**ay**loo

hair gel o gel para o cabelo Jehl p**a**roo

hairgrips a m**o**la para o cabelo

hair spray a l**a**ca

half a metade mit**a**d

half an hour meia hora m**ay**-a **o**ra

half a litre meio litro m**ay**-oo l**ee**troo

about half that mais ou menos metade disto m**ee**z oh m**ay**noosh mit**a**d-d**ee**shtoo

half board a meia pensão m**ay**-a payns**ow**ng

half-bottle a meia garrafa

half fare o meio bilhete m**ay**-oo bil-y**ay**t

half price metade do preço mit**a**d doo pr**ay**soo

ham o fiambre f-y**a**mbr

hamburger o hamburger amb**oo**rger

hammer o martelo mart**eh**loo

hand a mão m**ow**ng

handbag a mala de mão di

handbrake o travão de mão trav**ow**ng

handkerchief o lenço l**ay**nsoo

handle (on door) o fecho f**ay**shoo

(on suitcase etc) a pega p**eh**ga

hand luggage a bagagem de mão bag**a**Jayng

hang-gliding a asa-delta aza-d**eh**lta

hangover a ressaca ris**a**ka

I've got a hangover estou de ressaca shtoh di

happen acontecer akontis**ay**r

what's happening? o que se passa? oo ki si

what has happened? o que aconteceu? oo ki-akoontis**ay**-oo

happy contente kont**ay**nt

I'm not happy about this não estou contente com isso n**ow**ng shtoh – kong **ee**soo

harbour o porto p**oh**rtoo

hard duro d**oo**roo

(difficult) difícil dif**ee**sil

hard-boiled egg o ovo cozido **oh**voo kooz**ee**edoo

hayfever a febre dos fenos
fehbr doosh **fay**noosh

hazelnuts as avelãs avel**a**ngsh

he ele el

head a cabeça kab**ay**sa

headache a dor de cabeça di

headlights o far**o**l

headphones os auscultadores
owshkooltad**oh**rish

health food shop a loja de
produtos naturais l**o**Ja di
prood**oo**toosh natoor**ī**sh

healthy saudável sowd**a**vil

hear ouvir ohv**ee**r

hearing aid o aparelho para a
surdez apar**ayl**-yoo – soord**ay**sh

heart o coração kooras**ow**ng

heart attack o enfarte aynf**a**rt

heat o calor kal**oh**r

heater o aquecedor akesid**oh**r

heating o aquecimento
akesim**ay**ntoo

heavy pesado piz**a**doo

heel (of foot) o calcanhar
kalkan-y**a**r
(of shoe) o s**a**lto

**could you put new
heels on these?**
podia pôr uns saltos

hard lenses as lentes rígidas
l**ay**ntsh r**ee**Jidash

hardly mal
hardly ever quase nunca
kwaz n**oo**nka

hardware shop a loja de
ferragens l**o**Ja di firra**J**ayngsh

hat o chapéu shap**eh**-oo

hate detestar ditisht**a**r

have ter tayr
can I have a...? pode dar-
me...? pod d**a**rmi
do you have...? tem...? tayng
what'll you have? o que vai
tomar? oo ki v**ī** toom**a**r
I have to leave now tenho de
ir agora t**ayn**-yoo deer
do I have to...? tenho de...? di
can we have some...? posso
ter...? p**o**soo tayr

novos? poodee-a pohr oongsh saltoosh novoosh

heelbar o sapateiro rápido sapatayroo rapidoo

height (of person) a altura altoora
(mountain) a altitude altitood

helicopter o helicóptero elikoptiroo

hello olá
(answer on phone) está shta

helmet (for motorcycle) o capacete kapasayt

help a ajuda aJooda
(verb) ajudar
help! socorro! sookohrroo
can you help me? pode ajudar-me? pod – mi
thank you very much for your help (said by man/woman) obrigado/obrigada pela sua ajuda obrigadoo – pila soo-a

helpful prestável preshtavil

hepatitis a hepatite epateet

her: I haven't seen her não a vi nowng a vee
to her para ela ehla
with her com ela kong
for her para ela
that's her é ela eh
that's her towel esta é a toalha dela ehshta-eh – dehla

herbal tea o chá de ervas sha dehrvash

herbs as ervas

here aqui akee
here is/are… aqui está/ estão… shta/shtowng
here you are aqui tem tayng

hers dela dehla
that's hers isso é dela eesoo eh

hey! eh!

hi! (hello) olá! oola

hide esconder shkondayr

high alto altoo

highchair a cadeira de bébé kadayra di bebeh

highway a autoestrada owtooshtrada

hill o monte mohnt

him: I haven't seen him não o vi nowng oo vee
to him para ele ayl
with him com ele kong
for him para ele
that's him é ele eh

hip a anca

hire alugar aloogar
for hire para alugar
where can I hire a bike? onde posso alugar uma bicicleta? ohnd posoo

his: it's his car é o carro dele eh-oo karroo dayl
that's his isto é dele eeshtweh

hit bater batayr

hitch-hike andar à boleia boolay-a

hobby o passatempo –taympoo

hold segurar sigoorar

hole o buraco boorakoo

holiday as férias fehr-yash
on holiday de férias shtoh di

Holland Holanda olanda

home a casa kaza
at home (in my house etc) em casa ayng

(in my country) no meu país
noo **may**-oo pa-**ee**sh

we go home tomorrow
vamos embora amanhã
vamoosh aym**bo**ra aman-yang

honest honesto on**eh**shtoo

honey o mel mehl

honeymoon a lua-de-mel
loo-a di

hood (US: of car) o capot kap**oh**

hope esperar shpir**ar**

I hope so espero que sim
shp**eh**roo ki s**ee**ng

I hope not espero que não
nowng

hopefully: hopefully… espero
que…

horn (of car) a buzina booz**ee**na

horrible horrível ohrr**ee**vil

horse o cavalo kav**a**loo

horse riding andar a cavalo

hospital o hospital oshpit**a**l

hospitality a hospitalidade
oshpitalid**a**d

**thank you for your
hospitality** (said by man/woman)
obrigado/obrigada pela sua
hospitalidade obrig**a**doo – p**i**la
s**oo**-a

hot quente kaynt

(spicy) picante pik**a**nt

I'm hot tenho calor
tayn-yoo kal**oh**r

it's hot today está imenso
calor hoje shta im**ay**nsoo – ohJ

hotel o hotel oht**eh**l

hotel room o quarto de hotel
kwartoo doht**eh**l

hour a hora **o**ra

house a casa k**a**za

house wine o vinho da casa
veen-yoo

how como k**oh**moo

how many? quantos?
kw**a**ntoosh

how do you do? muito
prazer mw**ee**ngtoo praz**ay**r

how are you? como está?
shta

fine, thanks, and you?
(said by man/woman) bem,
obrigado/obrigada, e você?
bayng obrig**a**doo – ee vos**ay**

how much is it? quanto é?
kwantw**eh**

it's 20 euros são vinte euros
sowng veent **ay**-ooroosh

I'll take it vou levar voh

humid húmido **oo**meedoo

hunger a fome fohm

hungry: are you hungry? tens
fome? taynsh

hurry apressar-se apris**ar**si

I'm in a hurry estou com
pressa shtoh kong pr**eh**sa

there's no hurry não há
pressa nowng a

hurry up! despacha-te!
dishp**a**shat

hurt doer dw**ay**r

it really hurts dói-me d**o**ymi

husband o meu marido **may**-oo
mar**ee**doo

hydrofoil o hydroplano idrooplanoo

hypermarket hipermercado eepermerkadoo

I

I eu **ay**-oo

ice gelo Jayloo

with ice com gelo kong

no ice, thanks (said by man/woman) sem gelo, obrigado/obrigada sayng – obrigadoo

ice cream o gelado Jiladoo

ice-cream cone o cone de gelado kohn di

iced coffee o café glacé kafeh glasay

ice lolly o gelado Jiladoo

ice rink o rinque de patinagem reenk di patinaJayng

ice skates os patins de gelo pateenJ di Jayloo

idea a ideia iday-a

idiot o idiota id-yota

if se si

ignition a ignição ignisowng

ill doente dwaynt

I feel ill sinto-me doente seentoomi

illness a doença dwaynsa

imitation (leather etc) a imitação imitasowng

immediately imediatamente imed-yatamaynt

important importante impoortant

it's very important é muito importante eh mweengtoo

it's not important não é importante nowng

impossible impossível impooseevil

impressive impressionante impris-yoonant

improve melhorar mil-yorar

I want to improve my Portuguese quero melhorar o meu português kehroo – oo may-oo poortoogaysh

in: it's in the centre fica no centro feeka noo sayntroo

in my car no meu carro noo may-oo karroo

in Beja em Beja ayng behJa

in two days from now daqui a dois dias dakee a do-iJ dee-ash

in five minutes em cinco minutos ayng seenkoo minootoosh

in May em Maio mī-oo

in English em inglês inglaysh

in Portuguese em português poortoogaysh

is he in? ele está? el shta

inch a polegada pooligada

include incluir inklweer

does that include meals? isso inclui as refeições? eesoo inkloo-i refaysoyngsh

is that included? isso está incluído no preço? shta inklweedoo noo praysoo

inconvenient pouco conveniente pohkoo konvin-yaynt

incredible incrível inkreevil

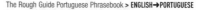

Indian (*adj*) indiano ind-yanoo

indicator o indicador indikad**ohr**

indigestion a indigestão indiJisht**owng**

indoor pool a piscina coberta pish-**see**na koobe**hr**ta

indoors dentro de casa d**a**yntroo di k**a**za, em recinto fechado ayng ris**ee**ntoo fish**a**doo

inexpensive barato bar**a**too

infection a infecção infehs**owng**

infectious infeccioso infehs-y**oh**zoo

inflammation a inflamação inflamas**owng**

informal informal info**o**rmal

information a informação infoormas**owng**

    do you have any information about…? tem alguma informação sobre…? tayng alg**oo**ma – sohbr

information desk o balcão de informações balk**owng** dinfoormas**oy**ngsh

injection a injecção inJehs**owng**

injured ferido fir**ee**doo

    she's been injured ela ficou ferida **eh**la fik**oh** fir**ee**da

in-laws os sogros oosh s**o**groosh

inner tube (for tyre) a câmara de ar k**a**ma-ra dar

innocent inocente inoos**a**ynt

insect o insecto ins**eh**too

insect bite a picada de insecto dins**eh**too

    do you have anything for insect bites? tem alguma

coisa p**a**ra picada de insectos? tayng alg**oo**ma koh-iza – ins**eh**toosh

insect repellent o repele-insectos rip**eh**l ins**eh**toosh

inside dentro d**a**yntroo

    inside the hotel dentro do hotel dwoht**eh**l

    let's sit inside vamos sentar-nos lá dentro v**a**moosh sentar-noosh

insist insistir insisht**eer**

    I insist insisto ins**ee**shtoo

insomnia a insónia ins**o**n-ya

instant coffee o café instantâneo kaf**eh** inshtant**a**n-yoo

instead em vez ayng vaysh

    give me that one instead dê-me antes aquele daym antsh ak**a**yl

    instead of… em vez de… di

insulin a insulina insool**ee**na

insurance o seguro sig**oo**roo

intelligent inteligente intili**J**aynt

interested: I'm interested in… (said by a man/woman) estou muito interessado/interessada em… shtoh mw**ee**ngtoo intris**a**doo – ayng

interesting interessante intris**a**nt

    that's very interesting isso é muito interessante **ee**soo eh mw**ee**ngtoo

international internacional intayrnas-yoonal

Internet Internet intirn**eh**t

interpret interpretar interprit**a**r

interpreter (*male/female*) o/a
intérprete int**eh**rprit

intersection o cruzamento
kroozam**ay**ntoo

interval (at theatre) o intervalo
interv**a**loo

into p**a**ra

  I'm not into... não me
  interesso por... nowng
  mintr**eh**soo poor

introduce apresentar aprizent**a**r

  may I introduce...? posso
  apresentar... p**o**soo

invitation o convite konv**ee**t

invite convidar konvid**a**r

Ireland a Irlanda eerl**a**nda

Irish irlandês eerland**ay**sh

  I'm Irish (*male/female*) sou
  irlandês/sou irlandesa soh –
  eerland**ay**za

iron (for ironing) o ferro de
engomar f**eh**rroo dayngoom**a**r

  can you iron these for me?
  pode engomar-me isto?
  pod ayngoom**a**rm **ee**shtoo

is é eh; está shta (*see note on p.8*)

island a ilha **ee**l-ya

it o oo, *f* a

  it is... é... eh; está... shta

  is it...? é...?; está...?

  where is it? onde é?
  ohnd**eh**; onde está?

  it's him é ele ayl

  it was... era... **eh**ra; estava...
  sht**a**va

Italian (*adj*, language) italiano
ital-y**a**noo

Italy Itália ital-ya

itch: it itches faz comichão
fash koomish**ow**ng

jack (for car) o macaco mak**a**koo

jacket o casaco kaz**a**koo

jam a comp**o**ta

jammed: it's jammed
está encravado shta aynkrav**a**doo

January Janeiro Jan**ay**roo

jar o j**a**rro

jaw a maxila maks**ee**la

jazz o jazz

jealous ciumento s-yoom**ay**ntoo

jeans os jeans

jellyfish a alforreca
alfoorr**eh**ka

jersey a camisola kamiz**o**la

jetty o pontão pont**ow**ng

jeweller's a ourivesaria
ohrivezar**ee**-a

jewellery a joalharia Jwal-yar**ee**-a

Jewish judaico Jood**ee**koo

job o emprego aympr**ay**goo

jogging o jogging

  to go jogging pratic**a**r
  jogging

joke a piada p-y**a**da

journey a viagem v-yaJayng

  have a good journey!
  boa viagem! b**oh**-a

jug o jarro J**a**rroo

  a jug of water um jarro de
  água oong – d**a**gwa

juice o sumo soomoo

July Julho Jool-yoo

jump pular poolar

jumper a camisola kamizola

jump leads os cabos para ligar a bateria kaboosh – batiree-a

junction o cruzamento kroozamayntoo

June Junho Joon-yoo

just (only) só saw

    just two só dois/duas

    just for me só para mim meeng

    just here aqui mesmo akee mayJmoo

    not just now agora não nowng

    we've just arrived acabámos de chegar akabamooJ di shigar

K

keep guardar gwardar

    keep the change guarde o troco gward oo trohkoo

    can I keep it? posso ficar com ele/ela? posoo fikar kong ayl/**eh**la

    you can keep it pode ficar com ele/ela pod

ketchup o ketchup

kettle a chaleira shalayra

key a chave shav

    the key for room 201, please a chave do quarto duzentos e um, faz favor doo kwartoo doozayntooz-yoong fash favohr

keyring o chaveiro shavayroo

kidneys (in body, food) os rins reengsh

kill matar

kilo o quilo keeloo

kilometre o quilómetro kilomitroo

    how many kilometres is it to…? quantos quilómetros são até…? kwantoosh kilomitroosh sowng ateh

kind (generous) amável

    that's very kind é muito amável eh mweengtoo

---

which kind do you want? que tipo deseja? ki teepoo disayJa

I want this/that kind desejo este/aquele tipo aysht/akayl

---

king o rei ray

kiosk o quiosque k-yoshk

kiss o beijo bayJoo

    (verb) beijar bayJar

kitchen a cozinha koozeen-ya

kitchenette a cozinha pequena pikayna

Kleenex os lenços de papel laynsoosh di papehl

knee o joelho Jwayl-yoo

knickers as cuecas de mulher ash kwehkaJ di mool-yehr

knife a faca faka

knock bater batayr

knock down atropelar atropilar

he's been knocked down ele foi atropelado *el foh-i atropiladoo*

knock over (object) derrubar *dirroobar*

(pedestrian) atropelar *atropilar*

know (somebody, a place) conhecer *koon-yisair*

(something) saber

I don't know não sei *nowng say*

I didn't know that não sabia isso *nowng sabee-a eesoo*

do you know where I can find...? sabe onde posso encontrar...? *sabohnd poswaynkontrar*

L

label (on clothes) a etiqueta *etikayta*

(on bottles etc) o rótulo *rotooloo*

ladies' room, ladies' (toilets) o quarto de banho das senhoras *kwartoo di ban-yoo dash sin-yorash*

ladies' wear a roupa de senhoras *rohpa di*

lady a senhora *sin-yora*

lager a cerveja *sirvay-Ja*

lake o lago *lagoo*

lamb (meat) o borrego *boorraygoo*

lamp o candeeiro *kand-yayroo*

lane (motorway) a faixa *fisha*

(small road) a viela *v-yehla*

language a língua *leengwa*

language course o curso de línguas *koorsoo di leengwash*

laptop o laptop

large grande *grand*

last o último *ooltimoo*

last week semana passada *simana*

last Friday sexta-feira passada *sayshta-fayra*

last night ontem à noite *ohntayng a noh-it*

what time is the last train to Fátima? a que horas parte o último comboio para Fátima? *kyorash part-yoo-ooltimoo komboh-yo*

late tarde *tard*

sorry I'm late desculpe o atraso *dishkoolp oo atrazoo*

the train was late o comboio estava atrasado *oo komboh-yo shtava atrazadoo*

we must go – we'll be late temos que ir – vamos atrasar-nos *taymoosh ki-eer – vamooz-atrazar noosh*

it's getting late está a ficar tarde *shta-a fikar*

later, later on mais tarde *mīsh*

I'll come back later volto mais tarde *voltoo*

see you later até logo *a-teh*

latest o último *ooltimoo*

by Wednesday at the latest quarta-feira o mais tardar *kwarta-fayra oo mīsh*

laugh rir *reer*

launderette a lavandaria automática lavanda**ree**-a owtoom**a**tika

laundromat a lavandaria automática lavanda**ree**-a owtoom**a**tika

> Travel tip Small pensions don't really like you doing your laundry in your room and hotel laundry services are usually pretty expensive, so you're better off taking your clothes to the local *lavandaria*, where you can get them washed, dried and even ironed at a very reasonable cost (they usually charge by weight).

laundry (clothes) a roupa para lavar **roh**pa

(place) a lavandaria lavanda**ree**-a

lavatory os lavabos lav**a**boosh

law a lei lay

lawn o relvado relv**a**doo

lawyer (*male/female*) o advogado advoog**a**doo, a advog**a**da

laxative o laxativo lashat**ee**voo

lazy preguiçoso prigis**oh**zoo

lead (electrical) o fio **fee**-oo

(*verb*) conduzir kondoo**zeer**

where does this lead to? onde vai ter esta estrada? ohnd vī tayr **eh**shta sht**ra**da

leaf a folha **foh**l-ya

leaflet o panfleto panfl**ay**too

leak a fuga f**oo**ga

(*verb*) ter uma fuga tayr **oo**ma

the roof leaks há uma fuga de água no telhado a – d**a**gwa noo til-y**a**doo

learn aprender apraynd**ay**r

least: not in the least de nenhum modo di nin-**yoo**ng m**o**doo

at least pelo menos p**i**loo m**a**ynoosh

leather o cabedal kabid**a**l

leave (depart) partir part**ee**r

(behind) deixar daysh**a**r

I am leaving tomorrow parto amanhã p**a**rtoo aman-y**a**ng

he left yesterday ele partiu ontem ayl part**ee**-oo **oh**ntayng

may I leave this here? posso deixar isto aqui? p**o**soo – eesh**t**wak**ee**

I left my coat in the bar deixei meu casaco no bar daysh**ay** m**a**y-oo kaz**a**koo noo

when does the bus for Lagos leave? quando parte o autocarro para Lagos? kw**a**ndoo p**a**rtoo owtook**a**rroo – l**a**goosh

leeks o alho francês **a**l-yoo frans**ay**sh

left esquerdo shk**a**yrdoo

on the left, to the left à esquerda a shk**a**yrda

turn left vire à esquerda v**ee**ra

there's none left não há mais nowng a m**ī**sh

left-handed canhoto kan-y**oh**too

left luggage (office) o depósito de bagagem dip**o**zitoo di bag**a**jayng

leg a perna pe**hr**na
lemon o limão li**mow**ng
lemonade a limonada limoo**na**da
lemon tea o chá de limão sha di li**mow**ng
lend emprestar aymprish**tar**

  will you lend me your...? empresta-me o seu...? aympre**h**shtamoo **say**-oo

lens (of camera) a objectiva obJe**tee**va
lesbian a lésbica le**h**Jbika
less menos **may**nosh

  less than menos do que doo ki
  less expensive mais barato m
īJ ba**ra**too

lesson a lição li**sow**ng
let (allow) deixar day**shar**

  will you let me know? diz-me depois? **dee**Jmi dip**oh**-ish
  I'll let you know depois digo-lhe **dee**gool-yi
  let's go for something to eat vamos sair p**a**ra comer alguma coisa v**a**moosh sa-**eer** – koom**ayr** alg**oo**ma k**oh**-iza

let off: will you let me off at...? é capaz de par**ar** em...? eh kap**a**J di – **ayng**

letter a c**a**rta

  do you have any letters for me? tem alguma c**a**rta p**a**ra mim? tayng alg**oo**ma – meeng

letterbox o m**a**rco de correio **ma**rkoo di koor**ay**-oo
lettuce a **a**lface **a**lfas
lever a alav**a**nca
library a biblioteca bibl-yoot**eh**ka

licence a licença lis**ay**nsa
lid a t**a**mpa
lie (verb: tell untruth) mentir maynt**eer**

  lie down deitar-se day**tar**si

life a vida v**ee**da
lifebelt o cinto de salvação s**ee**ntoo di salvas**ow**ng
lifeguard o banheiro ban-**yay**roo
life jacket o colete de salvação kool**ay**t di salvas**ow**ng
lift (in building) o elevador elevad**oh**r

  could you give me a lift? pode dar-me uma boleia? pod dar**moo**ma bool**ay**-a
  would you like a lift? quer uma boleia? kehr

light a luz loosh
(not heavy) leve lehv

  do you have a light? (for cigarette) tem lume? tayng loom
  light green verde claro v**ay**rd kl**a**roo

light bulb a l**â**mpada

  I need a new light bulb preciso duma l**â**mpada pris**ee**zoo d**oo**ma

lighter (cigarette) o isqueiro shk**ay**roo
lightning a trovoada troov**wa**da
like gostar goosh**tar**

  I like it gosto g**o**shtoo
  I like going for walks gosto de passear a pé di pas-**yar** a peh
  I like you gosto de si di see
  I don't like it não gosto nowng

do you like…? você gosta de…? vo**say** go**sh**ta di

I'd like a beer queria uma cerveja ki**ree**-a **oo**ma sir**vay**ja

I'd like to go swimming queria ir nadar eer

would you like a drink? gostaria duma bebida? goo**sh**ta**ree**-a d**oo**ma bi**bee**da

would you like to go for a walk? quer ir dar uma v**o**lta? kehr

what's it like? como é? k**oh**moo eh

I want one like this quero um como este **keh**roo oong kohm**way**sht

lime a lima **lee**ma

lime cordial o sumo de lima s**oo**moo di

line a linha l**ee**n-ya

  could you give me an outside line? dá-me uma linha? dam**oo**ma

lips os lábios l**a**b-yoosh

lip salve o baton p**a**ra o cieiro bat**o**ng – oo s-y**ay**roo

lipstick o baton bat**o**ng

liqueur o licor lik**oh**r

Lisbon Lisboa li**zboh**-a

listen escutar shk**oo**tar

litre o litro l**ee**troo

  a litre of white wine um litro de vinho branco di v**ee**n-yoo br**a**nkoo

little pequeno pik**ay**noo

  just a little, thanks só um pouco, por favor saw oong p**oh**koo poor fav**oh**r

a little milk pouco leite layt

a little bit more um pouquinho mais oong poh**kee**n-yoo mīsh

live (verb) viver viv**ay**r

  we live together vivemos juntos viv**ay**mooJ J**oo**ntoosh

where do you live? onde é que vive? ohnd**eh** ki veev

I live in London vivo em Londres **vee**vwayng l**oh**ndrish

lively animado anim**a**doo

liver (in body, food) o fígado f**ee**gadoo

loaf o pão powng

lobby (in hotel) o hall

lobster a lagosta lag**oh**shta

local local look**a**l

  can you recommend a local wine? pode recomendar um vinho da região? pod rikoomaynd**a**r oong v**ee**n-yoo da ri**J**-y**ow**ng

  can you recommend a local restaurant? pode recomendar um restaurante local? risht**a**wr**a**nt

lock a fechadura fishad**oo**ra

  (verb) fechar à chave fish**a**r a shav

  it's locked está fechado à chave shta fish**a**dwa shav

lock out: I've locked myself out (of room) fechei o quarto com a chave lá dentro fish**ay** oo kw**a**rtoo kong – d**ay**ntroo

locker (for luggage etc) o cacifo kas**ee**foo

lollipop o chupa-chupa sh**oo**pa–

London Londres l**oh**ndrish

long comprido kompr**ee**doo

how long will it take to fix it? quanto tempo vai demorar para consertar? kw**a**ntoo t**a**ympoo vī dimoor**a**r – konsirt**a**r

how long does it take? quanto tempo demora? dim**o**ra

a long time muito tempo mw**ee**ngtoo

one day/two days longer mais um dia/dois dias mīz oong d**ee**-a/do-iJ d**ee**-ash

long-distance call a chamada de l**o**nga distância sham**a**da di – dishtans-ya

look: I'm just looking, thanks (said by man/woman) estou só a ver, obrigado/obrigada shtoh saw a v**a**yr obrig**a**doo

you don't look well parece não estar bem par**eh**s nowng shtar b**a**yng

look out! cuidado! kwid**a**doo

can I have a look? posso ver? p**o**soo v**a**yr

look after tomar conta (de) toom**a**r k**oh**nta

look at olhar (para) ol-y**a**r

look for procurar prookoor**a**r

I'm looking for... procuro... prook**oo**roo

loose (handle etc) solto s**oh**ltoo

lorry o camião kam-y**ow**ng

lose perder pird**a**yr

I've lost my way perdi-me pird**ee**m

I'm lost, I want to get to... (said by man/woman) estou perdido/perdida, quero ir para... shtoh pird**ee**doo – k**eh**roo eer

I've lost my bag perdi o meu saco pird**ee** oo m**a**y-oo s**a**koo

lost property (office) a secção de perdidos e achados

sehks**ow**ng di pird**ee**dooz
ee-ash**a**doosh

lot: a lot, lots muito mw**ee**ngtoo

not a lot não muito n**ow**ng

a lot of people muita gente
mw**ee**ngta J**ay**ngt

a lot bigger muito maior
mī-**or**

I like it a lot gosto imenso
g**o**shtoo im**ay**nsoo

lotion a loção loos**ow**ng

loud alto **a**ltoo

lounge (in house, hotel) a sala
(in airport) a sala de espera
dishp**eh**ra

love o amor am**oh**r
(*verb*) am**a**r

I love Portugal adoro
Portugal ad**o**roo poort**o**gal

lovely (meal, food) delicioso dilis-
y**oh**zoo
(view) encantador aynkantad**oh**r
(weather) excelente ish-sil**ay**nt
(present) ador**á**vil

low baixo b**ī**shoo

luck a sorte sort

good luck! boa sorte! b**oh**-a

luggage a bagagem bag**a**Jayng

luggage trolley o carrinho de
bagagem karr**ee**n-yoo di

lump (on body) o inchaço insh**a**soo

lunch o almoço alm**oh**soo

lungs os pulmões poolm**oy**ngsh

luxurious (hotel, furnishings)
luxuoso loosh-w**oh**zoo

luxury o luxo l**oo**shoo

machine a máquina m**a**kina

mad (insane) doido d**oh**-idoo
(angry) zangado zang**a**doo

Madeira (place) a Madeira
mad**ay**ra
(wine) o (vinho da) Madeira
v**ee**n-yoo

magazine a revista riv**ee**shta

maid (in hotel) a criada kr-y**a**da

maiden name o nome de
solteira nohm di soolt**ay**ra

mail o correio koorr**ay**-oo
(*verb*) pôr no correio pohr noo

is there any mail for me?
há algum correio para mim? a
alg**oo**m – meeng

mailbox o marco de correio
markoo di koor**ay**-oo, a caixa do
correio k**ī**sha doo

main principal prins**i**pal

main course o prato principal
pr**a**too prins**i**pal

main post office a central de
correios sentr**a**l di koorr**ay**-oosh

main road (in town) a rua
principal r**oo**-a prins**i**pal
(in country) a estrada principal
shtr**a**da

mains switch o disjuntor
principal diJoont**oh**r

make (brand name) a marca
(*verb*) fazer faz**ay**r

I make it 50 euros calculo
que sejam cinquenta euros

kalk**oo**loo ki s**ay**Jowng sinkw**ay**nta **ay**-ooroosh

what is it made of? de que é feito? di k-yeh f**ay**too

make-up a maquilhagem makil-y**a**Jayng

man o homem **oh**mayng

manager o gerente Jer**ay**nt

can I see the manager? pode chamar o gerente? pod shamar

manageress a gerente

manual manual manw**a**l

many muitos mw**ee**ngtoosh

not many não muitos n**ow**ng

map o mapa

March Março m**a**rsoo

margarine a margarina margar**ee**na

market o mercado mirk**a**doo

> Travel tip A town's municipal market is the place to buy meat, fish, fruit, veg and bread. In larger towns they are open daily (not Sunday), usually from 7 or 8 a.m. until lunchtime; smaller towns might have a market just once or twice a week.

marmalade a comp**o**ta de laranja di lar**a**nJa

married: I'm married (said by a man/woman) sou casado/cas**a**da soh kaz**a**doo

are you married? você é casado/casada? vos**ay** eh

mascara o rímel r**ee**mil

match (football etc) o jogo J**oh**goo

matches os fósforos f**osh**fooroosh

material (fabric) o tecido tis**ee**doo

matter: it doesn't matter não faz mal n**ow**ng faJ mal

what's the matter? o que se p**a**ssa? oo ki si

mattress o colchão koolsh**ow**ng

May Maio m**ī**-oo

may: may I have another one? (different one) pode dar-me outro/**ou**tra? pod d**a**rmi **oh**troo

may I come in? posso entrar? p**o**swayntrar

may I see it? posso vê-lo/vê-la? p**o**soo v**ay**loo/v**ay**la

may I sit here? posso sentar-me aqui? p**o**soo saynt**a**rm ak**ee**

maybe talvez talv**ay**sh

mayonnaise a maionese mi-on**eh**z

me mim meeng

that's for me isto é para mim **ee**shtweh p**a**ra meeng

send it to me envie-o/a para mim aynv**ee**-yoo

me too eu também **ay**-oo tamb**ay**ng

meal a refeição rifays**ow**ng

did you enjoy your meal? gostou da comida? goosht**oh** da koom**ee**da

it was excellent, thank you (said by man/woman) estava excelente, obrigado/obrigada sht**a**va ish-sel**ay**nt obrig**a**doo

mean: what do you mean? o
que quer dizer? oo ki kehr diz**ayr**

**what does this word
mean?** o que significa esta
palavra? oo ki signif**ee**ka
ehshta

it means… in English
significa… em inglês
ayng ingl**ay**sh

measles o sarampo sar**a**mpoo

meat a carne karn

mechanic o mecânico
mek**a**nikoo

medicine o remédio rim**eh**d-yoo

Mediterranean o Mediterrâneo
miditirr**a**n-yoo

medium médio m**eh**d-yoo

medium-dry meio seco m**ay**-oo
s**ay**koo

medium-rare médio m**eh**d-yoo

medium-sized de tamanho
médio di tam**a**n-yoo

meet encontrar aynkontr**a**r

nice to meet you muito
prazer mw**ee**ngtoo praz**ayr**

where shall I meet you?
onde nos encontramos?
ohnd noozaynkontr**a**moosh

meeting a reunião r-yoon-y**ow**ng

meeting place o local de
encontro look**a**l daynk**oh**ntroo

melon o melão mil**ow**ng

memory stick a pen

men os homens **oh**mayngsh

mend consertar konsirt**a**r

could you mend this for

me? pode consertar-me isto?
pod konsirt**a**rm **ee**shtoo

menswear a roupa de homens
r**oh**pa d**oh**mayngsh

mention mencionar mayns-yoon**a**r

don't mention it não tem de
quê nowng tayng di kay

menu a ementa em**ay**nta

**may I see the menu,
please?** posso ver a ementa,
faz favor p**o**soo vayr im**ay**nta
fash fav**ohr**

see **menu reader**

message o recado rik**a**doo

**are there any messages
for me?** há algum recado para
mim? a alg**oo**ng – meeng

**I want to leave a message
for…** gostava de deixar um
recado para… g**oo**sht**a**va di
daysh**a**r oong

metal o metal mit**a**l

metre o metro m**eh**troo

microwave (oven) microondas
mikroo-**oh**ndash

midday o meio-dia m**ay**-oo d**ee**-a

at midday ao meio-dia ow

middle: in the middle no meio
noo m**ay**-oo

in the middle of the night
no meio da noite n**oh**-it

the middle one o/a do meio
oo/a doo

midnight a meia-noite m**ay**-a
n**oh**-it

at midnight à meia-noite

might: I might go pode ser que
eu vá pod sayr ki-**ay**-oo

I might not go pode ser que eu não vá *nowng*

I might want to stay another day sou capaz de querer ficar mais um dia *soh kapaJ di kirayr fikar mish oong dee-a*

migraine a enxaqueca *aynshakayka*

mild (taste) suave *swav*

(weather) ameno *amaynoo*

mile a milha *meel-ya*

milk o leite *layt*

milkshake o batido *bateedoo*

millimetre o milímetro *mileemitroo*

minced meat a carne picada *karn pikada*

mind: never mind não faz mal *nowng faJ mal*

I've changed my mind mudei de ideias *mooday diday-yash*

do you mind if I open the window? importa-se se abrir a janela? *importasi s-yabreer a Janehla*

no, I don't mind não, não me importo *nowng mimportoo*

mine: it's mine é meu *eh may-oo*

mineral water a água mineral *agwa*

mints as pastilhas de mentol *pashteel-yaJ di*

minute o minuto *minootoo*

in a minute dentro de um momento *dayntroo doong moomayntoo*

just a minute um momento *oong*

mirror o espelho *shpayl-yoo*

Miss a Senhora *sin-yora*

Miss! se faz favor! *si fash favohr*

miss: I missed the bus perdi o autocarro *pirdee oo-owtookarro*

missing falta

there's a suitcase missing falta uma mala *ooma*

mist a névoa *nehvwa*

mistake o erro *ayrroo*

I think there's a mistake julgo que há um erro *Joolgoo k-ya oong*

sorry, I've made a mistake desculpe, enganei-me *dishkoolp aynganaym*

misunderstanding o mal-entendido *malayntayndeedoo*

mix-up: sorry, there's been a mix-up desculpe, houve uma confusão *ohvooma konfoozowng*

mobile phone o telemóvel *telemovil*

modern moderno *moodehrnoo*

modern art gallery a galeria de arte moderna *galiree-a dart moodehrna*

moisturizer o creme hidratante *kraymeedratant*

moment: I won't be a moment não demoro nada *nowng dimoroo*

monastery o mosteiro mooshtayroo

Monday segunda-feira segoonda fayra

money o dinheiro deen-yayroo

month o mês maysh

monument o monumento moonoomayntoo

moon a lua loo-a

Moor o mouro moh-ooroo

Moorish mourisco moreeshkoo

moped a motorizada mootoorizada

more mais mïsh

  can I have some more water, please? mais água, por favor mïz agwa poor favohr

  more expensive mais caro maïsh karoo

  more interesting mais interessante mïzintrisant

  more than 50 mais de cinquenta mïz di sinkwaynta

  more than that mais do que isso mïz doo ki eesoo

  a lot more muito mais mweengtoo mïsh

would you like some more? deseja um pouco mais? disayJa oong pohkoo mïsh

no, no more for me, thanks (said by man/woman) não, não mais para mim, obrigado/obrigada nowng – meeng obrigadoo

how about you? e você? ee vosay

I don't want any more, thanks (said by man/woman) não quero mais, obrigado/obrigada nowng kehroo mïsh

morning a manhã man-yang

  this morning esta manhã ehshta

  in the morning de manhã di

Morocco o Marrocos marrokoosh

mosquito o mosquito mooshkeetoo

mosquito repellent o repele-mosquitos ripehl mooshkeetoosh

most: I like this one most of all gosto mais deste goshtoo mïJ daysht

  most of the time a maior parte do tempo a mï-or part doo taympoo

  most tourists a maioria dos turistas mï-ooree-a doosh tooreeshtash

mostly principalmente prinsipalmaynt

mother a mãe mayng

motorbike a motocicleta mootoosiklehta

motorboat o barco a motor barkwa mootohr

motorway a autoestrada owtooshtrada

mountain a montanha montan-ya

  in the mountains nas montanhas naJ montan-yash

mountaineering o alpinismo alpineeJmoo

mouse o rato ratoo

moustache o bigode big**o**d

mouth a boca b**oh**ka

mouth ulcer a **a**fta

move (one's car, house etc) mudar
mood**a**r

> **he's moved to another
> room** mudou-se para outra
> sala mood**oh**si para **oh**tra

> **could you move your car?**
> podia mudar o s**eu** c**a**rro?
> pood**ee**-a

> **could you move up a little?**
> pode chegar um pouquinho
> p**a**ra lá? pod shig**a**r oong
> pohk**ee**n-yoo

> **where has it moved to?**
> p**a**ra onde se mudou? **oh**ndsi
> mood**oh**

movie o filme feelm

movie theater o cinema sin**ay**ma

MP3 format o formato MP3
form**a**too ehm-pay-traysh

Mr o Senhor sin-y**oh**r

Mrs a Senhora sin-y**o**ra

much muito mw**ee**ngtoo

> **much better/worse** muito
> melhor/pior mil-y**o**r/pi-**o**r

> **much hotter** muito mais
> quente m**ī**sh k**ay**nt

> **not (very) much** não muito
> n**o**wng

> **I don't want very much** não
> quero muito k**eh**roo

mud a l**a**ma

mug (for drinking) a caneca kan**eh**ka

> **I've been mugged** (said by
> man/woman) fui assaltado/
> assalt**a**da fwee asalt**a**doo

mum a mamã mam**a**ng

mumps a papeira pap**ay**ra

museum o museu mooz**ay**-oo

> **Travel tip** Museums,
> churches and monuments
> usually open from 10am
> to 12.30 p.m. and 2/2.30
> p.m. to 6 p.m., though
> the larger ones stay open
> through lunchtime. Almost all
> museums and monuments,
> however, are closed on
> Mondays (or Wednesdays
> for palaces), as well as on
> public holidays. Entry is fairly
> inexpensive, but it pays to
> take along any student or
> youth discount cards you
> may be entitled to.

mushrooms os cogumelos
kogoom**eh**loosh

music a música m**oo**zika

musician (man) o músico
m**oo**zikoo

Muslim (adj) muçulmano
moosoolm**a**noo

mussels os mexilhões
mishil-y**oy**ngsh

must: I must... tenho de...
t**ay**n-yoo di

> **I mustn't drink alcohol** não
> devo beber álcool nowng d**ay**voo
> bib**ay**r **a**lko-ol

mustard a mostarda moosht**a**rda

my o meu m**ay**-oo, a minha m**ee**n-
ya; (pl) os meus m**ay**-oosh, as
minhas m**ee**n-yash

myself: I'll do it myself (said by
man/woman) eu mesmo/m**e**sma

faço isso **ay**-oo may**J**moo – fa**s**oo **ee**soo

by myself (said by man/woman) sozinho so**z**een-yoo/sozinha

N

nail (finger) a unha **oo**n-ya

(metal) o prego **preh**goo

nailbrush a escova de unhas sh**koh**va **doo**n-yash

nail varnish o verniz de unhas vir**nee**J **doo**n-yash

name o nome nohm

my name's John o meu nome é John oo **may**-oo nohm eh

what's your name? como se chama? **koh**moo si **sha**ma

what is the name of this street? qual é o nome desta rua? kawl**eh** oo nohm d**eh**shta **roo**-a

napkin o guardanapo gwarda**na**poo

nappy a fralda

narrow (street) estreito sh**tray**too

nasty (person) mau mow, *f* má

(weather, accident) grave grav

national nacional nas-yoo**nal**

nationality a nacionalidade nas-yoonali**da**de

natural natural na**too**ral

nausea as náuseas **now**z-yash

navy (blue) azul-marinho a**zool** mar**een**-yoo

near perto **peh**rtoo

is it near the city centre? é perto do centro da cidade? eh – doo **say**ntroo da si**dad**

do you go near the Paço Real? passa perto do Passo Real? **peh**rtoo doo **pa**soo ri-**al**

where is the nearest...? onde fica o/a... mais próximo/ próxima...? ohnd **fee**ka oo/a... mish **pro**simoo

nearby perto daqui pe**hr**too da**kee**

nearly quase kwaz

necessary necessário nisi**sar**-yoo

neck o pescoço pish**koh**soo

necklace o colar koo**lar**

necktie a gravata gra**va**ta

need: I need... preciso de... pris**ee**zoo di

do I need to pay? preciso de pag**ar**?

needle a agulha ag**ool**-ya

neither: neither (one) of them nenhum deles nin-**yoo**ng **day**lish

neither... nor... nem... nem... nayng

nephew o sobrinho soo**breen**-yoo

net (in sport) a rede rayd

Netherlands a Holanda o**lan**da

network map o mapa **ma**pa

never nunca **noo**nka

new novo n**oh**voo

news (radio, TV etc) as notícias
noot**ee**s-yash

newsagent's a tabacaria
tabak**ar**ee-a

newspaper o jornal Joorn**al**

newspaper kiosk o quiosque de
jornais k-y**osh**k di Joorn**i**sh

New Year Ano Novo **a**noo n**oh**voo

Happy New Year! Feliz Ano
Novo! fil**ee**z **a**noo n**oh**voo

New Year's Eve a véspera do
dia de Ano Novo v**eh**shpira doo
d**ee**-a d**a**noo

New Zealand Nova Zelândia
n**o**va zil**a**nd-ya

**New Zealander: I'm a New
Zealander** (*male/female*) sou
neo-zelandês/neo-zelandesa
soh n**eh**-o zil**a**nd**ay**sh/n**eh**-o
zil**a**nd**ay**za

next próximo pr**o**simoo

**the next corner/street on
the left** a próxima esquina/
rua à esquerda shk**ee**na/r**oo**-a a
shk**ay**rda

at the next stop na próxima
paragem par**a**Jayng

next week na próxima
semana sim**a**na

next to próximo de di

nice (food, person) agrad**á**vel

(looks, view etc) bonito
boon**ee**too

niece a sobrinha soobr**ee**n-ya

night a noite n**oh**-it

at night à noite

good night boa noite b**oh**-a

**do you have a single
room for one night?**
tem um quarto individual
para uma noite? t**ayn**-yoong
kw**a**rtwindiv**i**dwal para **oo**ma

yes, madam sim, senhora
seeng sin-y**o**ra

how much is it per night?
quanto é por noite?
kw**a**ntw**eh** poor

it's 35 euros for one night
são trinta e cinco euros por
uma noite sowng tr**ee**nti-
s**ee**nkoo **ay**-ooroosh poor **oo**ma

thank you, I'll take it (said
by man/woman) obrigado/
obrig**a**da, fico com ele
obrig**a**doo – f**ee**koo kong ayl

---

nightclub a boite bwat

nightdress a camisa de dormir
kam**ee**za di doorm**ee**r

night porter o porteiro da noite
poort**ay**roo da n**oh**-it

no não nowng

I've no change não tenho
troco t**ay**n-yoo tr**oh**koo

there's no... left não há
mais... a m**i**sh

no way! de maneira
nenhuma! di man**ay**ra
nin-y**oo**ma

oh no! (upset) oh não! nowng

nobody ninguém ning**ayng**

there's nobody there não há
ninguém lá nowng a – l**a**

noise o barulho bar**oo**l-yoo

noisy: it's too noisy é

barulhento demais eh
barool-**yay**ntoo dim**ī**sh

non-alcoholic não alcoólico
nowng alk**wo**likoo

none nenhum nin-**yoo**ng

nonsmoking carriage
a carruagem **p**ara não
fumadores karrwa**J**ayng – nowng
foomad**oh**rish

noon o meio-dia **may**-oo d**ee**-a

no-one ninguém ning**ay**ng

nor: nor do I nem eu nayng **ay**-oo

normal normal

north o n**o**rte nort

in the north no norte noo

to the north ao norte ow

north of Braga ao norte de
Br**a**ga di

northeast o nordeste noord**eh**sht

northern setentrional
set**ay**ntr-yoon**al**

Northern Ireland a Irlanda do
Norte eerl**a**nda doo nort

northwest o noroeste norw**eh**sht

Norway a Noruega noorw**eh**ga

Norwegian (*adj*) noruguês
noorweg**ay**sh

nose o nariz nar**ee**sh

nosebleed a hemorragia nasal
emoorra**J**ee-ya naz**al**

not não nowng

no, I'm not hungry não, não
tenho fome t**ay**n-yoo fohm

**I don't want anything,
thank you** (said by man/woman)
não quero n**a**da, obrig**a**do/
obrig**a**da k**eh**roo – obrig**a**doo

it's not necessary não é
necessário eh nese**sa**r-yoo

I didn't know that não sabia
sab**ee**-a

not that one – this one esse
não – este ays – aysht

note (banknote) a n**o**ta

notebook o bloco de
apontamentos bl**o**koo
dapontam**ay**ntoosh

notepaper (for letters) o papel de
c**a**rta pap**eh**l di

nothing n**a**da

nothing for me, thanks
(said by man/woman) nada p**a**ra

mim, obrigado/obrigada meeng
obrigadoo

nothing else mais nada mīʃ

novel o romance roomans

November Novembro
noovaymbroo

now agora

number o número noomiroo

I've got the wrong number
enganei-me no número
aynganaym noo

**what is your phone
number?** qual é o número do
seu telefone? kwaleh oo – doo
say-oo telefohn

number plate a chapa da
matrícula shapa da matreekoola

nurse (*male/female*) o enfermeiro
aynfirmayroo, a enfermeira

nut (for bolt) a porca

nuts a noz nosh

O

occupied (toilet, telephone)
ocupado okoopadoo

o'clock horas orash

October Outubro ohtoobroo

odd (strange) estranho shtran-yoo

of de di

off (lights) desligado diʃligadoo

**it's just off Praça do
Comércio** mesmo ao lado da
Praça do Comércio meʃmoo ow
ladoo da prasa doo koomehrs-yoo

we're off tomorrow partimos
amanhã parteemoozaman-yang

offensive (language, behaviour)
ofensivo ofaynseevoo

office (place of work) o escritório
shkritor-yoo

officer (said to policeman) Senhor
Guarda sin-yohr gwarda

often muitas vezes
mweengtaʃ vayzish

not often não muitas vezes
nowng

how often are the buses?
com que frequência há
autocarros? kong ki frikwaynsya
a owtookarroosh

oil (for car, for cooking) o óleo ol-yoo

ointment a pomada
poomada

OK está bem shta bayng

are you OK? você está bem?
vosay shta bayng

is that OK with you? está
bem para si? see

is it OK to…? pode-se…?
podsi

that's OK thanks (said by man/
woman) está bem obrigado/
obrigada obrigadoo

I'm OK, thanks (I've got
enough) não quero, obrigado/
obrigada nowng kehro

(I feel OK) sinto-me bem
seentoom

is this train OK for…? este
comboio vai para… aysht
kombohyoo vī

I'm sorry, OK? desculpe-me,
está bem? dishkoolpimi

old velho vehl-yoo

how old are you? que idade
tem? keed**ad** tayng

I'm 25 tenho vinte-e-cinco
anos **tayn**-yoo v**ee**ntiseenkoo

and you? e você? ee vos**ay**

old-fashioned antiquado
antikw**a**doo

old town (old part of town) a
cidade antiga sid**ad** ant**ee**ga

in the old town na cidade
antiga

olive oil o azeite az**ay**t

olives a azeitona azayt**oh**na

black/green olives as
azeitonas pretas/verdes
azayt**oh**nash pr**ay**tash/v**ay**rdsh

omelette a omeleta omil**ay**ta

on sobre sohbr

on the street/beach na
pr**a**ia/r**u**a

is it on this road? é nesta
rua? eh n**eh**shta

on the plane no avião nwav-
y**ow**ng

on Saturday no sábado noo

on television na televisão

I haven't got it on me não o
tenho comigo nowng oo **tayn**-
yoo koom**ee**goo

this one's on me (drink) esta
bebida sou eu que pago **eh**shta
bib**ee**da soh **ay**-oo kih p**a**goo

the light wasn't on a luz não
estava acesa looJ nowng sht**a**va
as**ay**za

what's on tonight? qual é
o programa para esta noite?

kwal**eh** oo proogr**a**ma
par**eh**shta n**oh**-it

once (one time) uma vez
ooma vaysh

at once (immediately)
imediatamente imid-yatam**ay**nt

one um oong, uma **oo**ma

the white one o/a branco/
branca oo/a br**a**nkoo

one-way ticket o bilhete
simples bil-y**ay**t s**ee**mplish

onion a cebola sib**oh**la

online (book, check) online

only só saw, somente som**ay**nt

only one só um/uma oong/
ooma

it's only 6 o'clock ainda são
só seis horas a-**ee**nda sowng saw
sayz **o**rash

I've only just got here acabei
de chegar akab**ay** di shig**ar**

on/off switch o interruptor de
ligar/desligar intirroopt**ohr** di
lig**ar**/diJlig**ar**

open (adj) aberto ab**eh**rtoo
(verb) abrir abr**ee**r

when do you open? quando
abre? kw**a**ndwabr

I can't get it open
não consigo abrir nowng
kons**ee**gwabr**ee**r

in the open air ao ar livre ow
ar leevr

opening times as horas de
abertura **o**rash dabirt**oo**ra

open ticket o bilhete em aberto
bil-y**ay**tayng ab**eh**rtoo

opera a ópera **o**pira

operation (medical) a operação
opiras**ow**ng

operator (telephone: man/woman)
o/a telefonista telefoon**ee**shta

**opposite: the opposite
direction** na direcção oposta
direhs**ow**ng op**o**shta

the bar opposite o bar do
outro lado doo **oh**troo l**a**doo

opposite my hotel em frente
ao meu hotel ayng fraynt ow

optician o oculista okool**ee**shta

or ou oh

orange (fruit) a laranja lar**a**nJa

(colour) cor de laranja kohr di

orange juice (fresh) o sumo de
laranja s**oo**moo

(fizzy) a laranjada com gás
lar**a**nJada kong**a**sh

(diluted) o refresco de laranja
rifr**ay**shkoo di

orchestra a orquestra ork**eh**shtra

order: can we order now?
(in restaurant) podemos pedir
ag**o**ra? pood**ay**moosh pid**ee**r

**I've already ordered,
thanks** (said by man/woman)
já pedi, obrigado/obrig**a**da Ja
pid**ee** obrig**a**doo

I didn't order this não pedi
isto nowng – **ee**shtoo

out of order avariado
avar-y**a**doo

ordinary vulgar voolg**a**r

other outro **oh**troo

the other one o outro oo

the other day outro dia
d**ee**-a

I'm waiting for the others
estou a esperar outras pessoas
stoh a shpir**a**r **oh**trash pis**oh**-ash

do you have any others?
tem mais algum/alguma?
tayng mīsh alg**oo**ng/alg**oo**ma

otherwise doutro modo
d**oh**troo m**o**doo

our nosso n**o**soo, nossa n**o**sa; (pl)
nossos n**o**soosh, nossas n**o**sash

ours nosso, nossa; (pl) nossos,
nossas

out: he's out saiu sa-**ee**-oo

**three kilometres out of
town** a três quilómetros da
cidade traysh kil**o**mitrooJ da sid**a**d

outdoors fora de casa di k**a**za

outside do lado de fora
doo l**a**doo di

can we sit outside?
podemos sentar-nos lá fora?
pood**ay**moosh saynt**a**rnoosh

oven o forno f**oh**rnoo

over: over here aqui ak**ee**

over there ali al**ee**

over five hundred mais de
quinhentos/quinh**e**ntas mīsh di

it's over terminado tirmin**a**doo

**overcharge: you've
overcharged me** você
vendeu-me mais caro vos**ay**
vend**ay**-oomi mīsh k**a**roo

overcoat o sobretudo
soobrit**oo**doo

**overlooking: I'd like a room
overlooking the courtyard**
queria um quarto que dê para
o pátio kir**ee**-a oong kw**a**rtoo ki
day paroo p**a**t-yoo

overnight (travel) de noite di n**oh**-it

overtake ultrapassar ooltrapas**ar**

owe: how much do I owe you? quanto lhe devo? kw**a**ntoo l-yi d**ay**voo

own: my own... o meu próprio... oo m**ay**-oo pr**o**pr-yoo

  are you on your own? (to man/woman) está sozinho/sozinha? shta saw**zee**n-yoo

  I'm on my own (said by man/woman) estou sozinho/sozinha shtoh

owner (*male/female*) o dono d**oh**noo, a d**o**na

oysters as ostras **oh**shtrash

P

pack fazer as malas faz**ay**r aⅉ m**a**lash

  a pack of... um pacote de... oong pak**o**t di

package (parcel) a encomenda aynkoom**ay**nda

package holiday a excursão organizada shkoors**ow**ng organiz**a**da

packed lunch o almoço embalado alm**oh**sw-aymbal**a**doo

packet: a packet of cigarettes o maço de cigarros m**a**soo di sig**a**rroosh

padlock o cadeado kad-y**a**doo

page (of book) a página p**a**ⅉina

  could you page Mr...? pode chamar o Sr...? pod sham**ar** oo sin-y**oh**r

pain a dor dohr

  I have a pain here tenho uma dor aqui t**ay**n-yoo **oo**ma dohr ak**ee**

painful doloroso dooloor**oh**zoo

painkillers os analgésicos analⅉ**eh**zikoosh

paint a tinta t**ee**nta

painting a pintura pint**oo**ra

pair: a pair of... um par de... oong di

Pakistani (*adj*) paquistanês pakishtan**ay**sh

palace o palácio pal**a**s-yoo

pale pálido p**a**lidoo

  pale blue azul claro az**oo**l kl**a**roo

pan a panela pan**eh**la

panties as cuecas kw**eh**kash

pants (underwear) as cuecas kw**eh**kash

  (US) as calças k**a**lsash

pantyhose os collants kool**a**nsh

paper o papel pap**eh**l

  (newspaper) o jornal ⅉoorn**a**l

  a sheet of paper uma folha de papel **oo**ma f**oh**lya di

paper handkerchiefs os lenços de papel l**ay**nsoosh

paragliding o parapentismo parapaynt**ee**ⅉmoo

parcel a encomenda aynkoom**ay**nda

pardon (me)? (didn't understand/hear) desculpe? dishk**oo**lp, como? k**oh**moo

parents os pais pish

parents-in-law os sogros sohgroosh

park o jardim público Jardeeng pooblikoo
(*verb*) estacionar shtas-yoonar
can I park here? posso estacionar aqui? posoo – akee

parking lot o parque de estacionamento park di shtas-yoonamayntoo

part a parte part

partner (boyfriend/girlfriend) o companheiro kompan-yayroo, a companheira

party (group) o grupo groopoo
(celebration) a festa fehshta

pass (in mountains) o desfiladeiro dishfiladayroo

passenger (*male/female*) o passageiro pasaJayroo, a passageira

passport o passaporte pasaport

password a senha sayn-ya

past: in the past no passado noo pasadoo
just past the information office logo a seguir ao escritório de informações logoo a sigeer owshkritor-yoo dinfoormasoyngsh

path o caminho kameen-yoo

pattern o desenho dizayn-yoo

pavement o passeio pasay-oo
on the pavement no passeio noo

pavement café o café de esplanada kafeh dishplanada

pay pagar
can I pay, please? por favor, queria pagar poor favohr kiree-a
it's already paid for já está pago Ja shta pagoo

pay phone o telefone público telefohn pooblikoo

peaceful tranquilo trankweeloo

peach o pêssego paysigoo

peanuts os amendoins amayndweensh

pear a pêra payra

peas as ervilhas irveel-yash

peculiar (taste, custom) estranho shtran-yoo

pedestrian crossing o passagem de peões pasaJayng di p-yoyngsh, a pasadeira de peões pasadayra

pedestrian precinct a zona para peões zohna para p-yoyngsh

peg (for washing) a mola
(for tent) a cavilha kaveel-ya

pen a caneta kanayta

pencil o lápis lapsh

penfriend (*male/female*) o/a correspondente koorrishpondaynt

penicillin a penicilina penisileena

penknife o canivete kanive**ht**

pensioner (*male/female*)
o reformado rifoorm**a**doo,
a reform**a**da

people a gente J**ay**nt

**the other people in the
hotel** as outras pessoas no
hotel az**oh**trash pis**oh**-ash
nwoht**eh**l

too many people gente
demais dim**ee**sh

pepper (spice) a pimenta pim**ay**nta
(vegetable) o pimento pim**ay**ntoo

peppermint (sweet) a hortelã-
pimenta ortil**a**ng pim**ay**nta

per: per night por noite
poor n**oh**-it

how much per day? quanto
é por dia? kwantw**eh** poor d**ee**-a

per cent por cento s**ay**ntoo

perfect perfeito pirf**ay**too

perfume o perfume pirf**oo**m

perhaps talvez talv**ay**sh

perhaps not talvez não nowng

period (of time, menstruation)
o período pir**ee**-oodoo

perm a permanente pirman**ay**nt

permit a licença lis**ay**nsa

person a pessoa pis**oh**-a

petrol a gasolina gazool**ee**na

petrol can a lata de gasolina di
gazool**ee**na

petrol station a bomba de
gasolina b**oh**mba di

pharmacy a farmácia farm**a**s-ya

phone o telefone telef**oh**n
(*verb*) telefonar telefoon**a**r

phone book a lista telefónica
le**e**shta telef**oh**nika

phone box a cabina telefónica
kabe**e**na

phonecard o cartão de telefone
kart**ow**ng di telef**oh**n

phone charger o carregador de
telemóvel karrigad**oh**r di telem**o**vil

phone number o número de
telefone n**oo**miroo

photo a fotografia footoografe**e**-a

**excuse me, could you take
a photo of us?** faz favor, pode
tirar-nos uma fotografia? fash
fav**oh**r pod tirarn**oo**z **oo**ma

phrasebook o livro de
expressões le**e**vroo dishpris**oy**ngsh

piano o piano p-y**a**noo

pickpocket (*male/female*) o/a
carteirista kartayre**e**shta

**pick up: will you be there to
pick me up?** estarás lá para
apanhar-me? shtara**J** – apan-
y**a**rmi

picnic o piquenique pikin**ee**k

picture (drawing, painting) a
pintura peent**oo**ra
(photograph) a fotografia
footoografe**e**-a

pie a tarte tart

piece o pedaço pid**a**soo

a piece of... um bocado de...
oong book**a**doo di

pilchards as sardinhas
sarde**e**n-yash

pill a pílula pe**e**loola

I'm on the pill estou a tomar a
pílula sht**oh** a toom**a**r

pillow a almofada almoo**f**ada

pillow case a fronha da almofada fr**oh**n-ya

pin o alfinete alfin**ay**t

pineapple o ananás anan**ash**

pineapple juice o sumo de ananás s**oo**moo danan**ash**

pink cor de rosa kohr di r**o**za

pipe (for smoking) o cachimbo kash**ee**mboo

(for water) o cano k**a**noo

pipe cleaner o desentupidor de cachimbo dizayntoopid**ohr** di kash**ee**mboo

pity: it's a pity é uma pena eh **oo**ma p**ay**na

pizza a pizza

place o lugar loo**g**ar

at your place na sua casa s**oo**-a k**a**za

at his place na casa dele dayl

plain (not patterned) liso l**ee**zoo

plane o avião av-y**ow**ng

by plane de avião dav-y**ow**ng

plant a planta

plaster cast o gesso J**ay**soo

plasters o adesivo adiz**ee**voo

plastic o plástico pl**ash**tikoo

plastic bag o saco de plástico s**a**koo di

plate o prato pr**a**too

platform o cais kīsh

which platform is it for Fátima? qual é o cais para Fátima? kwal**eh** oo

play (verb) jogar Joo**g**ar

(in theatre) a peça de teatro p**eh**sa di t-y**a**troo

playground o pátio de recreio pat-yoo di rikr**ay**-oo

pleasant agrad**á**vel

please se faz favor si fash fav**ohr**, por favor poor

yes please sim, por favor seeng

could you please…? por favor, pode…? pod

please don't por favor, não faça isto nowng f**a**sa **ee**shtoo

pleased: pleased to meet you (said to man/woman) muito prazer em conhecê-lo/ conhecê-la mw**ee**ngtoo praz**ayr** ayng koon-yis**ay**loo

pleasure: my pleasure de n**a**da di

plenty: plenty of… muito… mw**ee**ngtoo

there's plenty of time temos muito tempo t**ay**mooJ – t**ay**mpoo

that's plenty, thanks (said by man/woman) chega, obrigado/ obrigada sh**ay**ga obrig**a**doo

pliers o alicate alik**a**t

plug (electrical) a tomada toom**a**da

(for car) a vela v**eh**la

(in sink) a tampa do ralo doo r**a**loo

plumber o canalizador kanalizad**ohr**

p.m. da tarde tard

poached egg o ovo escalfado **oh**voo shkalf**a**doo

pocket o bolso oo b**oh**lsoo

point: two point five dois virgula cinco d**oh**-iJ v**ee**rgoola s**ee**nkoo

there's no point não vale a
pena nowng val-ya payna

points (in car) os platinados
platinadoosh

poisonous venenoso vininohzoo

police a polícia poolees-ya

  call the police! chamem a
  polícia! shamayng

policeman o polícia
oo poolees-ya

police station o Posto da Polícia
pohshtoo

policewoman a mulher-polícia
mool-yehr

polish (for shoes) a pomada para
calçados poomada
para kalsadoosh

polite bem-educado bayng
idookadoo

polluted contaminado
kontaminadoo

pony o pónei ponay

pool (for swimming) a piscina
pish-seena

poor (not rich) pobre pobr
(quality) mau mow, f má

pop music a música pop moozika

pop singer (male/female) o cantor
pop kantohr, a cantora pop

popular popular poopoolar

population a população
poopoolasowng

pork a carne de porco
karn di pohrkoo

port (for boats) o porto
pohrtoo
(drink) o vinho do Porto
veen-yoo doo

porter (in hotel) o porteiro
poortayroo

portrait o retrato ritratoo

Portugal Portugal poortoogal

Portuguese (adj) português
poortoogaysh
(language) português
(man) o português
(woman) a portuguesa

  the Portuguese os
  portugueses poortoogayzish

posh (restaurant, people) chique
sheek

possible possível pooseevil

  is it possible to…? é
  possível…? eh

  as… as possible tão…
  quanto possível towng…
  kwantoo

post (mail) o correio koorray-oo
(verb) pôr no correio pohr noo

  could you post this for me?
  podia-me pôr isto no correio?
  poodee-ami – eeshtoo noo

postbox a caixa do correio
kīsha doo

postcard o postal pooshtal

postcode o código postal
kodigoo pooshtal

poster (for room) o poster
(in street) o cartaz kartash

poste restante a posta-restante
poshta rishtant

post office os correios
koorray-oosh

potato a batata

potato chips as batatas fritas
batatash freetash

pots and pans as panelas e tachos pan**eh**lazee ta**shoosh**

pottery (objects) a loiça de barro l**oh**-isa di b**a**rroo

pound (money, weight) a libra l**ee**bra

power cut o corte de energia kort denir**J**ee-a

power point a tomada too**ma**da

practise: I want to practise my Portuguese quero praticar o meu português k**eh**roo pratika**r**oo m**a**y-oo poortoog**a**ysh

prawn a gamba

prefer: I prefer… prefiro… prif**ee**roo

pregnant gr**á**vida

prescription (for medicine) a receita ris**a**yta

present (gift) o presente priz**a**ynt

president (of country: man/woman) o/a presidente prizid**a**ynt

pretty bonito boon**ee**too

it's pretty expensive é muito caro mw**ee**ngtoo k**a**roo

price o preço pr**a**ysoo

priest o padre padr

prime minister (*male/female*) o primeiro ministro prim**a**yroo min**ee**shtroo, a prim**ei**ra min**i**stra

printed matter os impressos impr**eh**soosh

priority (in driving) a prioridade pr-yoorid**a**d

prison a cadeia kad**a**y-a

private privado priv**a**doo

private bathroom a casa de banho privativa k**a**za di ban-yoo priva**tee**va

probably provavelmente proovavilm**a**ynt

problem o problema proobl**a**yma

no problem! tudo bem! t**oo**doo bayng

program(me) o programa proog**ra**ma

promise: I promise prometo proom**a**ytoo

pronounce: how is this pronounced? como se pronuncia? k**oh**moo si proonoons**ee**-a

properly (repaired, locked etc) bem bayng

protection factor (of suntan lotion) o factor de protecção fat**oh**r di prooteh**sow**ng

Protestant protestante prooti**sh**tant

public convenience a casa de banho pública k**a**za di ban-yoo p**oo**blika

public holiday o feriado fir-y**a**doo

pudding (dessert) a sobremesa sobrim**a**yza

pull puxar poo**shar**

pullover o pullover

puncture o furo f**oo**roo

purple roxo r**oh**shoo

purse (for money) a carteira kart**a**yra

(US) a mala de mão di

push empurrar aympoo**rrar**

pushchair o carrinho de bebé kar**ee**n-yoo di beb**eh**

put pôr pohr

   where can I put...? onde
   posso pôr...? ohnd **po**soo

   **could you put us up for
   the night?** pode dar-nos
   acomodação para uma noite?
   pod **da**rnooz akoomoodas**ow**ng
   para **oo**ma

pyjamas o pijama pi**J**ama

Q

quality a qualidade kwali**da**d

quarantine a quarentena
kwarayn**tay**na

quarter a quarta parte
kwarta part

quayside: on the quayside no
cais noo kish

question a pergunta pirg**oo**nta

queue a bicha b**ee**sha

quick rápido **ra**pidoo

   that was quick! que rápido
   que foi! ki – foh-i

   **what's the quickest way
   there?** qual é o caminho
   mais rápido para lá? kwal**eh** oo
   kam**een**-yoo mish **ra**pidoo

quickly depressa dipr**eh**sa

quiet (place, hotel) silencioso
silayns-y**oh**zoo

   quiet! cale-se! **ka**lsi

quite (fairly) bastante bash**ta**nt

   (very) muito mw**een**gtoo

   that's quite right está certo
   shta s**eh**rtoo

   quite a lot bastante

R

rabbit o coelho kwa**yl**-yoo

race (for runners, cars) a corrida
koor**ree**da

racket (tennis, squash) a raqueta
rak**eh**ta

radiator (of car, in room)
o radiador rad-yad**oh**r

radio o rádio rad-yoo

   on the radio no rádio noo

rail: by rail por caminho de ferro
poor kam**een**-yoo di **feh**rroo

railway o caminho de ferro

rain a chuva sh**oo**va

   in the rain à chuva

   it's raining está a chover
   shta-a shoov**ay**r

raincoat o impermeável
impirm-y**a**vil

rape a violação v-yoolas**ow**ng

rare (uncommon) raro r**a**roo

   (steak) mal passado pas**a**doo

rash (on skin) a erupção eroops**ow**ng

raspberry a framboesa
frambw**ay**za

rat a ratazana rataz**a**na

rate (for changing money) o câmbio
k**a**mb-yoo

rather: it's rather good
é bastante bom/boa
eh bash**ta**nt bong/**boh**-a

   I'd rather... prefiro... prif**ee**roo

razor (electric) a máquina de
barbear m**a**kina di barb-y**a**r

razor blades as lâminas para
barbear l**a**minash

read ler layr

ready pronto pro**h**ntoo

   are you ready? (said to man/
woman) estás pronto/
pro**n**ta? shtash pro**h**ntoo

   I'm not ready yet (said by
man/woman) ainda não estou
pronto/pronta a-**ee**nda
nowng shtoh

   when will it be ready?
quando estará pronto?
kwandoo shtar**a**

   **it should be ready in a
couple of days** deve ficar
pronto em dois dias dehv
fikar – ayng do**h**-iJ dee-ash

real verdadeiro virdad**ay**roo

really realmente r-yalm**ay**nt

   I'm really sorry lamento
imenso lam**ay**ntoo im**ay**nsoo

that's really great isso é
fantástico eesw**eh** fant**a**shtikoo

really? (doubt) de verdade?
di virdad

(polite interest) sim? seeng

rear lights as luzes de trás
l**oo**zish di trash

rearview mirror o espelho
retrovisor shp**ay**l-yoo ritroovizohr

reasonable (prices etc) razoável
razw**a**vil

receipt o recibo ris**ee**boo

recently há pouco a p**oh**koo

reception (in hotel, for guests)
a recepção risehs**ow**ng

   at reception na recepção

reception desk o balcão da
recepção balk**ow**ng

receptionist (male/female)
o/a recepcionista
risehs-yoon**ee**shta

recognize reconhecer rikoon-yisayr

recommend: could you recommend...? podia recomendar...? poodee-a rikoomayndar

record (music) o disco deeshkoo

red vermelho virmayl-yoo

red wine o vinho tinto veen-yoo teentoo

refund o reembolso ri-aymbohlsoo

can I have a refund? pode dar-me o reembolso? pod darmoo

region a região riJ-yowng

registered: by registered mail por correio registado poor koorray-oo riJishtadoo

registration number a matrícula matreekoola

relative (noun: male/female) o/a parente paraynt

religion a religião riliJ-yowng

remember: I remember lembro-me laymbroomi

I don't remember não me lembro nowng mi laymbroo

do you remember? lembra-se? laymbrasi

rent (noun: for apartment etc) o aluguer aloogehr

(verb: car etc) alugar

to rent para alugar

rented car o carro de aluguer karroo daloogehr

repair reparar

can you repair this? pode reparar isto? pod riparar eeshtoo

repeat repetir ripiteer

could you repeat that? podia repetir? poodee-a

reservation a reserva rizehrva

I'd like to make a reservation queria fazer uma reserva kiree-a fazayr ooma

I have a reservation tenho uma reserva tayn-yoo ooma

yes sir, what name please? sim senhor, que nome, por favor? seeng sin-yohr ki nohm poor favohr

reserve (verb) reservar rizirvar

can I reserve a table for tonight? posso reservar uma mesa para esta noite? posoo – ooma mayza para ehshta noh-it

yes madam, for how many people? sim senhora, para quantas pessoas? seeng sin-yora para kwantash pisoh-ash

for two para duas doo-ash

and for what time? e para que hora? i – ki-ora

for eight o'clock para as oito horas azoh-itorash

and could I have your name, please? pode dizer-me o seu nome, por favor? pod dizayrmoo say-oo nohm poor favohr

see **alphabet** for spelling

rest: I need a rest preciso

dum descanso pris**ee**zoo doong
dishk**a**nsoo

the rest of the group o resto
do grupo r**eh**shtoo doo gr**oo**poo

restaurant o restaurante
risht**o**wrant

restaurant car a carruagem
restaurante karrwa**J**ayng
risht**o**wrant

rest room a casa de banho k**a**za
di b**a**n-yoo

see **toilet**

retired: I'm retired (said by man/
woman) estou reformado/
reform**a**da shtoh rifoorm**a**doo

return: a return to... um bilhete
de ida e v**o**lta a... oong bil-y**a**yt
d**ee**da ee

return ticket o bilhete de ida
e volta

see **ticket**

reverse charge call a chamada
p**a**ga no destinatário sham**a**da –
noo dishtinat**a**r-yoo

reverse gear a marcha atrás
marshatr**a**sh

revolting repugnante ripoogn**a**nt

rib a costela koosht**eh**la

rice o arroz arr**oh**sh

rich (person) rico r**ee**koo

(food) forte fort

ridiculous ridículo rid**ee**kooloo

right (correct) certo s**eh**rtoo

(not left) direito dir**ay**too

you were right tinhas razão
teen-ya**J** raz**ow**ng

that's right está certo shta

this can't be right isto não

pode estar certo **ee**shtoo nowng
pod shtar

right! está bem! bayng

is this the right road for...?
esta é a estrada certa para...?
ehshta eh a shtr**a**da

on the right à direita dir**ay**ta

turn right vire à direita veer

right-hand drive com volante à
direita kong v**oo**lant

ring (on finger) o anel an**eh**l

I'll ring you eu telefono-lhe
ay-oo telef**oh**nool-yi

ring back volt**a**r a telefonar
telefoon**a**r

ripe (fruit) maduro mad**oo**roo

rip-off: it's a rip-off isso é um
roubo **ee**soo eh oong r**oh**boo

rip-off prices os preços
exorbitantes pr**ay**sooz
ezoorbit**a**ntsh

risky arriscado arr**i**shk**a**doo

river o rio r**ee**-oo

> **Travel tip** An unsung glory
> of central and northern
> Portugal is its river beaches
> – look out for the signs (*praia
> fluvial*) directing you to quiet
> bends in the local river or to
> weirs or dramatic gorges.
> The local municipality
> often erects a bar during
> the summer, and there are
> usually picnic and barbecue
> areas, and public toilets.

road (in town) a rua r**oo**-a

(in country) a estrada shtr**a**da

is this the road for...? é esta
a estrada para...? ehshta

it's just down the road é
aqui perto eh akee pehrtoo

road accident o acidente de
viação asidaynt di v-yasowng

road map o mapa das estradas
daz shtradash

roadsign o sinal

rob: I've been robbed
(said by man/woman) fui
roubado/roubada fwee
rohbadoo

rock a rocha rosha

(music) a música rock moozika

on the rocks (with ice) com
gelo kong Jayloo

roll (bread) o paposseco
papoosaykoo

roof (of house) o telhado til-yadoo

(of car) o tejadilho tiJadeel-yoo

roof rack o porta-bagagens no
tejadilho porta bagaJayngsh

room o quarto kwartoo

in my room no meu quarto
noo may-oo

room service o serviço de
quartos sirveesoo di kwartoosh

rope a corda

rosé (wine) rosé roozay

roughly (approximately)
aproximadamente
aproosimadamaynt

round: it's my round é a minha
rodada eh a meen-ya roodada

roundabout (for traffic) a rotunda
rootoonda

round trip ticket o bilhete de

ida e volta bil-yayt deeda ee
see **ticket**

route o trajecto trajehtoo

what's the best route? qual
é o melhor trajecto? kwal eh-oo
mil-yor

rubber (material, eraser)
a borracha boorrasha

rubber band o elástico ilashtikoo

rubbish (waste) o lixo leeshoo

(poor quality goods) o refugo
rifoogoo

rubbish! (nonsense)
que disparate! ki dishparat

rucksack a mochila moosheela

rude grosseiro groosayroo

ruins as ruínas rweenash

rum o rum roong

a rum and Coke uma cuba
livre ooma kooba leevr

run (verb: person) correr koorrayr

**how often do the buses
run?** de quanto em quanto
tempo há autocarros?
di kwantoo ayng kwantoo taympoo
a owtookarroosh

I've run out of money o meu
dinheiro acabou oo may-oo din-
yayroo akaboh

rush hour a hora de ponta
ora di pohnta

S

sad triste treesht

saddle a sela sehla

safe (adj) seguro sigooroo

safety pin o alfinete de
segurança alfin**ayt** di sigoor**an**sa

sail a vela ve**h**la
(*verb*) velejar vili**J**ar

sailboard a prancha de windsurf
pr**an**sha di

sailboarding praticar windsurf
pratik**ar**

salad a salada

salad dressing o tempero da
sal**a**da taymp**ay**roo

sale: for sale à venda
v**ay**nda

salmon o salmão salm**ow**ng

salt o sal

same: the same o mesmo
may**J**moo

the same as this igual a este
igw**al** a **ay**sht

the same again, please o
mesmo, por favor poor fav**oh**r

it's all the same to me tanto
faz t**a**ntoo fash

sand a areia ar**ay**-a

sandals as sandálias sand**al**-yash

sandwich a sandes sandsh

sanitary napkins/towels
os pensos higiénicos
p**ay**nsooz i**J**-ye**h**nikoosh

sardine a sardinha sard**een**-ya

Saturday sábado s**a**badoo

sauce o molho m**oh**l-yoo

saucepan a panela pan**eh**la

saucer o pires peersh

sauna a sauna s**ow**na

sausage a salsicha sals**ee**sha

say dizer diz**ay**r

**how do you say... in
Portuguese?** como se diz…
em português? k**oh**moo si
deez… ayng poortoog**ay**sh

what did he say? o que é que
ele disse? oo k-yeh kayl dees

he said... ele disse…

could you say that again?
pode repetir? pod ripit**eer**

scarf (for neck) o lenço de
pescoço l**ay**nsoo di pishk**oh**soo
(for head) o lenço de cabeça
kab**ay**sa

scenery a paisagem piza**J**ayng

schedule (US) o horário oo
or**ar**-yoo

scheduled flight o voo regular
v**oh**-oo rigool**ar**

school a escola shk**o**la

scissors: a pair of scissors a
tesoura tiz**oh**ra

scooter a motoreta mootoor**ay**ta

scotch o whisky w**ee**shkee

Scotch tape a fita gomada
f**ee**ta goom**a**da

Scotland a Escócia shk**o**s-ya

Scottish escocês shkoos**ay**sh

I'm Scottish (*male/female*) sou
escocês/escocesa
soh – shkoos**ay**za

scrambled eggs os ovos
mexidos **o**voosh mish**ee**doosh

scratch o arranhão arran-y**ow**ng

screw o parafuso paraf**oo**zoo

screwdriver a chave de fendas
shav di f**ay**ndash

sea o mar

by the sea à beira-mar b**ay**ra

seafood os mariscos
mar**ee**shkoosh

seafood restaurant
a marisqueira marishk**ay**ra

seafront a praia prī-a

on the seafront junto à praia
J**oo**ntwa

seagull a gaivota gīv**o**ta

search procurar prook**oo**rar

seashell a concha do mar
k**oh**nsha doo

seasick: I feel seasick (said
by man/woman) estou enjoado/
enjo**a**da shtoh aynJw**a**doo

I get seasick enjoo sempre
aynJ**oh**-oo saympr

seaside: by the seaside à beira
do mar b**ay**ra doo

seat o assento as**ay**ntoo

is this seat taken? este lugar
está ocupado? aysht loog**a**r
shta okoop**a**doo

seat belt o cinto de segurança
s**ee**ntoo di sigoor**a**nsa

sea urchin o ouriço-do-mar
ohr**ee**soo doo

seaweed a alga

secluded retirado ritir**a**doo

second (*adj*) segundo sig**oo**ndoo

(of time) o segundo

just a second! espere
um momento! shp**ay**roong
moom**ay**ntoo

second class (travel) segunda
classe sig**oo**nda klas

second floor o segundo andar
sig**oo**ndoo

(US) o primeiro andar prim**ay**roo

second-hand em segunda mão
ayng sig**oo**nda mowng

see ver vayr

can I see? posso ver? p**o**soo

have you seen the...?
viu o/a...? v**ee**-oo

I saw him this morning
vi-o esta manhã v**ee**-oo **eh**shta
man-y**a**ng

see you! até logo! at**eh** l**o**goo

I see (I understand) percebo
pirs**ay**boo

self-catering apartment
o aparthotel apartoht**eh**l

self-service o self-service

sell vender vaynd**ay**r

do you sell...? vende...?
vaynd

Sellotape a fita gomada
f**ee**ta goom**a**da

send mandar

**I want to send this to
England** quero mandar isto
para Inglaterra k**eh**roo – **ee**shtoo
paringlat**eh**rra

senior citizen (*male/female*)
o cidadão de terceira idade
sidad**ow**ng di tirs**ay**ra id**a**d,
a cidadã de terceira idade
sidad**a**ng

separate separado sipar**a**doo

separated: I'm separated (said
by man/woman) estou separado/
separ**a**da shtoh

separately (pay, travel)
separadamente siparadam**ay**nt

September Setembro sit**ay**mbroo

septic séptico s**eh**ptikoo

serious sério se**h**r-yoo

service charge (in restaurant) a taxa de serviço tasha di sirvee**soo**

service station a estação de serviço shtasowng

serviette o guardanapo gwardana**poo**

set menu a ementa fixa ema**y**nta fe**e**ksa

several vários va**r**-yoosh

sew coser kooza**y**r

> **could you sew this back on?** podia coser-me isto? poodee-a kooza**y**rm ee**sh**too

sex o sexo se**h**xoo

sexy sexy se**h**xi

shade: in the shade à sombra so**h**mbra

shallow (water) pouco profundo po**h**koo proof**oo**ndoo

shame: what a shame! que pena! ki pa**y**na

shampoo o champô shampo**h**

> **shampoo and set** lavagem e mise lava**J**ayng i me**e**zi

share (room, table etc) partilhar partil-ya**r**

sharp (knife) afiado af-ya**d**oo

> (taste) ácido a**s**idoo

> (pain) agudo ag**oo**doo

shattered (very tired) estafado shtafa**d**oo

shaver a máquina de barbear makina di barb-ya**r**

shaving foam a espuma de barbear shp**oo**ma

shaving point a tomada para a

máquina de barbear toomada para makina

she ela e**h**la

> **is she here?** ela está aqui? shta ak**ee**

sheet (for bed) o lençol layns**o**l

shelf a prateleira pratila**y**ra

shellfish os mariscos maree**sh**koosh

sherry o vinho de Xerêz vee**n**-yoo di shira**y**sh

ship o navio nave**e**-o

> **by ship** de navio di

shirt a camisa kame**e**za

shit! merda! me**h**rda

shock o choque shok

> **I got an electric shock from the...** apanhei um choque eléctrico do... apan-ya**y** oong – ele**h**trikoo doo

shock-absorber o amortecedor amoortisido**h**r

shocking chocante shookant

shoe os sapatos sapa**t**oosh

> **a pair of shoes** um par de sapatos oong par di

shoelaces os atacadores atakado**h**rish

shoe polish a graxa para sapatos grasha para sapa**t**oosh

shoe repairer o sapateiro sapata**y**roo

shop a loja l**o**Ja

shopping: I'm going shopping vou às compras voh ash ko**h**mprash

shopping centre o centro comercial sa**y**ntroo komayrs-ya**l**

shop window a montra m**oh**ntra

shore (of sea, lake) a margem mar**J**ayng

short (person) baixo b**ī**shoo

(time, journey) curto k**oo**rtoo

shortcut o atalho at**a**l-yoo

shorts os calções kals**oy**ngsh

should: what should I do? que devo fazer? ki d**ay**voo faz**ay**r

he should be back soon ele deve voltar logo ayl dehv vo**o**ltar l**o**goo

you should... devia div**ee**-a

you shouldn't... não devia... n**ow**ng

shoulder o ombro **oh**mbroo

shout gritar

show (in theatre) o espetáculo shpit**a**kooloo

could you show me? podia mostrar-me? pood**ee**-a moosht**ra**rmi

shower (in bathroom) o duche doosh

(of rain) o aguaceiro agwas**ay**roo

with shower com duche kong

shower gel o gel de duche **J**ehl di doosh

shrimp a gamba g**a**mba

shut (verb) fechar fish**a**r

when do you shut? a que horas fecha? k-y**o**rash f**eh**sha

when does it shut? a que horas fecha?

it's shut está fechado/ fechada shta fish**a**doo

I've shut myself out fechei

a p**o**rta e deixei a chave dentro fish**ay** – i daysh**ay** a shav d**ay**ntroo

shut up! cale-se! k**a**lisi

shutter (on camera) o obturador obtoorad**oh**r

(on window) os postigos poosht**ee**goosh

shy tímido t**ee**midoo

sick (unwell) doente dw**ay**nt

I'm going to be sick (vomit) vou vomitar voh voomit**a**r

side o lado l**a**doo

the other side of the street o outro lado da rua oo **oh**troo – r**oo**-a

sidelights as luzes de presença a**J** loo**z**i**J** di priz**ay**nsa

side salad a salada a acompanhar akompan-y**a**r

side street a rua secundária r**oo**-a sikoondar-ya

sidewalk o passeio pas**ay**-oo

sight: the sights of... os centros de interesse de... oosh s**ay**ntroosh dintr**ay**s di

sightseeing: we're going sightseeing vamos ver os lugares de interesse v**a**moosh vayr oosh loog**a**rish

sightseeing tour o circuito turístico sirk**oo**-eetoo toor**ee**shtikoo

sign (roadsign etc) o sinal

signal: he didn't give a signal (driver, cyclist) ele não deu um sinal ayl nowng d**ay**-oo oong

signature a assinatura asinat**oo**ra

signpost o poste indicador posht indikad**oh**r

silence o silêncio sil**ayn**s-yoo

silk a seda s**ay**da

silly tolo t**oh**loo

silver a pr**a**ta

silver foil o papel de alumínio pap**eh**l daloom**ee**n-yoo

similar semelhante simil-y**a**nt

simple (easy) simples s**ee**mplish

since: since last week desde a semana passada d**ay**Jda sim**a**na

since I got here desde que cheguei d**ay**Jd ki shig**ay**

sing cant**a**r

singer (male/female) o cantor kant**oh**r, a cant**o**ra

single: a single to... uma bilhete simples para... **oo**ng bil-y**ay**t s**ee**mplish

I'm single (said by man/woman) sou solteiro/solt**ei**ra soh soolt**ay**roo

single bed a cama individual individw**a**l

single room o quarto individual kw**a**rtoo

single ticket o bilhete simples bil-y**ay**t s**ee**mplish

sink (in kitchen) a lava-louça lava l**oh**sa

sister a irmã eerm**a**ng

sister-in-law a cunhada koon-y**a**da

sit: can I sit here? posso sentar-me aqui? p**o**soo saynt**a**rmi ak**ee**

is anyone sitting here? está alguém sentado aqui? shta alg**ay**ng saynt**a**doo ak**ee**

sit down sentar-se saynt**a**rsi

sit down sente-se s**ay**ntsi

size o tamanho tam**a**n-yoo

skin a pele pehl

skin-diving mergulhar mirgool-y**a**r

skinny magricela magris**eh**la

skirt a saia s**ī**-ya

sky o céu s**eh**-oo

sleep dormir doorm**ee**r

did you sleep well? dormiu bem? doorm**ee**-oo b**ay**ng

sleeper (on train) a carruagem-cama karrw**a**Jayng k**a**ma

sleeping bag o saco de dormir s**a**koo di doorm**ee**r

sleeping car (on train) a carruagem-cama karrw**a**Jayng k**a**ma

sleeping pill o comprimido para dormir komprim**ee**doo para doorm**ee**r

sleepy: I'm feeling sleepy estou com sono shtoh kong s**oh**noo

sleeve a m**a**nga

slide (photographic) o diapositivo d-yapoozit**ee**voo

slip (garment) a combinação kombinas**ow**ng

slippery escorregadio shkoorrigad**ee**-oo

slow lento l**ay**ntoo

slow down! (driving) mais devagar! m**ī**J divag**a**r

slowly devag**a**r

very slowly muito devagar mw**ee**ngtoo

could you speak more slowly? pode falar mais devagar? pod – mij

small pequeno pikaynoo

smell: it smells (smells bad) cheira mal shayra

smile sorrir soorreer

smoke o fumo foomoo

do you mind if I smoke? importa-se que fume? importasi ki foomi

I don't smoke não fumo nowng

do you smoke? fuma? fooma

snack: just a snack só um snack saw oong

sneeze o espirro shpeerroo

snorkel o snorkel

snow a neve nehv

it's snowing está a nevar shta

so: it's so good! é tão bom! eh towng bong

it's so expensive! é tão caro! karoo

not so much não tanto nowng tantoo

it's not so bad não é tão mau/má eh towng mow

so am I, so do I eu também ay-oo tambayng

so-so mais ou menos mizohmaynoosh

soaking solution (for contact lenses) a solução para as lentes de contacto sooloosowng paraj layntsh di kontatoo

soap o sabonete saboonayt

soap powder o detergente deterjaynt

sober sóbrio sobr-yoo

sock a peúga p-yooga

socket (electrical) a tomada toomada

soda (water) a soda

sofa o sofá soofa

soft (material etc) mole mol

soft-boiled egg o ovo quente ohvoo kaynt

soft drink a bebida não alcoólica bibeeda nowng alko-olika

soft lenses as lentes gelatinosas layntsh jilatinozash

sole (of shoe, of foot) a sola

could you put new soles on these? pode pôr-lhes solas novas? pod pohrl-yish solash novash

some: can I have some water? pode trazer-me água? trazayrm

can I have some of this? pode dar-me um pouco disto? darmoong pohkoo deeshtoo

somebody, someone alguém algayng

something alguma coisa algooma koh-iza

something to eat alguma coisa para comer koomair

sometimes às vezes ash vayzish

somewhere nalguma parte nalgooma part

son o filho feel-yoo

song a canção kansowng

son-in-law o genro jaynroo

soon em breve ayng brev

  I'll be back soon estarei
de volta em breve shtaray di
vohltayng

  as soon as possible logo
que possível logoo ki pooseevil

sore: it's sore dói-me doymi

sore throat a dor de garganta
dohr di

sorry: (I'm) sorry tenho muita
pena tayn-yoo mweengta payna

  sorry? (didn't understand)
como? kohmoo

sort: what sort of...? que tipo
de...? ki teepoo di

soup a sopa sohpa

sour (taste) azedo azaydoo

south o sul sool

  in the south no sul noo

South Africa a África do Sul doo

South African (adj) sul-africano
soolafrikanoo

  I'm South African (male/
female) sou sul-africano/sul-
africana soh

southeast o sudeste soodehsht

southwest o sudoeste
soodwehsht

souvenir a lembrança laymbransa

Spain a Espanha shpan-ya

Spanish espanhol shpan-yol

spanner a chave de porcas
shav di porkash

spare part a peça sobresselente
pehsa sobrisilaynt

spare tyre o pneu sobresselente
pnay-oo

spark plug a vela vehla

sparkling wine o vinho
espumante veen-yooshpoomant

speak: do you speak English?
fala inglês? inglaysh

  I don't speak... não falo...
nowng faloo

can I speak to Roberto?
posso falar com o Roberto?
posoo – kong oo

who's calling? quem fala?
kayng

it's Patricia é Patricia eh

**I'm sorry, he's not in,
can I take a message?**
desculpe, ele não está, quer
deixar um recado?
dishkoolp ayl nowng shta kehr
dayshar oong rikadoo

**no thanks, I'll call back
later** não, obrigada, ligarei
mais tarde ligaray mish tard

please tell him I called
por favor, diga-lhe que
telefonei poor favohr deegal-
yi ki telefoonay

spectacles os óculos okooloosh

speed a velocidade viloosidad

speed limit o limite de
velocidade limeet di

speedometer o velocímetro
vilooseemitroo

spell: how do you spell it?
como é que se soletra?
kohmoo eh ki si soolehtra

  see **alphabet**

spend gastar gashtar

spider a aranha ar**a**n-ya

spin-dryer o secador de roupa sikad**oh**r di r**oh**pa

splinter a pua p**oo**-a

spoke (in wheel) o raio rĩ-oo

spoon a colher kool-y**eh**r

sport o desporto dishp**oh**rtoo

sprain: I've sprained my… torci o… toors**ee** oo

spring (season) a Primavera primav**eh**ra

(of car, seat) a mola m**o**la

square (in town) a praça pr**a**sa

squash o squash

stairs a escada shk**a**da

stale (bread) duro d**oo**roo

stall: the engine keeps stalling o motor está sempre a falhar oo moot**oh**r shta s**ay**mpra fal-y**a**r

stamp o selo s**ay**loo

DIALOGUE

a stamp for England, please um selo para Inglaterra, faz favor oong s**ay**loo para inglat**eh**rra fash fav**oh**r

what are you sending? o que vai enviar? oo ki vĩ aynv-y**a**r

this postcard este postal aysht poosht**a**l

standby standby

star a estrela shtr**ay**la

(in film: man/woman) o actor principal at**oh**r prinsip**a**l, a actriz principal atr**ee**sh

start o começo koom**ay**soo

(*verb*) começar koomis**a**r

when does it start? quando
começa? kwandoo koom=**eh**sa

the car won't start o carro
não pega oo k**a**rroo nowng p**eh**ga

starter (of car) o motor de
arranque moot**oh**r darr**a**nk

(food) a entrada ayntr**a**da

starving: I'm starving (said by
man/woman) estou morto/
m**o**rta de fome shtoh m**oh**rtoo
– di fohm

state (country) o estado sht**a**doo

the States (USA) os Estados
Unidos sht**a**dooz oon**ee**doosh

station a estação shtas**ow**ng

statue a estátua sht**a**twa

stay: where are you staying?
(to man/woman) onde está
hospedado/hospedada?
ohnd sht**a** oshpid**a**doo

I'm staying at... (said by man/
woman) estou hospedado/
hospedada em... shtoh – **a**yng

**I'd like to stay another two
nights** gostaria de ficar mais
duas noites gooshtar**ee**-a di fik**a**r
mish d**oo**-aJ n**oh**-itsh

steak o bife beef

steal roubar rohb**a**r

my bag has been stolen
roubaram-me a mala
rohb**a**rowng m-ya m**a**la

steep (hill) íngreme **ee**ngrim

steering a direcção direhs**ow**ng

step: on the step no degrau
digr**ow**

stereo a aparelhagem (de som)
aparil-y**a**Jayng (di song)

sterling as libras esterlinas
l**ee**braz ishtirl**ee**nash

steward (on plane) o comissário
de bordo koomis**a**r-yoo di b**o**rdoo

stewardess a hospedeira
oshpid**a**yra

sticking plaster o adesivo
adiz**ee**voo

sticky tape a fita-cola f**ee**ta k**o**la

still: I'm still here ainda estou
aqui a-**ee**nda shtoh ak**ee**

is he still there? ele ainda
está aí? ayl – shta a-**ee**

keep still! fique quieto!
feek k-y**eh**too

sting: I've been stung (said by
man/woman) fui picado/pic**a**da
fwee pik**a**doo

stockings as meias m**a**y-ash

stomach o estômago sht**oh**magoo

stomach ache a dor de
estômago dohr disht**oh**magoo

stone (rock) a pedra p**eh**dra

stop par**a**r

please, stop here (to taxi
driver etc) pare aqui, por favor
par ak**ee** poor fav**oh**r

do you stop near...? p**á**ra
perto de...? p**eh**rtoo di

stop it! pare com isso!
kong **ee**soo

stopover a paragem par**a**Jayng

storm a tempestade taympisht**a**d

straight (whisky etc) puro
p**oo**roo

it's straight ahead sempre
em frente s**a**ymprayng fraynt

straightaway em seguida ayng sigeeda

strange (odd) esquisito shkizeetoo

stranger (*male/female*) o estranho shtran-yoo, a estranha

  I'm a stranger here sou de fora soh di

strap (on watch) a pulseira poolsayra

  (on dress) a alça alsa

  (on suitcase) a correia koorray-a

strawberry o morango moorangoo

stream o ribeiro ribayroo

street a rua roo-a

  on the street na rua

streetmap o mapa da cidade sidad

string o cordel koordehl

strong forte fort

stuck emperrado aympirradoo

  it's stuck está emperrado shta

student (*male/female*) o/a estudante shtoodant

stupid estúpido shtoopidoo

suburb os arredores arredorish

subway (US) o metro mehtroo

suddenly subitamente soobitamaynt

suede a camurça kamoorsa

sugar o açúcar asookar

suit o fato fatoo

  it doesn't suit me (jacket etc) não me fica bem nowng mi feeka bayng

  it suits you fica-lhe bem feekal-yi

suitcase a mala mala

summer o Verão virowng

  in the summer no Verão noo

sun o sol

  in the sun ao sol ow

  out of the sun à sombra sohmbra

sunbathe tomar banho de sol toomar ban-yoo di

sunblock (cream) o creme écran total kraym ekrang tootal

sunburn a queimadura de sol kaymadoora di

sunburnt queimado de sol kaymadoo

Sunday domingo doomeengoo

sunglasses os óculos de sol okooloosh di

sun lounger a cadeira reclinável kadayra reklinavil

sunny: it's sunny está (a fazer) sol shta (a fazayr) sol

sunroof o tejadilho de abrir tijadeel-yoo dabreer

sunset o pôr do sol pohr doo

sunshade o chapéu de sol shapeh-oo di

sunshine a luz do sol looj doo

sunstroke a insolação insoolasowng

suntan o bronzeado bronz-yadoo

suntan lotion a loção de bronzear loosowng di bronz-yar

suntanned bronzeado bronz-yadoo

suntan oil o óleo de bronzear ol-yoo di

super óptimo *otimoo*

supermarket o supermercado *soopermerkadoo*

supper o jantar *Jantar*

supplement (extra charge) o suplemento *sooplimayntoo*

sure: are you sure? tem a certeza? *tayng a sirtayza*

sure! claro! *klaroo*

surname o apelido *apileedoo*

swearword a asneira *aJnayra*

sweater a camisola *kamizola*

sweatshirt a sweatshirt

Sweden a Suécia *swehs-ya*

Swedish (*adj*, language) sueco *swehkoo*

sweet (taste) doce *dohs*

(dessert) a sobremesa *sobrimayza*

sweets os rebuçados *riboosadoosh*

swelling o inchaço *inshasoo*

swim nadar

I'm going for a swim vou nadar *voh*

let's go for a swim vamos nadar *vamoosh*

swimming costume o fato de banho *fatoo di ban-yoo*

swimming pool a piscina *pish-seena*

swimming trunks os calções de banho *kalsoyngsh di ban-yoo*

Swiss (*adj*) suíço *sweesoo*

switch o interruptor *intirooptohr*

switch off (engine, TV) desligar *diJligar*

(lights) apagar

switch on (engine, TV) ligar

(lights) acender *asayndayr*

Switzerland a Suíça *sweesa*

swollen inchado *inshadoo*

T

table a mesa *mayza*

a table for two uma mesa para duas pessoas *ooma – doo-ash pisoh-ash*

tablecloth a toalha de mesa *twal-ya di mayza*

table tennis o ténis de mesa *tehnish*

table wine o vinho de mesa *veen-yoo*

tailback (of traffic) a fila de carros *feela di karroosh*

tailor a alfaiataria *alfi-ataree-a*

take (lead) levar

(accept) aceitar *asaytar*

can you take me to the…? pode levar-me ao…? *pod levarmow*

do you take credit cards? aceita cartões de crédito? *asayta kartoyngsh di krehditoo*

fine, I'll take it está bem, fico com ele *shta bayng feekoo kong ayl*

can I take this? (leaflet etc) posso levar isto? *posoo – eeshtoo*

how long does it take? quanto tempo leva? *kwantoo taympoo lehva*

it takes three hours leva três horas tray*zo*rash

is this seat taken? este lugar está ocupado? aysht loo*gar* shta okoo*pa*doo

hamburger to take away o hamburger *pa*ra levar

can you take a little off here? (to hairdresser) pode cortar um pouco aqui? pod koor*tar* oong *poh*koo a*kee*

talcum powder o pó de talco paw di *tal*koo

talk fa*lar*

tall alto *al*too

tampons os tampões tamp*oyng*sh

tan o bronzeado bronz-*ya*doo

to get a tan bronzear-se bronz-*yar*si

tank (of car) o depósito di*po*zitoo

tap a torneira toor*nay*ra

tape (for cassette) a fita *fee*ta

tape measure a fita métrica *me*htrika

tape recorder o gravador grava*dohr*

taste o sabor sa*bohr*

can I taste it? posso provar? *po*soo pro*var*

taxi o táxi

will you get me a taxi? pode chamar-me um táxi? pod shama*r*moong

where can I find a taxi? onde posso encontrar um táxi? ohnd *po*soo*way*nkontrar

to the airport/Borges Hotel, please para o aeroporto/Hotel Borges, se faz favor pa*roo*-ayroo*pohr*too/oh*tehl* bor*J*ish si fash fa*vohr*

how much will it be? quanto vai custar? *kwan*too vī koosh*tar*

ten euros dez euros dehz **ay**-ooroosh

that's fine right here, thanks aqui está bem, obrigado/obrigada a*kee* shta bayng obriga*doo*

taxi-driver o pracista pra*see*shta

taxi rank a praça de táxis *pra*sa di *tax*ish

tea (drink) o chá sha

tea for one/two, please chá *pa*ra um/dois, por favor oong/*doh*-ish poor fa*vohr*

teabags os saquinhos de chá sa*keen*-yooJ di sha

teach: could you teach me? pode ensinar-me? pod aynsi*nar*mi

teacher (*male/female*) o professor proofes*ohr*, a professo*r*a

team a equipa e*kee*pa

teaspoon a colher de chá kool-*yehr* di sha

tea towel o pano de cozinha *pa*noo di kooz*een*-ya

teenager o/a adolescente adoolish-*say*nt

telephone o telefone tele*fohn*
see **phone**

television a televisão televi*zowng*

tell: could you tell him…?
pode dizer-lhe…?
pod diz**ayrl**-yi

temperature (weather) a
temperatura taympirat**oo**ra
(fever) a febre fehbr

tennis o ténis teh**nish**

tennis ball a b**o**la de ténis di

tennis court o campo de ténis
k**a**mpoo

tennis racket a raqueta de ténis
rak**eh**ta

tent a tenda (de campismo)
t**ay**nda (di kamp**ee**Jmoo)

term (at school) o período escolar
p**ee**r**ee**-oodoo shkool**a**r

terminus (rail) o terminal tirm**ina**l

terrible terrível tirr**ee**vil

terrific (weather) esplêndido
shpl**ay**ndidoo
(food, teacher) excelente
ish-sel**ay**nt

text o SMS ehs-em-ehs
(verb) enviar um SMS a
ayngvee-**a**r oong

than do que doo ki

smaller than mais pequeno
do que mïsh pik**ay**noo

thanks, thank you (said by man/
woman) obrigado/obrig**a**da
obrig**a**doo

thank you very much muito
obrigado/obrigada mw**ee**ngtoo

thanks for the lift obrigado/
obrigada pela boleia
p**i**la bool**ay**-a

no thanks não obrigado/
obrigada n**o**wng

DIALOGUE

thanks (said by man/woman)
obrigado/obrigada

that's OK, don't mention it
está bem, não se preocupe
com isso shta b**ay**ng n**o**wng si
pri-ook**oo**p kong **ee**soo

that: that… esse/essa… ays/**eh**sa
(further away) aquele/aquela…
ak**ayl**/ak**eh**la

that one esse/essa/isso **ee**soo
(further away) aquele/aquela/
aquilo ak**ee**loo

I hope that… espero que…
shp**eh**ro ki

that's nice! que bom! bong

is that…? isso é…? eh

that's it (that's right) certo
s**eh**rtoo

the o oo, f a ;
(pl) os oosh, as ash

theatre o teatro t-y**a**troo

their deles d**ay**lish, delas d**eh**lash

theirs deles, delas

them os oosh,
f as ash

for them para eles/elas ayIsh/
ehlash

with them com eles/elas kong

to them para eles/elas

who? – them quem? – eles/
elas k**ay**ng

then (at that time) então aynt**o**wng
(after that) depois dip**oh**-ish

there ali al**ee**, lá

over there ali adiante ad-y**a**nt

up there ali acima as**ee**ma

is there/are there...? há...? a

there is/there are... há...

there you are (giving something) tome lá tohm

thermometer o termómetro tir**moh**mitroo

Thermos flask o termo **tay**rmoo

these: these men estes homens **ay**shtiz**oh**mayngsh

these women estas mulheres **eh**shtaJ mool-**yeh**rish

I'd like these queria estes/ estas kir**ee**-a **ay**shtish/**eh**shtash

they (male) eles **ay**lish

(female) elas **eh**lash

thick espesso shp**ay**soo

(stupid) estúpido sht**oo**pidoo

thief (*male/female*) o ladrão ladr**ow**ng, a l**a**dra

thigh a coxa k**oh**sha

thin fino f**ee**noo

(person) magro m**a**groo

thing a coisa k**oh**-iza

my things as minhas coisas aJ m**ee**n-yash k**oh**-izash

think pensar payns**a**r

I think so acho que sim **a**shoo ki seeng

I don't think so acho que não nowng

I'll think about it vou pensar voh

third party insurance o seguro contra terceiros sig**oo**roo k**oh**ntra tirs**ay**roosh

thirsty: I'm thirsty tenho sede **tay**n-yoo sayd

this: this boy este menino aysht min**ee**noo

this girl esta menina **eh**shta min**ee**na

this one este aysht/esta **eh**shta/ isto **ee**shtoo

this is my wife esta é a minha mulher eh a m**ee**n-ya mool-y**eh**r

is this...? isto é...? **ee**shtweh

those: those... esses/essas... **ay**sish/**eh**sash

(further away) aqueles/aquelas... ak**ay**lish/ak**eh**lash

which ones? – those quais? – esses/essas kw**ee**sh

(further away) quais? – aqueles/ aquelas

thread o fio f**ee**-oo

throat a garganta garg**a**nta

throat pastilles as pastilhas para a garganta pasht**ee**l-yash

through por, através de atr**a**vehJ di

does it go through...? (train, bus) passa em...? ayng

throw atirar

throw away deitar fora dayt**a**r

thumb o polegar pool**e**gar

thunderstorm a trovoada troovw**a**da

Thursday quinta-feira k**ee**nta f**ay**ra

ticket o bilhete bil-y**ay**t

DIALOGUE

a return to Setúbal um bilhete de ida e volta para Setúbal oong – deedï – sitoobal

coming back when? quando volta? kwandoo

today/next Tuesday hoje/ na próxima terça-feira ohJ/ na prosima tayrsa fayra

that will be 6 euros são seis euros sowng sayz ay-ooroosh

ticket office (bus, rail) a bilheteira bil-yitayra

tide a maré mareh

tie (necktie) a gravata

tight (clothes etc) apertado apirtadoo

it's too tight está demasiado apertado shta dimaz-yadoo

tights os collants koolansh

till a caixa kïsha

time o tempo taympoo

what's the time? que horas são? k-yorash sowng

this time esta vez ehshta vaysh

last time a última vez ooltima

next time a próxima vez prosima

three times três vezes traysh vayzish

timetable o horário oo orar-yoo

tin (can) a lata

tinfoil o papel de alumínio papehl daloomeen-yoo

tin-opener o abre-latas abrilatash

tiny minúsculo minooshkooloo

tip (to waiter etc) a gorgeta goorJayta

tired cansado kansadoo

I'm tired (said by man/woman) estou cansado/cansada shtoh

tissues os lenços de papel laynsoosh di papehl

to: to Lisbon/London para Lisboa/Londres liJboh-a/ lohndrish

to Portugal/England para Portugal/Inglaterra poortoogal/ inglatehrra

we're going to the museum/to the post office vamos ao museo/aos correios vamooz ow moosay-oo/owsh koorray-oosh

toast (bread) a torrada toorrada

today hoje ohJ

toe o dedo do pé daydoo doo peh

together juntos Joontoosh

we're together (in shop etc) viemos juntos v-yaymoosh Joontoosh

toilet a casa de banho kaza di ban-yoo

where is the toilet? onde é a casa de banho? ohndeh

I have to go to the toilet tenho de ir à casa de banho tayn-yoo deer

toilet paper o papel higiénico papehl iJ-yehnikoo

tomato o tomate toomat

tomato juice o sumo de tomate soomoo di toomat

tomato ketchup o ketchup

tomorrow amanhã aman-yang

tomorrow morning amanhã de manhã aman-yang di man-yang

the day after tomorrow depois de amanhã dipoh-ish daman-yang

toner (cosmetic) o tónico tonikoo

tongue a língua leengwa

tonic (water) a água tónica agwa

tonight esta noite ehshta noh-it

tonsillitis a amigdalite ameegdaleet

too (excessively) demasiado dimaz-yadoo

(also) também tambayng

too hot demasiado quente kaynt

too much demais dimish

me too eu também ay-oo tambayng

tooth o dente daynt

toothache a dor de dentes dohr di dayntsh

toothbrush a escova de dentes shkohva

toothpaste a pasta de dentes pashta

top: on top of... em cima de... ayng seema di

at the top no alto noo altoo

at the top of... no topo de... tohpoo di

top floor o piso superior peezoo soopir-yohr

topless topless

torch a lanterna lantehrna

total o total tootal

tour a excursão shkoorsowng

is there a tour of...? há alguma excursão/visita guiada a...? algooma – vizeeta gee-ada

tour guide (male/female) o guia turístico gee-a tooreeshtikoo, a guia turística

tourist (male/female) o/a turista tooreeshta

tourist information office o turismo tooreeJmoo

tour operator o operador turístico opiradohr tooreeshtikoo

towards para

towel a toalha twal-ya

town a cidade sidad

in town na cidade

just out of town junto à cidade joontwa

town centre o centro da cidade sayntroo

town hall a câmara municipal moonisipal

toy o brinquedo breenkaydoo

track (US) o cais kish
see **platform**

tracksuit o fato de treino fatoo di traynoo

traditional tradicional tradis-yoonal

traffic o trânsito tranzítoo

traffic jam o engarrafamento ayngarrafamayntoo

traffic lights os semáforos simafooroosh

trailer (for carrying tent etc)
o reboque rib**o**k

(US) a roulotte rool**o**t

trailer park o parque de
campismo park di kamp**ee**Jmoo

train o comboio komb**oy**-oo

by train de comboio di

**is this the train for
Fátima?** é este o comboio
para Fátima? eh **ay**shtoo

sure com certeza kong sirt**ay**za

**no, you want that platform
there** não, tem que ir à
plataf**o**rma de lá nowng tayng
ki-**ee**r – di

trainers (shoes) os sapatos de
treino sap**a**toosh di tr**ay**noo

train station a estação de
comboios shtas**ow**ng di
komb**oy**-oosh

tram o eléctrico el**eh**trikoo

translate traduzir tradooz**ee**r

could you translate that?
pode traduzir isto? pod –
eeshtoo

translation a tradução
tradoos**ow**ng

translator (male/female) o
tradutor tradoot**oh**r, a tradut**o**ra

trash (waste) o lixo l**ee**shoo

trashcan o caixote de lixo
k**ee**sh**o**t di l**ee**shoo

travel viajar v-ya**J**ar

we're travelling around
estamos a viajar por aí
sht**a**mooz – poor a-**ee**

travel agent's a agência de
viagens a**J**aynsya di v-ya**J**ayngsh

traveller's cheque o cheque de
viagem shehk di v-ya**J**ayng

tray a travessa trav**eh**sa

tree a árvore **a**rvoori

tremendous bestial bisht-y**a**l

trendy à m**o**da

trim: just a trim, please (to
hairdresser) queria só cortar as
pontas, por favor kir**ee**-a saw
koort**a**r ash p**o**ntash poor fav**oh**r

trip (excursion) a excursão
shkoors**ow**ng

I'd like to go on a trip to…
gostava de ir numa viagem a…
goosht**a**va deer n**oo**ma v-ya**J**ayng

trolley o carrinho karr**ee**n-yoo

**trouble: I'm having trouble
with…** tenho tido problemas
com… t**ay**n-yoo t**ee**doo
pr**oo**bl**ay**mash kong

trousers as calças k**a**lsash

true verdadeiro virdad**a**yroo

   that's not true não é verdade nowng eh vird**a**d

trunk (US: of car) o porta-bagagens p**o**rta-bagaJayngsh

trunks (swimming) os calções de banho kals**o**yngsh di ban-yoo

try tent**a**r

   can I try it? posso experimentar? p**o**soo shpirimaynt**a**r

   (food) posso provar? proov**a**r

try on experiment**a**r

   can I try it on? posso experimentar? p**o**soo shpirimaynt**a**r

T-shirt a T-shirt

Tuesday terça-feira t**a**yrsa f**a**yra

tuna o atum at**oo**ng

tunnel o túnel t**oo**nil

turn: turn left/right vire à esquerda/direita v**ee**ra shk**a**yrda/dir**a**yta

turn off: where do I turn off? onde devo virar? ohnd d**a**yvoo

   can you turn the heating off? pode desligar o aquecimento? pod diJlig**a**r oo akesim**a**yntoo

turn on: can you turn the heating on? pode ligar o aquecimento?

turning (in road) a curva k**oo**rva

TV TV tay-vay

tweezers a pinça p**ee**nsa

twice duas vezes d**oo**-aJ v**a**yzish

twice as much o dobro oo d**oh**broo

twin beds as camas separadas k**a**mash sipar**a**dash

twin room o quarto com duas camas kw**a**rtoo kong d**oo**-ash

twist: I've twisted my ankle torci o meu tornozelo toors**ee** oo m**a**y-oo toornooz**a**yloo

type o tipo t**ee**poo

   a different type of... um tipo diferente de... oong – difir**a**ynt di

typical típico t**ee**pikoo

tyre o pneu pn**a**y-oo

U

ugly feio f**a**y-oo

UK Reino Unido raynoon**ee**doo

ulcer a úlcera **oo**lsira

umbrella o guarda-chuva gw**a**rda sh**oo**va

uncle o tio t**ee**-oo

unconscious inconsciente inkonsh-sy**a**ynt

under (in position) debaixo de dib**ī**shoo di

   (less than) menos de m**a**ynoosh di

underdone (meat) mal passado pas**a**doo

underground (railway) o metro m**eh**troo

underpants as cuecas kw**eh**kash

understand: I understand já percebi Ja pirsib**ee**

   I don't understand não percebo nowng pirs**a**yboo

do you understand? está a
compreender? shta a kompr-
ayndayr

unemployed desempregado
dizaymprigadoo

United States os Estados
Unidos shtadooz ooneedoosh

university a universidade
ooniversidad

unleaded petrol a gasolina
sem chumbo gazooleena
sayng shoomboo

unlimited mileage
quilometragem ilimitada
kilomitraJayng ilimitada

unlock abrir abreer

unpack desfazer as malas
dishfazayr aJ malash

until até a ateh

unusual pouco vulgar
pohkoo voolgar

up acima aseema

  up there lá em cima ayng seema

  he's not up yet (not out of bed)
  ele ainda não está levantado ayl
  a-eenda nowng shta levantadoo

  what's up? (what's wrong?)
  o que aconteceu? oo ki
  akontisay-oo

upmarket sofisticado
soofishtikadoo

upset stomach o desarranjo
intestinal dizarranJoo intishtinal

upside down de pernas para o
ar di pehrnash proo ar

upstairs lá em cima ayng seema

urgent urgente oorJaynt

us nos noosh

with us connosco konohshkoo

  for us para nós nosh

use usar oozar

  may I use...? posso usar...?
  posoo

useful útil ootil

usual usual oozwal

  the usual (drink etc)
  o de sempre oo di saympr

V

**vacancy: do you have any
vacancies?** (hotel) têm vagas?
tay-ayng vagash

vacation as férias fehr-yash

  on vacation de férias shtoh di

vaccination a vacinação
vasinasowng

vacuum cleaner o aspirador
ashpiradohr

valid (ticket etc) válido validoo

  **how long is it valid
  for?** até quando é válido?
  ateh kwandoo

valley o vale val

valuable (adj) valioso val-yohzoo

  **can I leave my valuables
  here?** posso deixar aqui os
  meus artigos de valor? posoo
  dayshar akee ooJ may-ooz
  arteegoosh di valohr

value o valor

van a furgoneta foorgoonayta

vanilla a baunilha bowneel-ya

  a vanilla ice cream
  um gelado de baunilha

oong Ji**la**doo di

vary: it varies varia va**ree**-a

vase a jarra **Ja**rra

veal a vitela vi**teh**la

vegetables os legumes li**goo**mish

vegetarian (*male/female*) o vegetariano vi**J**i**tar-ya**noo, a vegetari**a**na

vending machine a máquina de

> Travel tip Portuguese cuisine is tough on strict vegetarians and you'll be eating a lot of omelettes, salads and pizzas, though there are vegetarian restaurants in Lisbon, Porto and some parts of the Algarve. *Caldo verde* – a cabbage-and-potato broth – might come with a bit of sausage in it, but nearly everywhere does a basic vegetable soup.

venda ma**k**ina di **vay**nda

very muito m**wee**ngtoo

  very little for me muito pouco para mim po**h**koo para meeng

  I like it very much gosto muito disso go**sh**too – **dee**soo

vest (under shirt) a camisola interior kami**zo**la intir-y**oh**r

via via v**ee**-a

video (film) o vídeo v**eed**-yoo

video recorder o videogravador veed-yoogravad**oh**r

view a vista v**ee**shta

villa a vivenda viv**ay**nda

village a aldeia al**day**-a

vinegar o vinagre vin**ag**r

vineyard a vinha v**ee**n-ya

visa o visto v**ee**shtoo

visit visitar vizi**tar**

  I'd like to visit... gostaria de visitar... goosh**taree**-a di

vital: it's vital that... é imprescindível que... eh impresh-sind**ee**vil ki

vodka o v**o**dka

voice a voz vo**sh**

voltage a tensão tayn**sow**ng

vomit vomitar voo**mi**tar

W

waist a cintura sin**too**ra

waistcoat o colete ko**la**yt

wait esperar shpi**rar**

  wait for me espere por mim shpehr poor meeng

  don't wait for me não espere por mim nowng

  can I wait until my wife/ partner gets here? posso esperar até a minha mulher/ companheira chegar? pos shpi**rar** at**e**h a m**ee**n-ya mool-y**eh**r/kompan-y**ay**ra shi**gar**

  can you do it while I wait? pode fazer isso enquanto espero? pod fa**zayr ee**soo aynk**wa**ntoo shp**eh**roo

  could you wait here for me? pode esperar-me? pod shpi**rar**mi

waiter o empregado de mesa aympregadoo di mayza

waiter! se faz favor! si fash favohr

waitress a empregada de mesa aympregada di mayza

waitress! se faz favor! si fash favor!

wake: can you wake me up at 5.30? pode acordar-me às cinco meia? pod akoordarmi ash seenkwee may-a

wake-up call a chamada para despertar shamada para dishpirtar

Wales o País de Gales pa-eeJ di galish

walk: is it a long walk? é muito longe a pé? eh mweengtoo lohnJ a peh

it's only a short walk é perto a pé pehrtoo

I'll walk vou a pé voh

I'm going for a walk vou dar um passeio oong pasay-oo

wall (outside) o muro mooroo

(inside) a parede parayd

wallet a carteira kartayra

wander: I like just wandering around gosto de andar a ver goshtoo dandar a vayr

want: I want a... queria um... kiree-a oong

I don't want any... não quero... nowng kehroo

I want to go home quero ir para casa eer para kaza

I don't want to não quero

he wants to ele quer ayl kehr

what do you want? o que deseja? oo ki disayJa

ward (in hospital) a enfermaria aynfirmaree-a

warm quente kaynt

I'm so warm tenho tanto calor tayn-yoo tantoo kalohr

was: he was (ele) era (ayl) ehra; (ele) estava shtava

she was (ela) era (ehla); (ele) estava

it was era; estava (see note on p.8)

wash lavar

(oneself) lavar-se –si

can you wash these? pode lavar isto? pod – eeshtoo

washer (for bolt etc) a anilha aneel-ya

washhand basin o lavatório lavator-yoo

washing (clothes) a roupa para lavar rohpa

washing machine a máquina de lavar makina di

washing powder o detergente deterJaynt

washing-up liquid o detergente líquido leekidoo

wasp a vespa vayshpa

watch (wristwatch) o relógio (de pulso) riloJ-yoo (di poolsoo)

will you watch my things for me? pode tomar conta das minhas coisas? pod toomar kohnta daJ meen-yash koh-izash

watch out! cuidado! kwidadoo

watch strap a correia de relógio koorray-a di riloJ-yoo

water a água agwa

may I have some water? pode dar-me um pouco de água? pod darmoong pohkoo dagwa

waterproof (*adj*) à prova de água dagwa

waterskiing o esqui aquático shkee akwatikoo

wave (in sea) a onda ohnda

way: it's this way é por aqui eh por akee

it's that way é por ali alee

is it a long way to…? é muito longe até…? mweengtoo lohnJ ateh

no way! de maneira nenhuma! di manayra nin-yooma

could you tell me the way to…? pode indicar-me o caminho para…? podindikarmoo kameen-yoo

go straight on until you reach the traffic lights siga em frente até chegar ao semáforo seegayng fraynt ateh shigar ow semafooroo

turn left vire à esquerda veera shkayrda

take the first on the right vire na primeira à direita veer na primayra dirayta

see **where**

we nós nosh

weak fraco frakoo

weather o website

what's the weather forecast? qual é a previsão do tempo? kwaleh a privizowng doo taympoo

it's going to be fine vai estar bom vī shtar bong

it's going to rain vai chover shoovayr

it'll brighten up later vai melhorar mais tarde mil-yoorar mish tard

website o tempo taympoo

wedding o casamento kazamayntoo

wedding ring a aliança al-yansa

Wednesday quarta-feira kwarta fayra

week a semana simana

a week (from) today de hoje a uma semana dohJ a ooma

a week (from) tomorrow de amanhã a uma semana daman-yang

weekend o fim de semana feeng di

at the weekend no fim de semana noo

weight o peso payzoo

weird esquisito shkizeetoo

he's weird ele é esquisito ayl eh

welcome: welcome to… bem vindo a… bayng veendwa

you're welcome (don't mention it) não tem de quê nowng tayng di kay

well: I don't feel well não me
sinto muito bem mi **see**ntoo
mw**ee**ngtoo bayng

she's not well ela não está
bem **eh**la – shta

you speak English very well
f**a**la inglês muito bem ingl**ay**sh

well done! muito bem!

this one as well este também
aysht tamb**ay**ng

well well! (surprise) ah sim!
seeng

how are you? como está?
k**o**hmo shta

**very well, thanks, and
you?** (said by man/woman)
muito bem, obrigado/
obrig**a**da, e você? obrig**a**doo
– ee vos**ay**

well-done (meat) bem passado
bayng pas**a**doo

Welsh galês gal**ay**sh

I'm Welsh (*male/female*) sou
galês/galesa soh – gal**ay**za

were: we were éramos
ehramoosh; estávamos
sht**a**vamoosh

you were você era vos**ay** **eh**ra;
você estava sht**a**va

they were (eles/elas) eram
(aylsh/**eh**lash) **eh**rowng; (eles/
elas) estavam sht**a**vavowng
(*see note on p.8*)

west o oeste wesht

in the west no oeste noo

West Indian (*adj*) antilhano
antil-y**a**noo

wet molhado mool-y**a**doo

what? o quê? oo kay

what's that? o que é isso?
oo k-yeh **ee**soo

what should I do? o que
devo fazer? oo kay d**ay**voo faz**ay**r

what a view! que vista linda!
ki v**ee**shta l**ee**nda

what bus do I take?
que autocarro devo tomar?
ki owtook**a**rroo d**ay**voo toom**a**r

wheel a r**o**da

wheelchair a cadeira de rodas
kad**ay**ra di r**o**dash

when? quando? kw**a**ndoo

when we get back
quando nós voltarmos nosh
voolt**a**rmoosh

when's the train/ferry?
quando é o comboio/ferry?
kw**a**ndweh o komb**o**y-oo

where? onde? ohnd

I don't know where it is não
sei onde está nowng say ohndshta

where is the cathedral?
onde fica a catedral?
ohnd f**ee**ka

it's over there fica ali
adiante f**ee**kalee ad-yant

**could you show me where
it is on the map?** pode
mostrar-me onde está no
mapa? pod m**oo**shtrarmi
ohndsht**a** noo mapa

it's just here está bem aqui
sht**a** bayng ak**ee**

see **way**

which: which bus? qual
autocarro? kwal owtookarroo

DIALOGUE

which one? qual deles?
kwal daylish
that one aquele akayl
this one? este? aysht
no, that one não aquele ali
nowng – alee

while: while I'm here enquanto
estou aqui aynkwantoo
shtoh akee

whisky o whisky weeshkee

white branco brankoo

white wine o vinho branco
veen-yoo

who? quem? kayng

who is it? quem é? kayngeh
the man who... o homem
que... ohmayng ki

whole: the whole week toda a
semana tohda simana

the whole lot tudo isto
toodoo eeshtoo

whose: whose is this? de
quem é isto? di kayng eh eeshtoo

why? porquê? poorkay

why not? porque não? nowng

wide largo largoo

wife: my wife a minha mulher
meen-ya mool-yehr

Wi-Fi wifi wee-fee

will: will you do it for me?
fá-lo para mim? faloo para
meeng

wind o vento vayntoo

window a janela Janehla

(of shop) a montra mohntra

near the window ao pé da
janela ow peh

in the window (of shop)
na montra

window seat o lugar ao pé da
janela loogar ow peh da Janehla

windscreen o pára-brisas
para-breezash

windscreen wiper o limpa
pára-brisas leempa

windsurfing o windsurf

windy: it's so windy está muito
vento shta mweengtoo vayntoo

wine o vinho veen-yoo

**can we have some more
wine?** pode trazer mais vinho?
pod trazayr mīsh

wine list a lista dos vinhos
leeshta dooJ veen-yoosh

winter o Inverno invehrnoo

in the winter no Inverno noo

winter holiday as férias de
inverno fehr-yash dinvehrnoo

wire o arame aram

(electric) o fio fee-oo

wish: best wishes com os
melhores cumprimentos kong
ooJ mil-yorish koomprimayntoosh

with com kong

I'm staying with... estou na
casa do/da... shtoh na kaza doo

without sem sayng

witness a testemunha
tishtimoon-ya

**will you be a witness
for me?** quer ser minha
testemunha? kehr sayr meen-ya

woman a mulher mool-y**eh**r

wonderful (weather, holiday, person) maravilhoso maravil-y**oh**zoo

(meal) excelente ish-sel**ay**nt

won't: it won't start não pega nowng p**eh**ga

wood (material) a madeira mad**ay**ra

woods (forest) o bosque boshk

wool a lã lang

word a pal**a**vra

work o trabalho trab**a**l-yoo

it's not working não funciona nowng foons-y**oh**na

I work in... trabalho em... ayng

world o mundo m**oo**ndoo

worry: I'm worried (said by man/ woman) estou preocupado/ preocup**a**da shtoh pri-ookoop**a**doo

worse: it's worse está pior shta p-yor

worst o pior oo

worth: is it worth a visit? vale a pena uma visita? val a p**ay**na **oo**ma viz**ee**ta

would: would you give this to...? pode dar isto a...? pod dar **ee**shtwa

wrap: could you wrap it up? pode embrulhá-lo? aymbrool-y**a**loo

wrapping paper o papel de embrulho pap**eh**l daymbr**oo**l-yoo

wrist o pulso p**oo**lsoo

write escrever shkriv**ay**r

could you write it down? pode escrever isso? pod – **ee**soo

how do you write it? como é que escreve isso? k**oh**moo eh kishkr**eh**v

writing paper o papel de carta
pap**eh**l di

wrong: it's the wrong key
não é esta a chave nowng eh
ehshta shav

this is the wrong train
este não é o comboio aysht
nowng eh oo komb**oy**-oo

the bill's wrong a conta
está enganada k**oh**ntashta
aygan**a**da

sorry, wrong number
desculpe, enganei-me no
número dishk**oo**lp ayngan**ay**mi
noo n**oo**miroo

sorry, wrong room
desculpe, enganei-me no
quarto kw**a**rtoo

**there's something wrong
with...** passa-se qualquer coisa
com... p**a**sasi kwalk**eh**r k**oh**-iza
kong

what's wrong? o que se
p**a**ssa? oo ki si

X

X-ray o raio X ra-yoo sheesh

Y

yacht o iate yat
yard a jarda J**a**rda
year o ano **a**noo
yellow amarelo amar**eh**loo
yes sim seeng
yesterday ontem **oh**ntayng

yesterday morning ontem de
manhã di man-y**a**ng

the day before yesterday
anteontem anti**oh**ntayng

yet ainda a-**ee**nda, já Ja

yoghurt o iogurte yoog**oo**rt
you (*pol*) você vos**ay**
(more formal: to man/woman)
o senhor oo sin-y**oh**r, a senh**o**ra
(*fam*) tu too

this is for you isto é para si
eeshtweh para see
(*fam*) isto é para ti

with you consigo kons**ee**goo
(*fam*) contigo kont**ee**goo

young jovem J**o**vayng

your (*pol*) seu s**ay**-oo, sua s**oo**-a
(more formal: to man/woman)
do senhor sin-y**oh**r, da senhora
sin-y**o**ra
(*fam*) teu t**ay**-oo, tua t**oo**-a

yours (*pol*) seu s**ay**-oo, sua s**oo**-a
(more formal: to a man/woman)
do senhor sin-y**oh**r,
da senhora sin-y**o**ra
(*fam*) teu t**ay**-oo, tua t**oo**-a

youth hostel o albergue da
juventude alb**eh**rg
da Joovaynt**oo**d

Z

zero zero zehroo

zip o fecho éclair fayshwayklehr

  could you put a new zip on? pode pôr um fecho éclair novo? pod pohr oong – nohvoo

zipcode o código postal kodigoo pooshtal

zoo o jardim zoológico Jardeeng zwoloJikoo

zucchini a courgette

PORTUGUESE
→ **ENGLISH**

Colloquialisms

The following are words you might well hear. You shouldn't be tempted to use any of the stronger ones unless you are sure of your audience.

bestial! bisht-yal fantastic!

burro *m* boorroo thickhead

cabrão! kabrowng bastard!

está nas suas sete quintas shta nash soo-ash seht keentash he's/she's in his/her element

estou-me nas tintas shtoh-mi nash teentash I don't give a damn

filho da puta! poota son-of-a-bitch!

gajo *m* gaJoo bloke

grosso grohsoo pissed

imbecil imbeseel stupid

isso é canja eesweh kanJa piece of cake (literally: this is chicken soup)

louco lohkoo nutter

maçada masada bother

maluco malookoo barmy, nuts

merda! mehrda shit!

não faz mal nowng faJ it doesn't matter

não me diga! nowng mi deega you don't say!

ora essa! ora ehsa don't be stupid!

porreiro! poorrayroo bloody good!

que chatice! ki shatees oh no!, blast!

que disparate! dishparat rubbish!, nonsense!

que droga! droga blast!

raios o partam! ra-yooz oo partowng damn you!

rua! roo-a get out of here!

sacana! bastard!

tolo tohloo silly

vá à fava! go away!

vá para o caralho! paroo karal-yoo fuck off!

vá para o diabo! d-yaboo go to hell!

vá para o inferno! infehrno go to hell!

A

a the; to; her; it; to it; you

à to the

abaixo abīshoo below; down

mais abaixo mīz further down

abcesso *m* absehsoo abscess

aberto abehrtoo open; opened

aberto até às 19 horas open until 7 p.m.

aberto das ... às ... horas open from ... to ... o'clock

abertura *f* abirtoora opening

aborrecer aboorrisayr to annoy; to bore

aborrecido aboorriseedoo annoying; bored; annoyed

abre-garrafas *m* abrigarrafash bottle-opener

abre-latas *m* abrilatash
can-opener, tin-opener

Abril abreel April

abrir abreer to open; to unlock

a abrir brevemente open
soon

a/c c/o

acabar to finish

acalmar-se –si to calm down

acampar to camp

acaso: por acaso poor akazoo
by chance

aceitar asaytar to accept; to take

acelerador *m* asiliradohr
accelerator

acenda os médios switch on
dipped headlights

acenda os mínimos switch on
your parking lights

acender asayndayr to switch on;
to light

acento *m* asayntoo accent

aceso asayzoo on, switched on

acesso *m* asehsoo access

acetona *f* asitohna nail polish
remover

acho: acho que não ashoo ki
nowng I don't think so

acho que sim seeng I think so

acidente *m* asidaynt accident;
crash

acidente de viação di v-yasowng road accident

ácido asidoo sour; sharp

acima aseema up; above

acompanhar akompan-yar
to accompany

aconselhar akonsil-yar to advise

acontecer akontisayr to happen

o que aconteceu? oo
ki-akontisay-oo what has
happened?, what's up?, what's
wrong?

**o que é que está a
acontecer?** oo k-yeh kishta
what's happening?

acordado akoordadoo awake

acordar akoordar to wake,
to wake up

ele já acordou? ayl Ja
akoordoh is he awake?

acordo: de acordo com d-ya-
kohrdoo kong according to

A.C.P. a say pay Portuguese
Motoring Organization

acreditar to believe

acrílico *m* akreelikoo acrylic

actor *m* atohr, **actriz** *f* atreesh
actor; actress

adaptador *m* adaptadohr adapter

adega *f* cellar; old-style bar

adepta *f* adehpta, **adepto** *m*
adehptoo fan

adesivo *m* adizeevoo sticking
plaster, Bandaid

adeus aday-oosh goodbye

adeuzinho! aday-oozeen-yoo
cheerio!

adiantado ad-yantadoo
in advance

adiante: fica ali adiante
feekalee ad-yant it's over there

adoecer ad-wisayr to fall ill

adolescente *m/f* adoolish-saynt
teenager

adorar adoorar to adore

adorável adooravil lovely

adulta f adoolta, **adulto** m adooltoo adult

advogada f advoogada, **advogado** m advoogadoo lawyer

aeroporto m a-ayroopohrtoo airport

afiado af-yadoo sharp

afogador m choke

África f Africa

África do Sul doo sool South Africa

africano (m) afrikanoo African

afta f mouth ulcer

afundar afoondar to sink

agência f aJayns-ya agency

agência de viagens di v-ya-Jayngsh travel agency

agenda f aJaynda diary

agitar bem antes de usar shake well before using

agora agora now

agora não nowng not just now

Agosto agohshtoo August

agradável agradavil nice, pleasant

agradecer agradisayr to thank

agradecido agradiseedoo grateful

água f agwa water

aguaceiro m agwasayroo shower

água de colónia di eau de toilette

água destilada f agwa dishtilada distilled water

água fria free-a cold water

água potável pootavil drinking water

aguardar agwardar to wait for

agudo agoodoo sharp

agulha f agool-ya needle

aí a-ee there

ainda a-eenda yet, still

ainda mais... mish even more...

ainda não nowng not yet

ainda são só... sowng saw it's only...

ajuda f aJooda help

ajudar to help

al. avenue

alameda f alamayda avenue

alarme m alarm alarm

alarme de incêndios dinsaynd-yoosh fire alarm

alavanca f lever

alavanca das mudanças daJ moodansash gear lever

albergaria f albirgaree-a luxury hotel

albergue da juventude m albehrg da Joovayntood youth hostel

albergue juvenil youth hostel

alça f alsa strap

alcunha f alkoon-ya nickname

aldeia f alday-a village

aldeia de pescadores di pishkadohrish fishing village

além: além de alayng di apart from

para além de paralayng beyond

alemã (f) alimang German
Alemanha f aliman-ya Germany
alemão (m) alimowng German
alérgico a... alehrJikoo
  allergic to...
Alfa high-speed train
alfabeto m alfabehtoo alphabet
alfaiataria f alfi-ataree-a, **alfaiate**
  m alfi-at tailor
alfândega f alfandiga Customs
alfinete m alfinayt brooch; pin
alfinete de segurança m di
  sigooransa safety pin
alforreca f alfoorrehka jellyfish
alga f seaweed
algodão m algoodowng cotton
algodão em rama ayng cotton
  wool
alguém algayng anybody;
  somebody, someone
algum algoong, **alguma** algooma
  some; any
alguma coisa koh-iza
  something; anything
algumas algoomash, **alguns**
  algoonsh some; any
ali alee (over) there
  ali acima aseema up there
  ali adiante ad-yant over there
  é por ali eh poor it's that way
aliança f al-yansa wedding ring
alicate m alikat pliers
alicate de unhas doon-yash
  nail clippers
alimento m alimayntoo food
almoçar almoosar to have lunch
almoço m almohsoo lunch

almoço embalado
  almohswaymbaladoo
  packed lunch
almofada f almoofada cushion;
  pillow
alojamento m aloojamayntoo
  accommodation
alpinismo m alpineeJmoo
  mountaineering
altitude f altitood height
alto altoo high; tall; loud
  no alto noo at the top
altura f altoora height
altura máxima maximum
  headroom
alugam-se quartos rooms to
  let, rooms for rent
alugar aloogar to hire, to rent
aluga-se alooga-si for hire,
  to rent
aluguer m aloogehr rent
aluguer de automóveis
  dowtoomovaysh car hire,
  car rental
aluguer de barcos boat hire
aluguer de barracas sunshades
  for hire
aluguer de cadeiras beach
  chairs for hire
aluguer de gaivotas pedal
  boat hire
aluguer de parassóis beach
  umbrellas for hire
alvorada f alvoorada dawn
ama f childminder
amanhã aman-yang tomorrow
amanhã à tarde tard tomorrow
  afternoon

amanhã de manhã di man-yang
  tomorrow morning
amar to love
amarelo amarehloo yellow
amargo amargoo bitter
amável amavil kind; generous
ambos amboosh both
ambulância famboolans-ya
  ambulance
ameno amaynoo mild
América f America
americano amirikanoo American
amiga fameega friend
amigdalite fameegdaleet
  tonsillitis
amigo m ameegoo friend
amor m amohr love
amortecedor m amoortisidohr
  shock-absorber

amperes mpl ampehrish amps
ampliação fampl-yasowng
  enlargement
ampolas bebíveis fpl ampohlaJ
  bibeevaysh ampoules
analgésicos mpl analJehzeekoosh
  painkillers
análises de sangue fpl analiziJ
  di sang blood tests
anca fhip
âncora fanchor
andar (m) floor, storey; to walk
andar à boleia boolay-a to
  hitchhike
andar a cavalo kavaloo horse-
  riding
andar a pé peh to walk
anel m anehl ring
anilha faneel-ya washer
animado animadoo lively
aniversário de casamento
  m anivirsar-yoo di kazamayntoo
  wedding anniversary
aniversário natalício nataleees-
  yoo birthday
ano m anoo year
Ano Novo nohvoo New Year
anteontem anti-ohntayng
  the day before yesterday
antepassado m ancestor
anterior: dia anterior m dee-a
  antir-yohr the day before
antes antsh before
antibióticos mpl antib-yotikoosh
  antibiotics
anticongelante m –konJilant
  antifreeze
antigo anteegoo ancient, old

antiguidade *f* antigweedad antique

anti-histamínicos *mpl* –eesh- tam**ee**nikoosh antihistamines

antilaxante *m* anti-lash**a**nt medicine for diarrhoea

antiquado antikw**a**doo old-fashioned

anti-séptico *m* –s**eh**ptikoo antiseptic

anúncio *m* an**oo**ns-yoo advertisement

ao ow to the; at the

ao norte de north of

aos owsh to the; at the

apagar to switch off

apagar os máximos switch headlights off

apanhar apan-y**a**r to get on, to catch; to pick up

apanhar banhos de sol ban-yooj di to sunbathe

aparelhagem (de som) *f* aparel- y**a**Jayng (di song) stereo; audio equipment

aparelho *m* apar**ay**l-yoo device

aparelho auditivo hearing aid

aparelho para a surdez soord**ay**sh hearing aid

aparelhos eléctricos *mpl* apar**ay**l-yooz el**eh**trikoosh electrical appliances

apartamento *m* apartam**ay**ntoo apartment, flat

aparthotel *m* apartoht**eh**l self-catering apartment

apelido *m* apil**ee**doo surname; family name

apendicite *f* apendis**ee**t appendicitis

apertado apirt**a**doo tight

apertar to hold tight; to fasten

apertar o cinto de segurança fasten your seatbelt

apetecer apitis**ay**r to feel like

apetece-me apit**eh**simi I feel like

apetite *m* apit**ee**t appetite

apinhado apeen-y**a**doo crowded

aprender apraynd**ay**r to learn

apresentar apprizent**a**r to introduce

apressar-se apris**a**rsi to hurry

aproximadamente aproosimadam**ay**nt approximately, roughly

aquecedor *m* akesid**oh**r heater

aquecedor eléctrico el**eh**trikoo electric fire

aquecimento *m* akesim**ay**ntoo heating

aquecimento central saynt**ra**l central heating

aquela ak**eh**la, **aquele** ak**ay**l that, that one (further away)

aquelas ak**eh**lash, **aqueles** ak**ay**lish those (further away)

aqui ak**ee** (over) here

aqui embaixo aymb**ï**shoo down here

aqui está/estão... shta/ shtowng here is/are...

aqui mesmo may**J**moo just here

é por aqui eh por it's this way

aqui tem tayng here you are

aquilo akeeloo that; that one (further away)

ar *m* air

árabe arabi Arab; Arabic
os árabes the Arabs

arame *m* aram wire

aranha faran-ya spider

arco-íris *m* arkoo-eereesh rainbow

ar condicionado *m* kondis-yoonadoo air conditioning

arder ardayr to burn

areia faray-a sand

armário *m* armar-yoo cupboard

armazém *m* armazayng warehouse; big store

aroma artificial/natural artificial/natural fragrance

arq. architect

arqueologia fark-yolooJee-a archaeology

arquitecto *m* arkitehtoo architect

arraial *m* arrī-al local fair with fireworks, singing and dancing

arranhão *m* arran-yowng scratch

arranjos *mpl* arranJoosh repairs

arredores *mpl* arredorish suburb

arriscado arrishkadoo risky

arroba f at sign, @

arte f art art

artesanato *m* artizanatoo handicrafts, crafts

artificial artifis-yal artificial

artigos de bébé *mpl* arteegooJ di bebeh baby goods

artigos de campismo kampeeJmoo camping equipment

artigos de casa kaza household goods

artigos de desporto dishpohrtoo sports goods

artigos de luxo looshoo luxury goods

artigos de viagem v-yaJayng travel goods

artigos em cabedal ayng kabidal leather goods

artigos em cortiça koorteesa cork goods

artigos em pele pehl leather goods

artigos regionais regional goods, typical goods from the region

artista *m/f* arteeshta artist

árvore farvoori tree

as ash the; them; you

às to the; at the

asa f wing

asa-delta faza-dehlta hang-gliding

ascensor *m* ashsaynsohr lift, elevator

asma faJma asthma

asneira faJnayra nonsense; swearword

aspirador *m* ashpiradohr vacuum cleaner

aspirina fashpireena aspirin

assaltado asaltadoo mugged

assar to bake; to roast

assento *m* asayntoo seat

assim aseeng this way

assim está bem shta bayng
that'll do nicely

assim está bem? is that OK?

assinado signed

assinar to sign

assinatura f asinatoora signature

atacadores mpl atakadohrish
shoelaces

atalho m atal-yoo shortcut

ataque m atak fit; attack

ataque cardíaco kardee-akoo
heart attack

até ateh until

até amanhã aman-yang see
you tomorrow

até já Ja see you soon

até logo! logoo see you!, see
you later!

até mesmo... mayJmoo
even...

atenção please note; caution;
warning

atenção ao comboio beware
of the train

atenção: portas automáticas
warning: automatic doors

aterragem f atirraJayng landing

aterragem de emergência
emergency landing

aterrar to land

atirar to throw

Atlântico m Atlantic

atletismo m atleteeJmoo athletics

atraente atra-aynt attractive

atrás atrash at the back, behind

atrás de... di behind...

atrasado atrazadoo late, delayed

estar atrasado shtar to be late

atraso m atrazoo delay

através de atravehJ di through

atravessar to go through, to cross

atravesse go, walk

atropelar atropilar to knock over,
to knock down

auscultador m owshkooltadohr
receiver

auscultadores mpl
owshkooltadohrish headphones

australiano (m) owshtral-yanoo
Australian

autobanco m owtoobankoo cash
dispenser, ATM

autocarro m owtookarroo coach,
bus

autocarro do aeroporto
dwayroopohrtoo airport bus

autoestrada f owtooshtrada
motorway, highway, freeway

automático owtoomatikoo
automatic

automóvel m owtoomovil car

Automóvel Clube de Portugal
Portuguese Motoring
Organization

av. avenue

avance go, walk

avaria f avaree-a breakdown

avariado avari-adoo damaged;
faulty; out of order

avariar avari-ar to damage; to
break down

avarias avaree-ash
breakdown service

ave f avi bird

avenida *f* avin**ee**da avenue

avião *m* av-**yow**ng plane, airplane

de avião dav-**yow**ng by plane; by air

aviso av**ee**zoo warning; notice

avô *m* av**oh** grandfather

avó *f* av**aw** grandmother

azedo az**ay**doo sour

azul az**oo**l blue

azulejaria *f* azoolayJar**ee**-a tile maker's workshop

azul-marinho az**oo**l mar**ee**n-yoo navy blue

B

bagagem *f* baga**J**ayng luggage, baggage

bagagem de mão *f* di mowng hand luggage

baía *f* ba-**ee**-a bay

baile *m* b**ī**li dance

bairro *m* b**ī**rroo district

baixo b**ī**shoo low; short

balcão *m* balk**ow**ng counter

balcão de informações dinfoormas**oy**ngsh information desk

balcão da recepção riseh**sow**ng reception desk

balde *m* bowld bucket

banco *m* b**a**nkoo bank; stool

banco de poupança di poh**pa**nsa savings bank

banda *f* band

bandeira *f* band**ay**ra flag

banheira *f* ban-**yay**ra

bathtub, bath

banheiro *m* ban-**yay**roo lifeguard

banheiros ban-**yay**roosh toilets

banho *m* ban-yoo bath

banho de sol: tomar banho de sol toomar – di to sunbathe

barata *f* cockroach

barato bar**a**too cheap, inexpensive

barba *f* beard

barbatanas *fpl* barbat**a**nash flippers

barbeiro *m* barb**ay**roo men's hairdresser's, barber's shop

barco *m* b**a**rkoo boat

barco a motor barkwa moot**oh**r motorboat

barco a remos ray**moo**sh rowing boat

barco a vapor steamer

barco à vela sailing boat

barcos de aluguer boats for hire

barraca *f* beach hut

barro: louça de barro *f* l**oh**sa di b**a**rroo earthenware

barulhento barool-y**ay**ntoo noisy

barulho *m* bar**oo**l-yoo noise

bastante bash**ta**nt fairly; rather; quite (a lot)

bata (à porta) knock

batechapas bodywork repairs

bater bat**ay**r to hit, to knock

bateria *f* batir**ee**-a battery

baton *m* bat**o**ng lipstick

baton para o cieiro oo s-yay**r**oo lip salve

bêbado bayb**a**doo drunk

bebé *m* bebeh baby

beber bibayr to drink

bebida *f* bibeeda drink

beco sem saída cul-de-sac, dead end

bege beige

beijar bayJar to kiss

beijo *m* bayJoo kiss

beira: à beira do mar bayra doo at/by the seaside

beira-mar: à beira-mar by the sea

belga (*m/f*) Belgian

Bélgica *f* behlJika Belgium

beliche *m* bileesh berth, bunk; couchette; bunk beds

belo behloo beautiful

bem bayng fine, well, OK; properly

  bem aqui akee right here

  está bem shta that's fine

  estás bem? shtash are you all right?

bem-educado bayng idookadoo polite

bem passado pasadoo well-done

bem-vindo veendoo welcome

  bem-vindo a... welcome to...

bengaleiro *m* bengalayroo cloakroom, checkroom

berço *m* bayrsoo cot

bestial! bisht-yal fantastic!, tremendous!

bexiga *f* bisheega bladder

biberão *m* bibirowng baby's bottle

biblioteca *f* bibl-yootehka library

bicha *f* beesha queue, line

bicicleta *f* bisiklehta bicycle, bike

bifurcação *f* bifoorkasowng fork (in road)

bigode *m* bigod moustache

bilha de gás *f* beel-ya di gash gas cylinder

bilhete *m* bil-yayt ticket

bilhete de entrada dayntrada admission ticket

bilhete de excursão dishkoorsowng excursion ticket

bilhete de ida deeda single ticket, one-way ticket

bilhete de ida e volta deedī return ticket, round trip ticket

bilhete de lotaria di lootaree-a lottery ticket

bilhete em aberto bil-yaytayng abehrtoo open ticket

bilheteira *f* bil-yitayra box office, ticket office

bilhetes tickets

bilhete simples *m* bil-yayt seemplish single ticket, one-way ticket

bloco de apartamentos *m* blokoo dapartamayntoosh apartment block

bloco de apontamentos dapontamayntoosh notebook

blusa *f* blooza blouse

boa boh-a good

boa noite noh-it good evening; good night

Boas Festas! boh-ash fehshtash merry Christmas and a happy New Year!

boa sorte! sohrt good luck!

boa tarde tard good afternoon; good evening

boate f bwat nightclub; disco

boa viagem! v-yaJayng have a good journey!

boca f bohka mouth

bocadinho m bookadeen-yoo little bit

bocado m bookadoo piece

bochecha f booshaysha cheek

bóia f bo-ya buoy

boite f bwat nightclub; disco

bola f ball

bola de futebol di footbol football

boleia f boolay-a lift; ride

   dar (uma) boleia a to give a lift to

bolha f bohl-ya blister

bolinha f boleen-ya ball (small)

bolso m bohlsoo pocket

bom bong good; fine

bom apetite! bong apiteet enjoy your meal!

bomba f bohmba bomb; pump

bomba de ar air pump

bomba de gasolina di gazooleena garage, filling station, gas station; petrol pump

bombeiros mpl bombayroosh fire brigade

bom dia bong dee-a good morning

boné m booneh cap, hat

boneca f boonehka doll

bonito booneetoo beautiful; nice; pretty

borboleta f borboolayta butterfly

borda f edge

borracha f boorrasha rubber; eraser

bosque m boshk woods, forest

bota f boot (footwear)

botão m bootowng button

botas de borracha fpl wellingtons

bote de borracha m bot di boorrasha dinghy

braço m brasoo arm

branco brankoo white

Brasil m brazeel Brazil

brasileiro (m) brazilayroo Brazilian

breve brev brief

   em breve soon

briga f breega fight

brigar to fight

brilhante breel-yant bright; brilliant

brincadeira f breenkadayra joke

brincos mpl breenkoosh earrings

brinquedo m breenkaydoo toy

brisa f breeza breeze

britânico britanikoo British

brochura f broshoora leaflet

bronquite bronkeet bronchitis

bronzeado (m) bronz-yadoo tan; suntan; suntanned

bronzeador m suntan lotion

bronzear brohnz-yar to tan

bronzear-se –si to get a tan

bugigangas *mpl* booJigangash
bric-a-brac

bule *m* bool teapot

buraco *m* boorakoo hole

burro (*m*) boorroo donkey;
thickhead; stupid

buscar booshkar to collect;
to fetch

bússola *f* boosoola compass

buzina *f* boozeena horn

C

c/ with

cá here

cabeça *f* kabaysa head

cabedais *mpl* kabidīsh leather
goods

cabedal *m* kabidal leather

cabeleireiro *m* kabilayrayroo
hairdresser's

cabeleireiro de homens
dohmayngsh men's hairdresser

cabeleireiro de senhoras di
sin-yorash ladies' hairdresser

cabeleireiro unisexo
oonisehksoo unisex salon

cabelo *m* kabayloo hair

cabide *m* kabeed coathanger

cabina *f* kabeena cabin

cabina de provas di provash
fitting room

cabina telefónica kabeena
telefohnika phone box, phone
booth

cabos para ligar a bateria *mpl*
kaboosh – batiree-a jump leads

cabra *f* goat

cabrão! kabrowng bastard!

cabrona! bastard!

caça *f* kasa game (meat); hunting

caçarola *f* kasarola saucepan

cachimbo *m* kasheemboo pipe
(for smoking)

cacifo *m* kaseefoo locker

cada each; every

cadeado *m* kad-yadoo padlock

cadeia *f* kaday-a prison; chain

cadeira *f* kadayra chair

cadeira de bebé di bebeh
highchair

cadeira de lona lohna deckchair

cadeira de rodas rodash
wheelchair

cadeira reclinável reklinavil
sun lounger

cadeirinha de bebé *f* kadayreen-
ya di bebeh pushchair, buggy

caderneta *f* kadayrnayta
book of tickets

café *m* kafeh café; coffee

café de esplanada dishplanada
pavement café

cãibra *f* kaymbra cramp

cair ka-eer to fall

cais *m* kīsh quay; quayside;
platform, (US) track

caixa *f* kīsha box; cash desk,
till; cashier; cashpoint, ATM;
savings bank; building society

caixa automático
owtoomateekoo cashpoint, ATM

caixa de fusíveis di foozeevaysh
fusebox

caixa de mudanças moodansash
gearbox

caixa de primeiros socorros
primayroosh sookorroosh
first-aid kit

caixa de velocidades
viloosidadsh gearbox

caixa do correio doo koorray-oo
postbox; mailbox

caixa fechada till closed

caixote de lixo m kishot di
leeshoo bin, dustbin, trashcan

calçado m kalsadoo footwear

calcanhar m kalkan-yar
heel (of foot)

calças fpl kalsash trousers, (US)
pants

calções mpl kalsoyngsh shorts

calções de banho di ban-yoo
swimming trunks

calculadora f kalkooladohra
calculator

caldeira f kaldayra boiler

calendário m kalendar-yoo
calendar

cale-se! kalsi quiet!; shut up!

calmo kalmoo calm

calor m kalohr heat

   está imenso calor shta
   imaynsoo it's hot

   ter calor tayr to be hot

cama f bed

cama de bebé di bebeh cot

cama de campanha kampan-ya
campbed

cama de casal di kazal double
bed

cama de solteiro sooltayroo
single bed

cama dupla doopla double bed

cama individual f individwal
single bed

câmara f camera

câmara de ar f dar inner tube

câmara de vídeo f di veed-yoo
camcorder

câmara municipal f moonisipal
town hall

camarim m kamareeng
dressing room

camarote m kamarot cabin

camas separadas fpl kamash
siparadash twin beds

câmbio m kamb-yoo bureau de
change; exchange rate

câmbio do dia doo dee-a current
exchange rate

camião m kam-yowng truck

caminho m kameen-yoo path

caminho de ferro railway

**Caminhos de Ferro
   Portugueses** Portuguese
Railways

camioneta f kam-yoonayta coach,
bus; light truck

camisa f kameeza shirt

camisa de dormir di doormeer
nightdress

camisaria f kamizaree-a
shirt shop

camisola f kamizola jersey,
jumper, sweater

camisola interior intir-yohr
vest (under shirt)

campainha f kampa-een-ya bell

campismo *m* kampeeɹmoo
  camping
campo *m* kampoo field;
  countryside, country
campo de futebol di footbol
  football ground
campo de golfe golf golf course
campo de ténis tehnish
  tennis court
camurça *f* kamoorsa suede
canadiano (*m*) kanad-yanoo
  Canadian
canal *m* canal; channel
Canal da Mancha English
  Channel
canalizador *m* kanalizadohr
  plumber
canção *f* kansowng song
cancelado kansiladoo cancelled
cancelar kansilar to cancel
candeeiro *m* kand-yayroo lamp
caneca *f* kanehka mug
caneta *f* kanayta pen
caneta de feltro di fayltroo
  felt-tip pen
caneta esferográfica
  shfiroografika ballpoint pen
canhoto kan-yohtoo left-handed
canivete *m* kaniveht penknife
cano *m* kanoo pipe (for water)
canoa *f* kanoh-a canoe
canoagem *f* kanwaɹayng
  canoeing
cano de esgoto *m* kanoo
  diɹgohtoo drain
cansado kansadoo tired
cantar to sing

canto *m* kantoo corner
  no canto noo in the corner
cantor *m* kantohr, **cantora** *f*
  singer
cão *m* kowng dog
cão de guarda gwarda
  guard dog
capacete *m* kapasayt helmet
capaz: não seria capaz de...
  siree-a kapaɹ di I wouldn't be
  able to...
capela *f* kapehla chapel
capelista *f* kapeleeshta
  haberdasher
capô *m* kapoh bonnet (of car),
  (US) hood
cápsula *f* capsule
cara *f* face
caranguejo *m* karangayɹoo crab
caravana *f* caravan, (US) trailer
carburador *m* karbooradohr
  carburettor

careca karehka bald

carga máxima maximum load

carnaval *m* carnival

caro karoo expensive

carpete *f* karpeht carpet

carregador de telemóvel *m* karrigadohr di telemovil phone charger

carrinho *m* karreen-yoo trolley, (US) cart

carrinho de bagagem di bagaJayng luggage trolley, (US) baggage cart

carrinho de bebé bebeh pushchair; pram

carro *m* karroo car

de carro di by car

carroçaria *f* karroosaree-a bodywork

carro de aluguer *m* karroo daloogehr rented car

carro de mão di mowng trolley

carros de aluguer daloogehr car hire, car rental

carruagem *f* karrwaJayng carriage, coach

carruagem-cama *f* sleeper, sleeping car

carruagem para não fumadores *f* nowng foomadohrish nonsmoking carriage

carruagem restaurante ristowrant buffet car; restaurant car

carta *f* letter

carta de condução di kondoosowng driver's licence

carta de embarque daymbark boarding pass

carta de identidade didentidad ID card

cartão *m* kartowng card; pass; identity card; business card; cardboard

cartão bancário bankar-yoo cheque card

cartão de crédito di krehdeetoo credit card

cartão de débito dehbeetoo charge card

cartão de embarque daymbark boarding pass

cartão de garantia di garantee-a cheque card

cartão de telefone di telefohn phonecard

cartão de visitas di vizeetash business card

cartão Eurocheque Eurocheque card

carta por correio expresso poor koorray-oo shprehsoo express letter

cartas letters

carta verde vayrd green card (car insurance)

cartaz *m* kartash poster

carteira *f* kartayra purse; wallet

carteirista *m/f* kartayreeshta pickpocket

carteiro *m* postman

casa *f* kaza home; house

em casa ayng at home

na sua casa soo-a at your place

estar na casa do/da shtar … doo to stay with

ir para casa to go home

casaco *m* kazakoo jacket; coat

casaco de malha di mal-ya cardigan

casa de antiguidades *f* kaza dantigweedadsh antique shop

casa de banho di ban-yoo bathroom; toilet, rest room

casa de banho dos homens dooz ohmayngsh gents' toilet, men's room

casa de banho privativa privateeva private bathroom

casa de banho pública pooblika public convenience

casa de fados di fadoosh restaurant where traditional Portuguese fado songs are sung

casa de hóspedes doshpidsh guesthouse

casa de jantar di Jantar dining room

casa de pasto pashtoo canteen-style eating place, usually open at lunchtime and serving a cheap three-course menu

casa de saúde disa-ood clinic; nursing home

casado kazadoo married

casal *m* kazal couple

casamento *m* kazamayntoo wedding

casar-se kazarsi to get married

casas de banho *mpl* kazaɹ di ban-yoo toilets, rest rooms

caseiro kazayroo home-made

caso *m* kazoo case

em caso de in case of

castanho kashtan-yoo brown

castelo *m* kashtehloo castle

catarata *f* waterfall; cataract

catedral *f* katidral cathedral

categoria *f* katigooree-a category

católico (m) katolikoo Catholic

catorze katohrz fourteen

causa *f* kowza cause

por causa de poor – di because of

cautela take care

cavaleiro *m* kavalayroo horseman

cavalheiro *m* kaval-yayroo gentleman

cavalheiros *mpl* kaval-yayroosh gents' toilet, men's room

cavalo *m* kavaloo horse

cave *f* kav cellar; basement

caveira *f* kavayra skull

caverna *f* kavehrna cave

cavilha *f* kaveel-ya tent peg

c/c current account

CE *f* say eh EC

cedo saydoo early

mais cedo mish earlier

cego sehgoo blind

cem sayng hundred

cemitério *m* simitehr-yoo cemetery

centígrado *m* senteegradoo centigrade

centímetro *m* senteemitroo centimetre

cento e… sayntwee one hundred and…

central sen-tral central

central de correios f di koorray-oosh main post office

centro m sayntroo centre

centro comercial komayrs-yal shopping centre

centro da cidade sidad city centre, town centre

centro de enfermagem dingfirmaJayng clinic

centro de informação turística dinfoormasowng tooreestika tourist information office

centro de turismo di tooreeJmoo tourist information

cerâmicas fpl siramikash ceramics

cerca f sayrka fence

cerimónia f sirimohn-ya ceremony

de cerimónia di formal

certamente sirtamaynt certainly

certamente que não ki nowng certainly not

certeza: de certeza di sirtayza definitely

de certeza que não ki nowng definitely not

tem a certeza? tayng are you sure?

com certeza kong certainly, of course, sure

certidão f sirtidowng certificate

certo sehrtoo correct, right; sure

cervejaria f sirvayJaree-a beer house serving food

cesto m sayshtoo basket

cesto de compras di komprash shopping basket

céu m seh-oo sky

chaleira f shalayra kettle

chamada f shamada call

chamada de longa distância di lohnga dishtans-ya long-distance call

chamada internacional internas-yoonal international call

chamada interurbana interoorbana long-distance call

chamada local lookal local call

chamada paga no destinatário noo dishtinatar-yoo collect call, reverse charge call

chamada para despertar dishpirtar wake-up call

chamar shamar to call

chamar-se –si to be called

como se chama? kohmoo si shama what's your name?

champô m shampoh shampoo

chão m showng ground; floor

no chão noo on the floor; on the ground

chapa da matrícula f shapa da matreekoola licence plate

chapelaria f shapilaree-a hat shop

chapéu m shapeh-oo hat

chapéu de sol di beach umbrella, sunshade

charcutaria f sharkootaree-a delicatessen

charuto m sharootoo cigar

chateado shat-yadoo bored

chave f shav key

chave de fendas di fayndash
screwdriver

chave de porcas porkash
spanner

chave inglesa inglayza wrench;
spanner

chaveiro m shavayroo keyring

check-in: fazer o check-in to
check in

chávena f shavena cup

chefe da estação m shehf
dishtas-**ow**ng station master

chega shay**ga** that's plenty; that's
enough

chegada f shigada arrival

chegadas arrivals

chegar shigar to arrive, to get in;
to reach

cheio shay-oo full

cheirar shayrar to smell

cheiro m shayroo smell

cheque de viagem m shehk di
v-ya**J**ayng traveller's cheque

chinês (m) shinaysh Chinese

chique sheek posh; chic

chocante shook**ant** shocking

choque m shok shock

chorar shoorar to cry

chover shoovayr to rain

está a chover it's raining

chumbo m sh**oo**mboo lead; filling

chupa-chupa m sh**oo**pa-sh**oo**pa
lollipop

chupeta f shoopayta dummy

churrascada f shoorrashkada
barbecue

chuva f sh**oo**va rain

Cia. company

ciclismo m sikleeJmoo cycling

ciclista m/f sikleeshta cyclist

**cidadã/cidadão de terceira
idade** f/m sidadang/sidadowng di
tirs**ay**ra idad senior citizen

cidade f sidad town; city;
town centre

fora da cidade out of town

cidade antiga anteega old town

ciência f s-yayns-ya science

cigarro m sigarroo cigarette

cima: em cima de…
ayng s**ee**ma di on top of…

lá em cima up there; upstairs

cinco s**ee**nkoo five

cinquenta sinkw**ay**nta fifty

cinto m s**ee**ntoo belt

cinto de salvação di salvas**ow**ng
lifebelt

cinto de segurança sigoor**an**sa
seatbelt

cintura f sint**oo**ra waist

cinzeiro m sinz**ay**roo ashtray

cinzento sinz**ay**ntoo grey

circuito turístico m sirkoo-eetoo
toor**ee**shtikoo sightseeing tour

circule pela direita/esquerda
keep right/left

círculo m s**ee**rkooloo circle

ciumento s-yoom**ay**ntoo jealous

claro kl**a**roo pale; light; clear;

claro! sure!, of course!

claro que não ki-n**ow**ng
of course not

é claro eh of course

classe f klas class

classe económica ekoonohmika economy class

clima m kleema climate

clínica f kleenika clinic

clínica médica clinic

clínica veterinária veterinary clinic

clube m kloob club

clube de golfe di golf golf club

clube de ténis di tehnish tennis club

cobertor m koobirtohr blanket

cobra f snake

cobrar to cash

cobrir to cover

código m kodigoo code

código da estrada highway code

código postal m pooshtal, cod. postal postcode, zip code

coelho m kwayl-yoo rabbit

cofre m safe

coisa f koh-iza thing

cola f glue

colar m koolar necklace

colarinho m koolareen-yoo collar

colchão m koolshowng mattress

colchão de praia di prī-a beach mat

colecção f koolehsowng collection

colégio m koolehJ-yoo college

colete m koolayt waistcoat

colete de salvação di salvasowng life jacket

colher f kool-yehr spoon

colher de chá f di sha teaspoon

colisão f kooleezowng crash

collants mpl koolansh tights, pantyhose

com kong with

comandante m koomandant captain

combinação f kombinasowng combination; slip, underskirt

comboio m komboy-oo train

de comboio di by train

comboio rápido express train

começar koomesar to begin, to start

começo m koomaysoo start, beginning

comédia f koomehd-ya comedy

comer koomayr to eat

comerciante m/f koomayrs-yant business person

comichão f koomishowng itch

comida f koomeeda food; meal

comida congelada konJilada frozen food

comida de bebé f di bebeh baby food

comidas fpl food; meals

comissão f koomisowng commission

comissário de bordo m koomisar-yoo di bordoo steward

como kohmoo how; like; since, as

como? what?, pardon (me)?, sorry?

como é? eh what's it like?

como está? shta how are you?, how do you do?

como este kohmwaysht like this

como vai? vī how are things?

companheira f kompan-**yay**ra
partner, girlfriend

companheiro m kompan-**yay**roo
partner, boyfriend

companhia f kompan-**yee**-a
company

companhia aérea a-**ehr**-ya
airline

compartimento m
kompartim**ayn**too compartment

completamente komplitam**aynt**
completely

completo kompl**eh**too full

complicado komplik**a**doo
complicated

compra f k**oh**mpra purchase

comprar kompr**a**r to buy

Travel tip Don't expect to do
much in the way of haggling.
Prices are fixed in shops
everywhere, and although
open-air markets are a bit
more flexible, you won't be
able to negotiate a discount
on food, drink, clothes or
anything that has obviously
got a price attached to it.

compras fpl k**oh**mprash shopping

ir às compras eer ash to go
shopping

compreender kompr-yaynd**a**yr
to understand

comprido kompr**ee**doo long

comprimento m komprim**ayn**too
length

comprimido m komprim**ee**doo
tablet

comprimido para dormir
doorm**eer** sleeping pill

computador m kompootad**ohr**
computer

Comunidade Europeia
European Community

concerto m kons**ayr**too concert

concessionário m konsis-yoonar-
yoo agent

concha f k**oh**nsha shell

concha do mar doo seashell

concordar konkoord**a**r to agree

concordo konk**o**rdoo I agree

condições fpl kondis**oy**ngsh
conditions, terms

condução f kondoos**ow**ng
driving; transport

**condução enquanto
embriagado** aynkw**a**ntoo
aymbr-yag**a**doo drunken driving

condutor m kondoot**ohr**,
condutora f driver

conduza com cuidado drive
carefully

conduzir kondooz**eer** to lead; to
drive

cone de gelado m kohn di Jil**a**doo
ice-cream cone

confecções de criança fpl
konfehs-**oy**ngsh di kr-y**a**nsa
children's wear

confecções de homem
d**oh**mayng menswear

confecções de senhora di sin-
y**o**ra ladies' wear

confeitaria konfaytar**ee**-a sweet
shop, candy store

conferência f konfir**ayns**-ya
conference

confirmar konfirmar to confirm

confortável konfoortavil comfortable

confusão f konfoozowng confusion, mix-up

congelador m konJiladohr freezer

congestionamento m konJisht-yoonamayntoo traffic congestion

conhecer kon-yisayr to know

connosco konohshkoo with us

consciente konsh-syaynt conscious

consertar konsirtar to fix, to mend

conservar afastado da luz solar directa store away from direct sunlight

conservar no frio store in a cold place

consigo konseego with you

constipação f konshtipasowng cold

constipado: estou constipado shtoh konshtipadoo I have a cold

consulado m konsooladoo consulate

consulta f konsoolta appointment

consultório m konsooltor-yoo surgery, doctor's office

consultório dentário dental surgery

consumir dentro de … dias to be consumed within … days

conta f kohnta bill; account

conta bancária bankar-ya bank account

contactar to contact

contaminado kontaminadoo polluted

conta-quilómetros m konta-kilohmitroosh speedometer

contar to count; to tell

contente kontaynt happy; glad, pleased

contigo konteegoo with you

conto m kohntoo tale, story

contra against

contraceptivo m kontrasipteevoo contraceptive

contra-indicações fpl contraindications

contrário kontrar-yoo opposite

controlo de passaportes passport control

contusão f kontoozowng bruise

conveniente konvin-yaynt convenient

convento m konvayntoo convent

conversação f konversasowng conversation

convés m konvehsh deck

convidada f konvidada, **convidado** m konvidadoo guest

convidar konvidar to invite

convir konveer to suit; to be convenient

convite m konveet invitation

copo m kopoo glass; cup

cor f kohr colour

coração m koorasowng heart

corajoso kooraJohzoo brave

corda f rope

cordeiro m koordayroo lamb

cordel m koordehl string

cor de laranja kohr di laranJa orange (colour)

cor de rosa rozα pink

corpo *m* koh**r**poo body

corredor *m* koorrid**oh**r corridor

correia *f* koor**ray**-a strap

correia da ventoinha da
ventoow**ee**n-ya fan belt

correia de relógio di riloJ-yoo
watch strap

correio *m* koor**ray**-oo post, mail;
post office

  pôr no correio pohr noo to
  post, to mail

correio aéreo a-**eh**r-yoo airmail

correio azul az**oo**l express mail

correio expresso shpr**eh**soo
express mail, special delivery

correio registado riJishtad**oo**
registered mail

correios *mpl* koor**ray**-oosh post
office

Correios de Portugal S.A.
National Mail Service

corrente *f* koor**raynt** chain; current

corrente de ar koor**raynt** dar
draught

correr koor**ray**r to run

correspondente *m/f*
koorrishpond**aynt** correspondent;
penfriend

corrida *f* koor**ree**da race

cortado koortad**oo** cut; blocked

cortar to cut

corte *m* kort cut

corte de cabelo di kaba**yloo**
haircut

corte de energia denirJee-a
power cut

corte e brushing ee cut and
blow-dry

cortiça *f* koort**ee**sa cork

cortiças *fpl* koort**ee**sash cork goods

cortina *f* koort**ee**na curtain

cortinados *mpl* koortinad**oo**sh
curtains

coser kooz**ay**r to sew

cosméticos *mpl* kooJm**eh**tikoosh
cosmetics, make-up

costa *f* k**o**shta coast

  na costa on the coast

costas *fpl* k**o**shtash back (of body)

costela *f* koosht**eh**la rib

cotação cambial *f* kootas**ow**ng
kamb-y**a**l exchange rate

cotovelo *m* kootoova**yloo** elbow

couro *m* k**oh**roo leather

coxa *f* k**oh**sha thigh

coxia *f* koosh**ee**-a aisle

cozer kooz**ay**r to cook

cozinha *f* kooz**ee**n-ya kitchen

cozinhar kozeen-y**a**r to cook

cozinheiro *m* kozeen-y**ayr**oo cook

CP say pay Portuguese Railways

crédito *m* kr**eh**ditoo credit

creme *m* kraym cream, lotion

creme amaciador amas-yad**oh**r
conditioner

creme de barbear di barb-y**a**r
shaving cream

creme de base baz foundation
cream

creme de limpeza leempa**yz**a
cleansing lotion

creme écran total ekrang toot**a**l
sunblock

creme hidratante kraymeedrat**a**nt
moisturizer

crer krayr to believe

criada *f* kr-ya̱da maid

criada de quarto di kwartoo chambermaid

criança *f* kr-ya̱nsa child

crianças children; children crossing

crise *f* kreez crisis

crise de crédito *f* credit crunch

cru, crua kroo, kroo-a raw

cruzamento *m* kroozama̱yntoo junction, crossroads

cruzamento perigroso dangerous junction

cruzar kroozar to cross

cruzeiro *m* krooza̱yroo cruise

cruzeta *f* krooza̱yta coathanger

Cruz Vermelha Red Cross

CTT say tay tay National Mail Service

cuecas *fpl* kwe̱hkash underpants; pants, panties

cuecas de mulher kwe̱hkaJ di mool-ye̱hr pants, panties

cuidado *m* kwida̱doo care

cuidado! look out!, be careful!, take care!

cuidado com o cão beware of the dog

cuidadoso kwidado̱hzoo careful

cujo koo̱Joo of which; whose

culpa *f* koo̱lpa fault

é culpa minha/dele it's my/ his fault

culpado koolpa̱doo guilty

cumprimento *m* koomprima̱yntoo compliment

com os melhores cumprimentos with best wishes

cunhada *f* koon-ya̱da sister-in-law

cunhado *m* koon-ya̱doo brother-in-law

curar koorar to cure

curso *m* koorsoo course

curso de línguas di leengwash language course

curto koortoo short

curva *f* koorva turning; bend

curva perigosa dangerous bend

custar kooshtar to charge; to cost

cutelaria *f* kootilaree-a cutlery shop

c/v basement

D

d. right

da of the; from the

dá he/she/it gives; you give

damas *f* damash ladies' toilets, ladies' room

damos damoosh we give

dança *f* dansa dance

dança folclórica foolklorika folk dancing

dançar dansar to dance

dão downg they give; you give

daqui dakee from now

dar to give

das dash of the; from the

dás you give

data *f* date

data de validade di validad expiry date

de di from; of; by; in

de autocarro dowtookarroo by bus

de avião dav-yowng by air

de carro di karroo by car

de manhã di man-yang in the morning

debaixo de... dibīshoo di under...

decepcionado disips-yoonadoo disappointed

decepcionante disips-yonant disappointing

decidir disideer to decide

décimo dehsimoo tenth

decisão *f* disizowng decision

declaração *f* diklarasowng statement

dedo *m* daydoo finger

dedo do pé doo peh toe

defeito *m* difaytoo fault, defect

deficiente difis-yaynt disabled

deficientes físicos *mpl* disabled

degrau *m* digrow step

deitar fora daytar to throw away

deitar-se daytarsi to lie down; to go to bed

deixar dayshar to leave (behind); to let

deixar cair ka-eer to drop

dela dehla her; hers

delas dehlash their; theirs

dele dayl his

deles daylish their; theirs

delicioso dilis-yohzoo lovely, delicious

demais dimīsh too much

demasiado dimaz-yadoo too

demasiado grande too big

dê-me daymi give me

demora *f* delay

dentadura postiça *f* dentadoora pooshteesa dentures

dente *m* daynt tooth

dentista *m/f* denteeshta dentist

dentro de... dayntroo inside...

  dentro de ... dias di ... deeash in ... days' time

  dentro de um momento doong moomayntoo in a minute

  dentro de casa di kaza indoors

departamento *m* dipartamayntoo department

depende dipaynd it depends

  depende de... di it depends on...

depois dipoh-ish then, after that; afterwards

  depois de... di after...

  depois de amanhã damanyang the day after tomorrow

depósito *m* dipozitoo deposit; tank

depósito de bagagem di bagaJayng left luggage (office), baggage checkroom

depósitos *mpl* deposits

depressa diprehsa quickly

deprimido diprimeedoo depressed

dê prioridade give way, yield

derrubar dirroobar to knock over

desafio de futebol *m* dizafee-oo di footbol football match

desagradável dizagradavil unpleasant

desaparecer dizaparisayr to disappear

desapontado dizapontadoo disappointed

desarranjo intestinal *m* dizarranJoo intishtinal upset stomach

descansar dishkansar to relax

descanso *m* dishkansoo rest

descarregar dishkarrigar to download; to offload

descer dishsayr to go down; to get off

descobrir dishkoobreer to find out, to discover

descolagem *f* dishkoolaJayng take-off

descolar dishkoolar to take off, to unglue

descontar dishkontar to cash

desconto *m* dishkohntoo discount

descrição *f* dishkrisowng description

desculpar-se dishkoolparsi to apologize

desculpas *fpl* dishkoolpash apologies

desculpe dishkoolp I'm sorry, excuse me, pardon (me)

desde dayJdi since; from

desejar disayJar to want

  que deseja? ki disayJa how can I help you?

desempregado dizaymprigadoo unemployed

desenho *m* disayn-yoo drawing; pattern

desenvolver disaynvolvayr to develop

desfazer as malas dishfazayr aJ malash to unpack

desfiladeiro *m* dishfiladayroo pass

desfolhada *f* disfool-yada party held at threshing time

desgarradas *fpl* diJgarradash improvised popular songs

cantar à desgarrada to sing impromptu in competition

desinfectante *m* dizinfetant disinfectant

desligado diJligadoo off, switched off

desligar diJligar to turn off; to switch off

desligue o motor switch off your engine

desmaiar diJmī-ar to faint; to collapse

desmaquilhador de olhos *m* dishmakil-yadohr dol-yoosh eye make-up remover

desocupar antes das… vacate before…

desodorizante *m* dizohdoorizant deodorant

despacha-te! dishpashat hurry up!

despertador *m* dishpirtadohr alarm clock

desporto *m* dishpohrtoo sport

desportos náuticos *mpl* dishpohrtoosh nowtikoosh water sports

destinatário *m* addressee

destino *m* dishteenoo destination

desvio *m* diJvee-oo detour, diversion

detergente *m* deterJaynt soap powder, washing powder

detergente líquido leekidoo washing-up liquid

detergente para lavar a louça lohsa washing-up liquid

detestar ditishtar to hate

detestável ditishtavil obnoxious

Deus day-oosh God

devagar divagar slow; slowly

deve dehv you must, you have to

dever (*m*) divayr duty; to owe; to have to

devia divee-a you should

devolver divolvayr to give back

dez dehsh ten

dezanove dizanov nineteen

dezasseis dizasaysh sixteen

dezassete dizaseht seventeen

Dezembro dezaymbroo December

dezoito dizoh-ítoo eighteen

dia *m* dee-a day

diabética (*f*) d-yabehtika, **diabético** (*m*) d-yabehtikoo diabetic

dia de anos *m* dee-a danoosh birthday

dialecto *m* dialect

diamante *m* d-yamant diamond

diapositivo *m* d-yapooziteevoo slide

diária *f* d-yar-ya cost per day

diariamente d-yar-yamaynt daily

diário (*m*) d-yar-yo diary; daily

diarreia *f* d-yarray-a diarrhoea

dias de semana weekdays

dias verdes cheap travel days

dicionário m dis-yoonar-yoo dictionary

dieta f d-yehta diet

diferença f difiraynsa difference

diferente difiraynt different

difícil difeesil difficult, hard

dificuldade f difikooldad difficulty

digo I say

diluir num pouco de água dissolve in a little water

Dinamarca f dinamarka Denmark

dinamarquês dinamarkaysh Danish

dinheiro m deen-yayroo money; cash

> Travel tip The easiest way to get money is to use your bank debit card to withdraw cash from an ATM (known as a Multibanco), found in even the smallest towns. You can usually withdraw up to €300 a day and instructions are available in English.

dirá dira he/she will say; you will say

dirão dirowng they will say; you will say

dirás dirash you will say

direcção f direhsowng direction; steering

directo direhtoo direct

direi diray I will say

direita: à direita dirayta on the right

à direita (de) di on the right (of)

vire à direita veer turn right

direito diraytoo straight; right (not left)

direitos mpl diraytoosh rights

livre de direitos leevr di duty-free

diremos diraymoosh we will say

disco m deeshkoo disco; record

discoteca f dishkootehka disco; record shop

disjuntor principal m diJoontohr preensipal mains switch

disquete f dishkeht disk, diskette

disse dees I/he/she/it/you said

dissemos disaymoosh we said

disseram disehrowng you/they said

disseste disehsht you said

distância f dishtans-ya distance

distribuição f dishtribweesowng delivery

distribuidor m dishtribweedohr distributor

dito deetoo said

DIU m dee-oo IUD, coil

divertido divirteedoo fun, amusing, enjoyable

divertir-se divirteersi to enjoy oneself

divisas fpl foreign currency

divorciado divoors-yadoo divorced

dizer dizayr to say; to tell

o que quer dizer? oo ki kehr what do you mean?

do of the; from the

dobro dohbroo twice as much

doce dohs sweet

documento *m* dookoom**ay**ntoo document

doença *f* dw**ay**nsa disease, illness

doente dwaynt ill, sick, unwell

doer dwayr to hurt

doido d**oh**-idoo crazy, mad

dois d**oh**-ish two

doloroso doolooro**h**zoo painful

domingo doom**ee**ngoo Sunday

domingos e dias feriados Sundays and public holidays

Dona Mrs

dona *f* d**oh**na owner; respectful way of addressing a woman, precedes the first name

donde dohnd where from

donde é? dohnd**eh** where do you come from?

dono *m* d**oh**noo owner

do que doo ki than

dor *f* dohr ache, pain

dor de cabeça di kab**ay**sa headache

dor de dentes dayntsh toothache

dor de estômago disht**oh**magoo stomach ache

dor de garganta di garg**a**nta sore throat

dor de ouvidos dohv**ee**doosh earache

dormidas rooms to let (in a private house)

dormir doorm**ee**r to sleep

a dormir asleep

dor nas costas *f* dohr nash k**oh**shtash backache

dos of the; from the

dose *f* doz portion

dose para crianças *f* doz kr-yan-sash children's portion

dou doh I give

doutor *m* doht**oh**r, **doutora** *f* doht**o**ra doctor

doutro modo d**oh**troo m**o**doo otherwise

doze dohz twelve

droga *f* dr**o**ga drugs, narcotics

drogaria *f* droogar**ee**-a drugstore, shop selling toiletries

dto. right

duas vezes doo-aJ v**ay**zish twice

duche *m* doosh shower

com duche kong with shower

dunas *fpl* d**oo**nash sand dunes

duplo d**oo**ploo double

durante door**a**nt during

duro d**oo**roo hard; stale

duzentas doozaynt**a**sh, **duzentos** doozayntoosh two hundred

dúzia *f* d**oo**z-ya dozen

E

e ee and

e. left

é eh he/she/it is; you are

é…? is he/she/it…?; are you…?

écran *m* ekr**a**ng screen

edifício *m* idif**ee**s-yoo building

edredão *m* idrid**ow**ng duvet

efervescente ifirvish-**saynt**
effervescent, sparkling

eh! hey!

eixo *m* **ay**shoo axle

ela ehla she; her; it

elas ehlash they; them

elástico *m* ilashtikoo elastic;
elastic band

ele ayl he; him; it

electricidade *f* eletrisidad
electricity

electricista *m* eletris**ee**shta
electrician

eléctrico (*m*) ele**h**trikoo electric;
tram, streetcar

electro-domésticos *mpl*
doom**eh**shtikoosh electrical
appliances

eles aylish they; them

elevador *m* elevad**oh**r lift, elevator

em ayng in; at; on

embaixada *f* aymb**ī**shada
embassy

embaixo aymb**ī**shoo down,
downstairs; underneath

   embaixo de... di underneath...

   lá embaixo down there

embalagem económica *f*
economy pack

embalagem familiar family
pack

embaraçoso aymbaras**oh**zoo
embarrassing

embora aymbora although

   ir embora to go away

embraiagem *f* aymbrī-a**J**ayng

clutch

embrulhar aymbrool-**yar** to wrap

embrulho *m* aymbrool-yoo parcel

ementa *f* em**ay**nta menu

ementa fixa f**ee**ksa set menu

ementa turística tooreestika
today's menu, set menu

emergência *f* emir**J**ayns-ya
emergency

emergências casualty,
emergencies

emocionante emoos-yoon**a**nt
exciting

emperrado aympirr**a**doo stuck

empoeirado aympoo-ayr**a**doo
dusty

empolha *f* aymp**oh**l-ya blister

empregada *f* aympregada
waitress

empregada de balcão di
balk**ow**ng barmaid

empregada de mesa m**ay**za
waitress

empregada de quarto kwartoo
chambermaid, maid

empregado aympreg**a**doo *m*
employee

empregado (de mesa) *m* di
m**ay**za waiter

emprego *m* aympr**ay**goo job

empresa *f* aympr**ay**za company,
firm

**emprestado: pedir
emprestado** pid**ee**r
aymprisht**a**doo to borrow

emprestar aymprisht**ar** to lend

empurrar aympoorr**ar** to push

E.N. national highway

encantador aynkantadohr lovely

encaracolado aynkarakooladoo curly

encerrado aynsayrradoo closed

encher aynshayr to fill up, to fill

encomenda f aynkoomaynda package; parcel

encomendas fpl parcels, parcels counter

encontrar aynkontrar to find; to meet

encravado aynkravadoo jammed

endereço m ayndiraysoo address

enevoado inivwadoo foggy; misty; cloudy

enfarte m aynfart heart attack

enfermaria f aynfirmaree-a hospital ward

enfermeira f aynfirmayra, **enfermeiro** m aynfirmayroo nurse

enganado aynganadoo wrong

enganar-se aynganarsi to be wrong, to make a mistake

enganei-me aynganaym I've made a mistake

engarrafamento m ayngarrafamayntoo traffic jam

engolir ayngooleer to swallow

engraçado ayngrasadoo funny; amusing

enjoado aynjwadoo seasick

enorme enorm enormous

enquanto aynkwantoo while

ensinar aynsinar to teach

então ayntowng then, at that time

entrada f ayntrada entrance, way in; starter, appetizer; admission charge

entrada livre admission free

entrada proibida no entry

entrar ayntrar to go in, to enter

entre! come in!

entre ayntr among; between

entrega ao domicílio delivery service

entregar ayntrigar to deliver

entrevista ayntriveeshta appointment

entupido ayntoopeedoo blocked

envelope m aynvilop envelope

envelope de avião m dav-yowng airmail envelope

envergonhado aynvirgoon-yadoo ashamed

enviar aynv-yar to send

enviar posteriormente to forward

enxaqueca f aynshakayka migraine

época f ehpooka season; age

equipa f ekeepa team

equipamento m ekipamayntoo equipment

era ehra I was; he/she/it was; you were

eram ehrowng they were; you were

éramos ehramoosh we were

eras ehrash you were

ermida f ermeeda chapel

errado erradoo wrong

erro m ayrroo mistake, error

erupção f eroopsowng rash

ervanário *m* ervanar-yoo herbalist

és ehsh you are

esc. escudo (former Portuguese unit of currency)

escada *f* shkada ladder; stairs

escadas *fpl* shkadash stairs

escadas rolantes roolantsh escalator

escala *f* shkala intermediate stop

escalar shkalar to climb

escocês (*m*) shkoosaysh Scottish; Scotsman

escocesa (*f*) shkoosayza Scottish; Scots woman

Escócia *f* shkos-ya Scotland

escola *f* shkola school

escola de línguas *f* di leengwash language school

escolher shkool-yayr to choose

esconder shkondayr to hide

escorregadio shkoorrigadee-oo slippery

escova *f* shkohva brush

escova de cabelo di kabayloo hairbrush

escova de dentes dayntsh toothbrush

escova de unhas doon-yash nailbrush

escrever shkrivayr to write

escrito por... shkreetoo poor written by...

  por escrito in writing

escritório *m* shkritor-yoo office

escudo *m* shkoodoo escudo (former Portuguese unit of currency)

escurecer shkooresayr to get dark

escuro shkooroo dark

escutar shkootar to listen (to)

esferográfica *f* shfiroografika ballpoint pen

Espanha *f* shpan-ya Spain

espanhóis: os espanhóis shpan-**oy**sh the Spanish

espanhol shpan-yol Spanish

espantoso shpant**oh**zoo amazing, astonishing

especialidade *f* shpis-yalidad speciality

especialmente shpis-yalm**ay**nt especially

espectáculo *m* shpitakooloo show

espelho *m* shpayl-yoo mirror

espelho retrovisor ritroovizohr rearview mirror

esperar shpirar to expect; to hope; to wait

  espero que não shpehroo ki nowng I hope not

  espero que sim seeng I hope so

espere shpehr wait

espere pelo sinal wait for the tone

esperto shpehrtoo clever

espesso shpaysoo thick

espetáculo *m* shpitakooloo show

espigados *mpl* shpigadoosh split ends

espingarda *f* shpeengarda gun

espirrar shpirrar to sneeze

espirro *m* shpeerroo sneeze

esplanada *f* shplanada esplanade; pavement café

esplêndido shpl**ay**ndid**oo** terrific

esposa *f* shp**oh**za wife

espuma de barbear *f* shp**oo**ma di barb-y**ar** shaving foam

esq. left

esquadra da polícia *f* shkw**a**rda da pool**ee**s-ya police station

esquecer shkis**ay**r to forget

esqueci-me shkis**ee**mi I forget

esquerda: à esquerda shk**ay**rda on the left (of), to the left

vire à esquerda v**ee**ra turn left

esquerdo shk**ay**rdoo left

esqui aquático *m* shk**ee** akw**a**tikoo waterskiing

esquisito shkiz**ee**too weird, odd, strange

essa ehsa that; that one

essas ehsash those

esse ays that

essencial esayns-yal essential

esses aysish those

esta ehshta this; this one

está shta hello (on the phone); he/she/it is; you are

ele está? ayl is he in?

está… it is…

está…? is it…?; hello? (on the phone)

está bem bayng that's fine, all right

estação *f* shtas**ow**ng station; season

estação alta high season

estação baixa b**ī**sha low season

estação de autocarros dowtook**a**rroosh bus station

estação de caminho de ferro di kam**ee**n-yoo di f**eh**rroo railway station

estação de camionetas kam-yoon**ay**tash bus station, coach station

estação de comboios komb**oy**-oosh train station

estação de serviço di sirv**ee**soo service station

estação dos autocarros dooz owtook**a**rroosh bus station, coach station

estacionamento *m* shtas-yoonam**ay**ntoo car park, parking lot

estacionamento privado priv**a**doo private parking

estacionamento proibido no parking

estacionamento reservado aos hóspedes parking reserved for patrons, patrons only

estacionar shtas-yoonar to park

estadia f shtadee-a stay

estádio m shtad-yoo stadium

estado m shtadoo state

Estados Unidos (da América) mpl shtadooz ooneedooJ (damehrika) United States (of America)

estafado shtafadoo shattered, exhausted

estalagem f shtalaJayng luxury hotel

estamos shtamoosh we are

estância f shtans-ya timber yard

estão shtowng they are; you are

estar shtar to be

estará shtara he/she/it/you will be

estarão shtarowng you/they will be

estarás shtarash you will be

estarei shtaray I will be

estaremos shtaraymoosh we will be

estas ehshtash these

estás shtash you are

estátua f shtatwa statue

estava shtava I/he/she/it/you used to be

estavam shtavam you/they used to be

estávamos shtavamoosh we used to be

estavas shtavash you used to be

este aysht this; this one

este m ehsht east

estendal m shtendal clothes line

estes ayshtish these

esteve shtayv he/she/it was; you were

estive shteev I was

estivemos shtivaymoosh we were

estiveram shtivehrowng they were; you were

estiveste shtivehsht you were

estômago m shtohmagoo stomach

estou shtoh I am

estrada f shtrada road

estrada nacional nas-yoonal national highway

estrada principal preensipal main highway

estragado shtragadoo faulty; out of order

estragar shtragar to damage

estrangeira (f), **estrangeiro** (m) shtranJayroo foreign; foreigner

no estrangeiro noo abroad

estranha (f) shtran-ya, **estranho** (m) shtran-yoo stranger; peculiar; funny; strange

estreia f shtray-a first showing

estreito shtraytoo narrow

estrela f shtrayla star

estudante m/f shtoodant student

estupendo shtoopayndoo amazing

estúpido shtoopidoo stupid

etiqueta *f* etikayta label

eu ay-oo I

EUA USA

eu mesmo ay-oo mayЈmoo
myself

Europa *f* ay-ooropa Europe

europeia (*f*) ay-ooroopay-a,
europeu (*m*) ay-ooroopay-oo
European

exactamente! ezatamaynt exactly!

exacto ezatoo accurate, correct

exagerar ezagirar to exaggerate

exame *m* ezam exam, test

exausto ezowshtoo exhausted,
tired

excelente ish-selaynt excellent;
lovely

excepto ish-sehtoo except

  excepto aos domingos
  Sundays excepted

excesso de bagagem *m* ish-
  sehsoo di bagaЈayng
  excess baggage

excursão *f* shkoorsowng
  coach trip; trip

excursão com guia kong
  guided tour

excursão organizada
  organizada package holiday

excursões *fpl* shkoorsoyngsh
  excursions

exemplo *m* ezaymploo example

  por exemplo poor for example

exigir eziЈeer to demand

**Exmo. Sr. (Excelentíssimo
  Senhor)** Dear Sir

experiente shpir-yaynt
  experienced

experimentar shpirimayntar to
  try; to try on

explicar shplikar to explain

exposição *f* shpoozisowng
  exhibition

extensão *f* shtensowng extension;
  extension lead

extintor *m* shtintohr fire
  extinguisher

extraordinário shtra-ohrdinar-yoo
  extraordinary

extremamente shtremamaynt
  extremely

F

F cold (on tap)

fábrica *f* fabrika factory

fabricado em... made in…

faca *f* faka knife

fácil fasil easy

faço fasoo I do

factor de protecção *m* fatohr di
  prootesowng protection factor

factura *f* fatoora invoice

fadista *m/f* fadeeshta singer of
  traditional Portuguese fado
  songs

fado *m* fadoo traditional
  Portuguese song, usually sad
  and romantic

faiança *f* fi-ansa glazed
  earthenware

faixa *f* fisha lane

falar to speak; to talk

fala…? do you speak…?

não falo inglês I don't speak English

falido faleedo broke; bankrupt

falso falsoo fake; false

falta missing

faltar to be lacking; to be missing

família f fameel-ya family

famoso famohzoo famous

fantástico fantashtikoo fantastic

fará fara he/she/it/you will do

farão farowng you/they will do

farás farash you will do

farei faray I will do

faremos faraymoosh we will do

farmácia f farmas-ya pharmacy, chemist's

farmácias de serviço fpl di sirveesoo emergency pharmacies, duty chemists

faróis máximos mpl faroyJ masimoosh headlights

faróis médios dipped headlights

faróis mínimos meenimoosh sidelights

farol m headlight; lighthouse

farto fartoo fed up

fato m fatoo suit

fato de banho di ban-yoo swimming costume

fato de treino traynoo tracksuit

favorito favooreetoo favourite

favor: por favor favohr please

  se faz favor si fash please

  é favor fechar a porta please close the door

  favor não incomodar please do not disturb

fazem-se chaves keys cut here

fazer fazayr to do; to make

fazer a barba to shave

fazer amor amohr to make love

fazer as malas aJ malash to pack

fazer bicha beesha to queue, to stand in line

fazer brushing to blow-dry

fazer mudança moodansa to change (trains)

fazer surf to surf

fazer vela vehla to sail

fazer windsurf to windsurf

faz favor fash favohr please, excuse me

febre f fehbr temperature, fever

febre dos fenos fehbr doosh faynoosh hayfever

febril febreel feverish

fechado fishadoo shut, closed; reserved; overcast

fechado à chave fishadwa shav locked

fechado até… closed until…

fechado para balanço closed for stocktaking

fechado para férias closed for holidays

fechado para obras closed for repairs

fechadura f fishadoora lock

fechar fishar to close; to shut

fechar à chave shav to lock

fecho m fayshoo handle

fecho éclair zip, zipper

feio fay-oo ugly

feira *f* fayra funfair; trade fair

feiras das vilas local village fairs

feito faytoo made; done

feito à mão faytwa mowng handmade

feliz fileesh happy

feliz aniversário! fileez anivirsar-yoo happy birthday!

Feliz Ano Novo! anoo nohvoo Happy New Year!

felizmente filiJmaynt fortunately

Feliz Natal! fileeJ Merry Christmas!

feminista (*f*) femineeshta feminist

feriado *m* fir-yadoo public holiday

férias *fpl* fehr-yash holiday; vacation

　de férias di on holiday; on vacation

férias de inverno *fpl* dinvehrnoo winter holiday

férias grandes *fpl* grandsh summer holidays

ferida *f* fireeda wound

ferido fireedoo injured

ferragens *fpl* firraJayngsh ironmongery, hardware

ferramenta *f* firramaynta tool

ferro *m* fehrroo iron

ferro de engomar *m* dayngoomar iron

festa *f* fehshta party

　Boas Festas! boh-ash fehshtash merry Christmas and a happy New Year

festas dos santos populares feast days of saints

Fevereiro fivrayroo February

fez faysh he/she/it did, he/she/it has done; you did, you have done

fibras naturais natural fibres

ficar fikar to remain, to stay

　ficam dois feekowng doh-ish there are two left

　onde fica...? feeka where is...?

ficar com kong to keep

ficheiro *m* fishayroo file

fígado *m* feegadoo liver

fila *f* feela row; queue, line

filha *f* feel-ya daughter

filho *m* feel-yoo son

filho da puta! poota son-of-a-bitch!

filme *m* feelm film; movie

filme colorido *m* koolooreedoo colour film

filtro *m* feeltroo filter

filtros de café *mpl* feeltroosh di kafeh filter papers

fim *m* feeng end

　no fim de... noo – di at the end of...

　no fim eventually

fim de autoestrada end of motorway/highway

fim de estação end of season

fim de semana di simana weekend

finalmente finalmaynt at last

fino feenoo thin; fine

fio *m* fee-oo lead; thread; wire

fio de fusível *m* di foozee-vil fuse
wire

fio dentário *m* dentar-yoo dental
floss

fita *f* feeta tape, cassette

fita-cola *f* sticky tape

fita elástica *f* elashtika rubber
band

fita gomada goomada Sellotape,
Scotch tape

fita métrica mehtrika tape
measure

fiz feesh I did, I have done

fizemos fizaymoosh we did, we
have done

fizeram fizehrowng you/they did,
they have done

fizeste fizehsht you did, you have
done

flertar flirtar to flirt

flor *f* flohr flower

floresta *f* floorehshta forest

fluentemente flwentimaynt
fluently

fogão *m* foogowng cooker

fogo *m* fohgoo fire

fogos de artifício *mpl* fogoosh
dartifees-yoo fireworks

fogueira *f* foogayra fire, campfire

foi foh-i it was, he/she went, he/
she has left

folha *f* fohl-ya leaf; sheet

folha de prata silver foil

folheto *m* fool-yaytoo brochure;
leaflet

fome fohm hunger

  tenho fome tayn-yoo I'm
  hungry

  tens fome? taynsh are you
  hungry?

fomos fohmoosh we were, we have
been; we went, we have gone

fonte *f* fohnt fountain

fora: lá fora outside

  do lado de fora doo ladoo di
  outside

fora de casa di kaza outdoors

foram fohrowng you/they were,
you/they have been; you/they
went, you/they have gone

forcados *mpl* foorkadoosh group
of men who wrestle with the
bull during a bullfight

forma: em forma ayng forma fit

  de qualquer forma di
  kwalkehr anyway

formato MP3 *m* foormatoo ehm-
pay-traysh MP3 format

formiga *f* foormeega ant

forno *m* fohrnoo oven

forte fort strong; rich

fósforos *mpl* foshfooroosh
matches

foste fohsht you were, you have
been; you went, you have gone

fotocópias *fpl* footookop-yash
photocopies

fotografar footoografar to
photograph

fotografia *f* footoografee-a
photograph; photographic
goods

fotógrafo *m* footografoo
photographer

fraco frakoo weak

fractura *f* fratoora fracture

frágil fraJil fragile

fralda f fralda nappy, diaper

fraldas descartáveis fpl dishkartavaysh disposable nappies/diapers

França f fransa France

francês (m) fransaysh French; Frenchman

francesa (f) fransayza French; French woman

franquia f frankee-a postage

free-shop f duty-free shop

frente f fraynt front

    em frente ayng in front

    em frente a fraynta opposite; in front of

    na frente at the front

frequência f frikwayns-ya frequency

frequentado frikwayntadoo busy

frequente frikwaynt frequent

frequentemente frikwayn-temaynt frequently

fresco frayshkoo fresh; cool

frigideira f friJidayra frying pan

frigorífico m frigooreefikoo fridge

frio free-oo cold

    tenho frio tayn-yoo I'm cold

fritar fritar to fry

fronha da almofada f frohn-ya dalmoofada pillow case

fronteira f frontayra border, frontier

frutaria f frootaree-a fruit shop

fuga f fooga leak

fui fwee I went, I have gone; I was, I have been

fumadores mpl foomadohrish smokers, smoking

fumar foomar to smoke

    fuma? fooma do you smoke?

    não fumo nowng I don't smoke

fumo m foomoo smoke

funcionar foons-yonar to work

    não funciona nowng out of order

fundo (m) foondoo deep; bottom

funil m fooneel funnel

furado fooradoo flat (tyre)

furgão m foorgowng van

furgoneta f foorgoonayta van

furioso foor-yohzoo furious

furo m fooroo puncture

fusível m foozeevil fuse

futebol m footbol football

futuro m footooroo future

    no futuro noo in future

G

gado m gadoo cattle

gajo m gaJoo guy

galão m galowng gallon; milky coffee in a tall glass

galeria de arte f galiree-a dart art gallery

Gales m galish Wales

galês (m) galaysh Welsh; Welshman

galesa (f) galayza Welsh; Welsh woman

gama f range

ganhar gan-yar to win; to earn

ganso *m* ganso goose

garagem *f* garaJayng garage

garantia *f* garantee-a guarantee

garfo *m* garfoo fork

garganta *f* throat

garrafa *f* bottle

garraiadas *fpl* garrī-adash bull-running

gás *m* gash gas

gás Cidla *m* camping gas

gasóleo *m* gazol-yoo diesel

gasolina *f* gazooleena petrol, gasoline

gasolina-normal three-star petrol, regular gas

gasolina sem chumbo sayng shoomboo unleaded petrol

gasolina-super sooper four-star petrol

gás para campismo *m* gash para kampeeJmoo camping gas

gastar gashtar to spend

gato *m* gatoo cat

gaveta *f* gavayta drawer

G.B. Jay bay Great Britain

geada *f* J-yada frost

gelado (*m*) Jiladoo frozen; ice cream; ice lolly

gelataria *f* Jilataree-a ice-cream parlour

gel de duche *m* Jehl di doosh shower gel

gelo Jayloo ice

gel para o cabelo *m* Jehl par-oo kabayloo hair gel

gémeos *mpl* Jaym-yoosh twins

gengiva *f* JenJeeva gum

genro *m* Jaynroo son-in-law

gente *f* Jaynt people

   toda a gente tohda everyone

genuíno Jinweenoo genuine

geral Jeral general

geralmente Jeralmaynt usually

gerente *m/f* Jeraynt manager; manageress

gesso *m* Jaysoo plaster cast

ginásio *m* Jinaz-yoo gym

gira-discos *m* jeera-deeshkoosh record player

glutão glootowng greedy

G.N.R. Jay en err branch of the Portuguese police

golfe *m* golf golf

Golfo da Biscáia *m* gohlfoo da bishkī-a Bay of Biscay

gordo gohrdoo fat

gorduroso goordoorohzoo greasy

gorgeta *f* goorJayta tip

gostar gooshtar to like

   gosta de…? goshta di do you like…?

   gosto goshtoo I like, I like it

gostoso gooshtohzoo tasty; pleasant; nice

gota *f* gohta drop

gotas para os olhos *fpl* gohtash parooz ol-yoosh eye drops

governo *m* goovayrnoo government

Grã-Bretanha *f* gran britan-ya Great Britain

gradualmente gradwalmaynt gradually

grama *m* gram(me)

gramática *f* gramátika grammar

grande grand large, big

grandes armazéns *mpl* grandz armazáyngsh department store

granizo *m* graneezoo hail

gratuito gratoo-eetoo free (of charge)

gravador (de cassetes) *m* gravadohr (di kasehtsh) tape recorder

gravata *f* tie, necktie

grave grav nasty

grávida pregnant

graxa para sapatos *f* grasha para sapatoosh shoe polish

Grécia *f* grehs-ya Greece

grego *m* graygoo Greek

grelhador *m* gril-yadohr grill

gripe *f* greep flu

gritar gritar to shout

grosseiro groosayroo rude

grosso grohsoo pissed

grupo *m* groopoo group, party

grupo de sange di sang blood group

guarda *m/f* gwarda caretaker

guarda-chuva *m* gwarda shoova umbrella

Guarda Fiscal Customs police

Guarda Nacional Republicana branch of the Portuguese police

guardanapo *m* gwardanapoo napkin, serviette

guardar gwardar to keep

guerra *f* gehrra war

guia *f* gee-a guide, courier

guia turística *f* tooreeshtika, **guia turístico** *m* tooreeshtikoo tour guide

guichet *m* geeshay window; ticket window

H

h is not pronounced in Portuguese

H gents', men's room

há... a there is..., there are...

há...? is there...?, are there...?

há uma semana ooma simana a week ago

há pouco pohkoo recently

há vagas vacancies, rooms free

hábito *m* abeetoo custom; habit

hall *m* lobby

H.C. state hospital

hemorróidas *fpl* emoorroydash piles

hepatite *f* epateet hepatitis

hipermercado *m* eepermerkadoo hypermarket

história *f* ishtor-ya history; story

hoje ohJ today

Holanda *f* olanda Netherlands, Holland

holandês *m* olandaysh Dutch; Dutchman

holandesa *f* olandayza Dutch; Dutch woman

homem *m* ohmayng man

homens *mpl* ohmayngsh men; gents' toilet, men's room

honesto onehshtoo honest

hora *f* ora hour; time

hora de chegada di shigada arrival time

hora de partida parteeda departure time

hora de ponta pohnta rush hour

hora local local time

horário *m* orar-yoo timetable, (US) schedule

horário das consultas dash konsooltash surgery hours, (US) office hours

horas *fpl* orash hours; o'clock

às seis horas ash sayz orash at six o'clock

que horas são? k-yorash sowng what's the time?

horas de abertura *fpl* orash dabirtoora opening times

horas de visita *fpl* di vizeeta visiting hours

horrível orreevil awful, dreadful, horrible

hortelã-pimenta *f* ortilang pimaynta peppermint

hospedado oshpidadoo:

estar hospedado em shtar – ayng to be a guest at, to stay at

hospedaria *f* oshpidaree-a guesthouse

hospedar-se oshpidarsi to stay

hóspede *m/f* oshpidi guest

hospedeira (de bordo) *f* oshpidayra (di bordoo) stewardess, air hostess

Hospital Civil *m* state hospital

hospitalidade *f* oshpitalidad hospitality

houve ohv there has been

húmido oomeedoo damp; humid

humor *m* oomohr mood; humour

hydroplano *m* idrooplanoo hydrofoil

I

iate *m* yat yacht

ida: bilhete de ida bil-yayt deeda
single ticket, one-way ticket

idade *f* eedad age

que idade tem? keedad tayng
how old are you?

ideia *f* iday-a idea

idiota *m* id-yota stupid

ignição *f* ignisowng ignition

igreja *f* igrayJa church

igual igwal same

ilha *f* eel-ya island

imediatamente imid-yatamaynt
immediately, at once

imenso imaynsoo immensely,
a lot

imitação *f* imitasowng imitation

impermeável *m* impirm-yavil
raincoat

importante impoortant important

importar to matter, to be
important; to import

importa-se de…? importasi
will you…?

importa-se se…? si do you
mind if…?

não me importo nowng
mimportoo I don't mind

importuno importoonoo annoying

impossível impooseevil
impossible

imprescindível impresh-sindeevil
vital

impressionante impris-yoonant
impressive

impresso *m* imprehsoo
form, document

impressos *mpl* imprehsoosh
printed matter

incêndio *m* insaynd-yoo fire

inchaço *m* inshasoo lump, swelling

inchado inshadoo swollen

incluído inklweedoo included

incluir inklweer to include

inconsciente inkonsh-syaynt
unconscious

inconstante inkonshtant
changeable

incrível inkreevil incredible

indiano (*m*) ind-yanoo Indian

indicações indications

indicador *m* indikadohr indicator

indicativo *m* indikateevoo
dialling code, area code

indigestão *f* indiJishtowng
indigestion

indústria *f* indooshtr-ya industry

infecção *f* infehsowng infection

infeccioso infehs-yohzoo
infectious

infectado infehtadoo septic

infelizmente infiliJmayngt
unfortunately

inflamação *f* inflamasowng
inflammation

inflamável inflammable

informação *f* infoormasowng
information, piece of
information

informações *fpl* infoorm-
asoyngsh directory enquiries;
information

Inglaterra *f* inglat**eh**rra England

inglês (*m*) inglay**sh** English; Englishman

em inglês ayng in English

inglesa (*f*) inglay**za** English; English woman

ingleses: os ingleses inglay**zish** the English

ingredientes *mpl* ingrid-y**ay**ntsh ingredients

íngreme ee**ng**rim steep

início *m* inee**s**-yoo beginning

no início noo at the beginning

início de autoestrada start of motorway/highway

injecção *f* inJeh**sow**ng injection

inocente inoosay**nt** innocent

insecto *m* inse**h**too insect

insistir insisht**ee**r to insist

insolação *f* insoolas**ow**ng sunstroke

insónia *f* inson-ya insomnia

Instituto do Vinho do Porto *m* Port Wine Institute

inteiro intay**r**oo whole

inteligente intili**J**ay**nt** intelligent, clever

Intercidades fast train, Intercity train

interdito a menores de … anos no admission to those under … years of age

interessado intrisa**d**oo interested

interessante intris**a**nt interesting

internacional internas-yoon**al** international

interpretar interprit**a**r to interpret

intérprete *m/f* inteh**r**prit interpreter

interruptor *m* intiroopt**oh**r switch

interruptor de ligar/desligar *m* di ligar/diJligar on/off switch

intervalo *m* interval**oo** interval

intoxicação alimentar *f* intoksikas**ow**ng food poisoning

introduza a moeda na ranhura insert coin in slot

inundação *f* inoondas**ow**ng flood

Inverno *m* inve**h**rnoo winter

ir eer to go

ir buscar boosh**k**ar to get, to fetch

Irlanda *f* eerlanda Ireland

Irlanda do Norte *f* eerlanda doo nort Northern Ireland

irlandês (*m*) eerlanday**sh** Irish; Irishman

irlandesa (*f*) eerland**ay**za Irish; Irishwoman

irmã *f* eerma**ng** sister

irmão *m* eermo**w**ng brother

isqueiro *m* ishkay**r**oo cigarette lighter

isso ee**s**oo that; that one

isso é… eh that's…

isso é…? is that…?

isto ee**sh**too this; this one

isto é…? eesht**w**eh is this…?

Itália *f* ital-ya Italy

italiana (*f*) ital-yana Italian, **italiano** (*m*) ital-ya**noo** Italian

J

já Ja ever; already
Janeiro Janayro January
janela f Janehla window
jantar (m) Jantar evening meal,
  dinner; supper; to have dinner
jarda f Jarda yard
jardim m Jardeeng garden
jardim público pooblikoo park
jardim zoológico zwolojikoo zoo
jarra f Jarra vase
jarro m Jarroo jug; jar
joalharia f Jwal-yaree-a jewellery
joalheiro m Jwal-yayroo jeweller
joelho m Jwayl-yoo knee
jogar Joogar to play
jogar fora to throw away
jogo m Johgoo game, match
jóias fpl Jo-yash jewellery
jornal m Joornal newspaper
jovem Jovayng young
jovens mpl Jovayngsh
  young people
judaico Joodikoo Jewish
Julho Jool-yoo July
Junho Joon-yoo June
junta da culatra f Joonta da
  koolatra cylinder head gasket
junto da... Joontoo da
  beside the...
juntos Joontoosh together
justo Jooshtoo just, fair

L

lá over there, there
lã f lang wool
lábios mpl lab-yoosh lips
laca f hair spray
lado m ladoo side
  do outro lado doo-ohtroo
  opposite
  do outro lado de... doo ohtroo
  ladoo di across the...
ladra f, **ladrão** m ladrowng thief
lago m lagoo lake; pond
lama f mud
lamentar lamayntar to regret,
  to be sorry
lâminas para barbear fpl
  laminash para barb-yar
  razor blades
lâmpada f light bulb
lanterna f lantehrna torch,
  flashlight
lápis m lapsh pencil
lápis para as sobrancelhas
  parash sobransayl-yash eyebrow
  pencil
lápis para os olhos parooz
  ol-yoosh eyeliner
largo m largoo wide; square
lata f can; tin
lata de gasolina f di gazooleena
  petrol can
lavabos mpl lavaboosh toilets,
  rest rooms
lavagem a seco f lavaJayng a
  saykoo dry-cleaning

lavagem automática
owtoom**a**tika carwash

lavagem e mise ee m**ee**z
shampoo and set

lava-louça *f* lava l**oh**sa sink

lavandaria *f* lavand**ar**ee-a laundry
(place)

lavandaria automática
owtoom**a**tika launderette

lavar to wash

lavar à mão mowng to handwash

lavar a roupa r**oh**pa to do the
washing

lavar e pentear paynt-**y**ar
wash and set

lavar na máquina
machine wash

lavar-se –si to wash (oneself)

lavatório *m* lavat**or**-yoo
washhand basin

lavrador *m* lavrad**oh**r farmer

laxativo *m* lashat**ee**voo laxative

lei *f* lay law

leite *m* layt milk

leitaria *f* laytar**ee**-a shop selling
dairy products

Travel tip Mini-mercados,
smaller shops and cafés
generally only stock UHT
milk, which is what most
Portuguese kids drink. Fresh
milk is sold in large super-
markets, but it tends to sell
out by mid-afternoon, so get
there early – *gordo* is full-
fat, *meio-gordo* half-fat and
magro skimmed milk.

leite de limpeza *m* layt di
leemp**ay**za skin cleanser

leitor de CDs *m* layt**oh**r di say
daysh CD-player

lembrança *f* laymbr**a**nsa
gift; souvenir

lembrar-se –si to remember

lembra-se? l**a**ymbrasi do you
remember?

não me lembro n**o**wng mi
l**a**ymbroo I don't remember

lenço *m* l**a**ynsoo handkerchief

lenço de cabeça di kab**ay**sa
headscarf

lenço de pescoço pishk**oh**soo
scarf (for neck)

lençol *m* layns**o**l sheet

lenços de papel *mpl* l**a**ynsoosh
di pap**eh**l tissues, paper
handkerchiefs, Kleenex

lentes de contacto *fpl* layntsh di
kont**a**too contact lenses

lentes gelatinosas Jilatin**o**zash
soft lenses

lentes rígidas ree**J**idash hard
lenses

lentes semi-rígidas
simiree**J**idash gas permeable
lenses

lento l**a**yntoo slow

leque *m* lehk fan (handheld)

ler layr to read

lésbica *f* l**eh**Jbika lesbian

leste *m* lehsht east

no leste noo in the east

letra *f* l**ay**tra letter

letra de imprensa block letters

levada *m* country walkway along irrigation channels on Madeira

levantar-se livantarsi to get up

levante o auscultador lift the receiver

levar to take; to carry

  para levar to take away, to go (food)

leve lehv light (not heavy)

Lg. square

lhe l-yi (to) him; (to) her; (to) you

lhes l-yaysh (to) them; (to) you

libra *f* leebra pound

libras esterlinas *fpl* leebraz ishtirleenash pounds sterling

lição *f* lisowng lesson

licença *f* lisaynsa licence; permit

  com licença kong excuse me

licenciatura *f* lisayns-yatoora degree

liceu *m* lisay-oo secondary school, high school

ligação *f* ligasowng connection

ligação com... connects with...

ligadura *f* ligadoora bandage

ligar to turn on, to switch on

lima de unhas *f* leema doon-yash nailfile

limite de velocidade *m* limeet di viloosidad speed limit

limpa pára-brisas *m* leempa parabreezash windscreen wiper

limpar leempar to clean

limpeza a seco *f* leempayza a saykoo dry-clean; dry-cleaning

limpo leempoo clean

língua *f* leengwa language; tongue

linha *f* leen-ya line

liquidação sale

liquidação total clearance sale

Lisboa liJboh-a Lisbon

liso leezoo plain

lista *f* leeshta list

lista telefónica telefohnika phone book, telephone directory

litro *m* leetroo litre

livraria *f* livraree-a bookshop, bookstore

livre leevr free, vacant

livro *m* leevroo book

livro de cheques di shehksh cheque book

livro de expressões dishprisoyngsh phrasebook

livro de moradas di mooradash address book

livro-guia *m* gee-a guidebook

lixívia *f* lisheev-ya bleach

lixo *m* leeshoo rubbish, trash; litter

local de encontro *m* lookal daynkohntroo meeting place

localidade *f* lookalidad place

loção *f* loosowng lotion

loção de bronzear *f* di bronz-yar suntan lotion

loção écran total *f* ekrang tootal sunblock

loção para depois do sol *f* dipoh-ish doo aftersun cream

locomotiva *f* lokoomooteeva engine

logo logoo immediately, at once

logo que possível ki pooseevil
as soon as possible

loiça f loh-isa crockery

loiça de barro di barroo pottery

Travel tip You can buy rustic,
brown kitchen earthen-
ware in every market and
supermarket for just a few
euros, but Caldas da Rainha
in Estremadura is prob-
ably Portugal's best-known
ceramics town – producing
caricatured rustic figurines
and floral- and animal-
inspired plates and bowls
since the nineteenth century.

---

loja f loJa shop

loja de aluguer de automóveis
daloogehr dowtoomovaysh car
hire, car rental

loja de antiguidades f
dantigweedadsh antique shop

loja de artesanato dartizanatoo
craft shop, handicrafts shop

loja de artigos fotográficos
darteegoosh fotografikoosh
camera shop

loja de brinquedos di
breenkaydoosh toyshop

loja de desportos dishportoosh
sports shop

loja de ferragens di firraJayngsh
hardware store

loja de fotografia footoografee-a
photography shop

loja de lembranças
laymbransash gift shop

loja de malas malash handbag
shop

loja de peles pehlsh furrier

loja de produtos naturais
proodootoosh natoorish health
food shop

Londres lohndrish London

longe lohnJ far

  ao longe ow in the distance

  fica longe? feeka is it far away?

lotação esgotada all tickets
sold

louça: lavar a louça lohsa
to wash the dishes

louça de barro f di barroo
earthenware

louco lohkoo nutter

louro lohroo blond

lua f loo-a moon

lua-de-mel f loo-a di mehl
honeymoon

lugar m loogar greengrocer's;
seat; place

  em outro lugar ayng ohtroo
elsewhere

lugar ao pé da janela ow peh da
Janehla window seat

lugar de corredor di kooridohr
aisle seat

lugar de vegetais di vigitish
greengrocer's

lugares em pé standing room

**lugares reservados a
cegos, inválidos, grávidas
e acompanhantes de
crianças com menos de
4 anos** seats reserved for the
blind, disabled, expectant

mothers and those with
children under four

lume *m* loom light; fire

luvas *fpl* **loo**vash gloves

luxo *m* **loo**shoo luxury

de luxo di de luxe

luxuoso loosh-**woh**zoo luxurious

luz *f* loosh light

luz do sol *f*looJ doo sunshine

luzes de presença *fpl* **loo**ziJ di prizaynsa sidelights

luzes de trânsito traffic lights

luzes de trás **loo**zish di trash rear lights

Lx Lisbon

M

M. underground, (US) subway

má bad; nasty

macaco *m* makakoo jack

maçada *f* masada bother

maçador masadohr boring

maçaneta *f* masanayta door knob

machão *m* mashowng macho

machista masheeshta sexist

maço *m* masoo packet

madeira *f* madayra wood

madrasta *f* madrashta stepmother

madrugada *f* madroogada dawn

de madrugada di at dawn

maduro madooroo ripe

mãe *f* mayng mother

magricela magrisehla skinny

magro magroo slim; thin

Maio mī-oo May

maior mī-**or** greater; bigger, larger

o maior the biggest

a maior parte (de) part (di) most (of)

maioria: a maioria dos/das... mī-oo**ree**-a doosh/dash most...

mais mīsh more

mais alguma coisa? mīz al**goo**ma **koh**-iza anything else?

mais de... mīJ di more than..., over...

mais... do que... more... than...

mais um/uma mīz oong/**oo**ma an extra one

não há mais nowng a mīsh there's none left

mais longe mīJ lohnJ further

mais nada no more; nothing else

mais ou menos mīz oh **may**noosh about, approximately, more or less; average, so-so

mais tarde mīsh tard later, later on

mal hardly; badly

mala *f* bag; suitcase; handbag

fazer as malas fazayr aJ malash to pack one's bags

mala de mão di mowng handbag, (US) purse

mal cozido koo**zee**doo not cooked, undercooked

mal-entendido *m* malayntayn**dee**doo misunderstanding

maluco malookoo barmy, nuts

mamã f mamang mum

mamar: dar de mamar a to breastfeed

mancha f spot

mandar to send

manga f sleeve

manhã f man-yang morning

  às sete da manhã ash seht at seven a.m.

  de manhã di in the morning

  esta manhã ehshta this morning

manivela do motor f manivehla doo motohr crankshaft

manta f blanket

mantenha-se à direita, caminhe pela esquerda (cars) keep to the right, (pedestrians) walk on the left

mão f mowng hand

mapa m map

mapa da cidade m sidad street map

mapa das estradas m daz shtradash road map

maquilhagem f makil-yaJayng make-up

máquina f makina machine

máquina de barbear di barb-yar electric shaver

máquina de lavar lavar washing machine

máquina de venda di vaynda vending machine

máquina fotográfica footoografika camera

mar m sea

maravilhoso maravil-yohzoo wonderful

marca f make, brand name

marcação f markasowng appointment

marcar to dial

marca registada registered trademark

marcha f marsha candlelit procession

marcha atrás marshatrash reverse gear

Março marsoo March

marco de correio m markoo di kooray-oo letterbox, mailbox

maré f mareh tide

margem f marJayng shore

marido m mareedoo husband

marisqueira f marishkayra seafood restaurant

marque o número desejado dial the number you require

Marrocos m marrokoosh Morocco

martelo m martehloo hammer

mas mash but

matar to kill

maternidade f maternidad maternity hospital

matrícula f matreekoola registration number

mau mow bad; nasty

maxila f makseela jaw

me me; to me; myself

mecânico m mekanikoo mechanic

média: em média ayng me**h**d-ya
on average

médica *f* me**h**dika doctor

medicamento *m* midika**may**ntoo
drug

médico *m* me**h**dikoo doctor

medida *f* mi**dee**da size

médio me**h**d-yoo medium;
medium-rare

de tamanho médio di taman-
yoo medium-sized

Mediterrâneo *m* miditirran-yoo
Mediterranean

medo *m* **may**doo fear

meia dúzia *f* **may**-a d**oo**z-ya
half a dozen

meia hora *f* ora half an hour

meia-noite *f* noh-it midnight

meia pensão *f* payns**ow**ng half
board, American plan

meias *fpl* **may**-ash stockings;
socks

meias collants stockings

meias de vidro di **vee**droo
hosiery

meio *m* **may**-oo middle; half

no meio noo in the middle

meio bilhete *m* bil-**yay**t half fare

meio-dia *m* **may**-oo **dee**-a
midday, noon

ao meio-dia ow at midday

mel *m* me**h**l honey

melhor mil-**yo**r best; better

melhorar mil-yo**ra**r to improve

mencionar mayns-yoo**na**r to
mention

menina *f* mi**nee**na girl; young lady

menino *m* boy

menor mi**no**r smaller

menos may**noo**sh less

menos de di under, less than

menos do que doo ki less than

pelo menos at least

mentir mayn**tee**r to lie

menu de preço fixo di pray**soo**
feeksoo fixed-price menu

menu turístico tooree**sh**tikoo
tourist menu

mercado *m* mir**ka**doo market

mercearia *f* mirs-ya**ree**-a
grocery store

merceeiro *m* mirs-**yay**roo
grocery store

merda! me**h**rda shit!

mergulhar mirgool-**ya**r to dive

mergulho *m* mir**goo**l-yoo skin-
diving

mês *m* maysh month

mesa *f* **may**za table

mesma may**J**ma, **mesmo**
may**J**moo same; myself

o/a mesmo/mesma the same

ele mesmo himself

mesmo se... may**J**mo si even if...

metade *f* mi**ta**d half

metade do preço doo pray**soo**
half price

metro *m* me**h**troo metre;
underground, (US) subway

metropolitano *m* underground,
(US) subway

meu **may**-oo my; mine

meu próprio... propr-yoo
my own...

meus may-oosh my; mine
mexer mishayr to move
microondas *f* mikroo-**oh**ndash microwave (oven)
mil meel thousand
milha *f* meel-ya mile
milhão *m* mil-y**ow**ng million
milímetro *m* mil**ee**mitroo millimetre
mim meeng me
minha meen-ya, **minhas** meen-yash my; mine
ministério *m* minisht**eh**r-yoo ministry, government department
minúsculo min**oo**shkooloo tiny
minuto *m* min**oo**too minute
míope mee-oopi shortsighted

miradouro *m* scenic view, vantage point
missa *m* mee**sa** mass
misturar mishtoorar to mix
mobília *f* moobeel-ya furniture
mochila *f* moosheela rucksack, backpack
moda *f* fashion
   na moda fashionable
modas para senhoras *fpl* m**o**dash para sin-y**o**rash ladies' fashions
moderno mood**eh**rnoo modern
moeda *f* mw**eh**da coin
moinho (*m*) moo-**ee**n-yoo mill; dull (pain)
mola *f* spring (in seat); peg
mola de roupa di r**oh**pa clothes peg

mola para o cabelo paroo kab**ay**loo hairgrip

mole mol soft

molhado mool-y**a**doo wet

momento m moom**ay**ntoo moment

  um momento oong hold on, just a moment

montanha f montan-ya mountain

montar a cavalo kav**a**loo to go horse-riding

monte m mohnt hill

montra f m**oh**ntra shop window

monumento m moonoom**ay**ntoo monument

monumento nacional national monument

morada f moor**a**da address

morar moor**a**r to live

mordedura f moorded**oo**ra bite

morrer moorr**ay**r to die

morte f mort death

morto m**oh**rtoo dead

morto de fome di fohm starving

mosca f m**oh**shka fly

mosquito m mooshk**ee**too mosquito

mosteiro m moosht**ay**roo monastery

mostrar mooshtr**a**r to show

mota f, **motocicleta** f mootoosikl**eh**ta motorbike

motor m moot**oh**r engine

motor de arranque darrank starter motor

motoreta f mootoor**ay**ta scooter

motorista m/f mootoor**ee**shta driver; motorist

motorizada f mootooriz**a**da moped

mourisco mohr**ee**shkoo Moorish

mouro m m**oh**-ooroo Moor

  os mouros the Moors

móveis de cozinha mpl kitchen furniture

muçulmano moosoolm**a**noo Muslim

mudança f mood**a**nsa gear(s)

mudar mood**a**r to move

mudar de roupa di r**oh**pa to get changed

mudar em… change at…

muitas vezes mweengtaJ v**ay**zish often

muito mw**ee**ngtoo a lot, lots; plenty of; much; very (much); quite

  muito mais mish a lot more

  não muito nowng not (very) much; not a lot; not too much

  muito tempo t**ay**mpoo a long time

  muito bem bayng very well

  muito bem! well done!

  muito prazer praz**ay**r how do you do?, nice to meet you

  muito prazer em conhecê-lo ayng koon-yis**ay**loo very pleased to meet you

muitos mpl mweengt**oo**sh many

muletas fpl moolayt**a**sh crutches

mulher f mool-y**eh**r woman; wife

mulher-polícia f poolees-ya policewoman

multa f moolta fine

multa por uso indevido penalty for misuse

multidão f mooltidowng crowd

mundo m moondoo world

muro m mooroo wall

músculo m mooshkooloo muscle

museu m moozay-oo museum

música f moozika music

música folclórica foolklorika folk music

música pop pop music

música rock rock (music)

músico m moozikoo musician

N

n. number

na in the; at the; on the

  na casa do Américo at Américo's

  na quinta-feira by Thursday

  na televisão on television

nacional nas-yoonal national

nacionalidade f nas-yoonalidad nationality

nada nothing

  mais nada miJ nothing else

  de nada my pleasure, don't mention it

  nada a declarar nothing to declare

nadador salvador f nadadohr salvadohr lifeguard

nadar to swim

nalguma parte nalgooma part somewhere

namorada f namoorada girlfriend

namorado m namooradoo boyfriend

não nowng no; not

não aconselhável a menores de... anos not recommended for those under... years of age

não beber do not drink

não congelar do not freeze

não contém... does not contain...

não engolir do not swallow

não engomar do not iron

não exceder a dose indicada do not exceed the dose indicated

não faz mal faJ mal it doesn't matter, never mind; it's OK

não fumar no smoking

não funciona out of order

não há vagas no vacancies

não ingerir do not swallow

não me diga! mi deega you don't say!

não mexer do not touch

não... nada nothing; not... anything

não... nenhum nin-yoong none; not... any

não... ninguém ningayng nobody, no-one; not... anybody, not... anyone

não... nunca noonka never

não pendurar do not hang, dry flat

não pisar a relva please keep off the grass

não secar na máquina do not spin-dry

não sei say I don't know

não tem de quê tayng di kay don't mention it, you're welcome

não torcer do not wring

nariz *m* nareesh nose

nas nash in the; at the; on the

nascer nash-sayr to be born

   nasci em... nash-see ayng I was born in...

Na. Sra. (Nossa Senhora) Our Lady

natação *f* natasowng swimming

Natal *m* Christmas

natural natooral natural

natureza *f* natoorayza nature

náuseas *fpl* nowz-yash nausea

navio *m* navee-o ship

   de navio di by ship

necessário nisisar-yoo necessary

negativo *m* nigateevoo negative

negócio *m* nigos-yoo deal; business

nem eu nayng ay-oo nor do I

nem... nem... nayng neither... nor...

nenhum nin-yoong, **nenhuma** nin-yooma none; no...

   de maneira nenhuma! di manayra no way!

   de nenhum modo modoo not in the least

   nenhum deles daylsh neither of them

neo-zelandês *m* neh-o zilandaysh, **neo-zelandesa** *f* zilandayza New Zealander

nervoso nirvohzoo nervous

neta *f* nehta granddaughter

neto *m* nehtoo grandson

nevar nivar to snow

neve *f* nehv snow

névoa *f* nehvwa mist

nevoeiro *m* nivwayroo fog

ninguém ningayng nobody, no-one

nível de óleo *m* neevil dol-yoo oil level

no noo in; in the; at the; on the

   no alto at the top

   no fundo de at the bottom of

   no hotel at the hotel

   no sábado on Saturday

no. number

nódoa *f* nodwa stain

noite *f* noh-it evening; night

   à noite in the evening; at night

   de noite at night

   esta noite ehshta this evening; tonight

noite de Santo António 13th June: Saint's day with music, fireworks and processions

noite de São João 24th June: Saint's day with music, fireworks and processions

noite de São Pedro 29th June: Saint's day with music, fireworks and processions

noiva (*f*) noh-iva engaged; fiancée

noivo (*m*) noh-ivoo engaged; fiancé

nojento nooJayntoo disgusting; filthy

nome *m* nohm name

nome de solteira di sooltayra maiden name

nome próprio propr-yoo Christian name, first name

nono nohnoo ninth

nora *f* daughter-in-law

nordeste *m* noordehsht northeast

noroeste *m* noorwehsht northwest

norte *m* nort north

  ao norte ow to the north

  no norte noo in the north

Noruega *f* noorwehga Norway

norueguês (*m*) noorwegaysh, **norueguesa** (*f*) noorwegayza Norwegian

nos noosh in the; at the; on the; us; to us; ourselves

nós nosh we; us

No. Sr. (Nosso Senhor) Our Lord

nossa, nossas nosash, **nosso** nosoo, **nossos** nosoosh our; ours

nota *f* note; banknote, (US) bill

notas falsas *fpl* notash falsash forged banknotes

notícias *fpl* nootees-yash news

noutro nohtroo in another; on another

nova morada *f* moorada forwarding address

Nova Zelândia ziland-ya New Zealand

nove nov nine

novecentas novesayntash,

novecentos novesayntoosh nine hundred

Novembro noovaymbroo November

noventa noovaynta ninety

novidades *fpl* noovidadsh news

novo nohvoo new

nu noo, **nua** noo-a naked

num noong, **numa** nooma in a

número *m* noomiroo number

número de telefone di telefohn phone number

número de voo noomiroo di voh-oo flight number

nunca noonka never

nuvem *f* noovayng cloud

O

o oo the; him; it; to it; you

objectiva *f* obJeteeva lens (of camera)

objectos de escritório *mpl* office supplies

objectos perdidos lost property, lost and found

obliterador *m* oblitiradohr ticket-stamping machine

obra *f* work

obras (na estrada) *fpl* roadworks

obrigada, obrigado obrigadoo thanks, thank you

  muito obrigado/obrigada mweengtoo thank you very much

observar obsirvar to watch

obturador *m* obtooradohr shutter

óbvio obv-yoo obvious

Oceano Atlântico os-yanoo atlantikoo Atlantic Ocean

Travel tip Supertubos, on the south side of Peniche, is the original surf destination in Portugal, though the currents and the raw power of the swell require a high level of expertise. Ericeira, also on the Estremadura coast, attracts highly talented local surfers and travelling pros, but the more protected west coast of the Algarve, around Sagres, is excellent for beginners and experienced surfers alike.

---

oculista *m* okooleeshta optician

óculos *mpl* okooloosh glasses, spectacles

óculos de sol di sunglasses

óculos protectores prootetohrish goggles

ocupado okoopadoo engaged; busy; occupied

oeste *m* wesht west

 no oeste noo in the west

ofender ofayndayr to offend

ofensivo ofaynseevoo offensive

oferecer ofrisayr to get; to offer

oferta especial special offer

oiço oh-isoo I hear

oitavo oh-itavoo eighth

oitenta oh-itaynta eighty

oito oh-itoo eight

oitocentas oh-itoosayntash, **oitocentos** oh-itoosayntoosh eight hundred

olá! oola hi!, hello!

óleo *m* ol-yoo oil

óleo de bronzear di brohnz-yar suntan oil

oleoso ol-yohzoo oily

olhar para ol-yar to look at

olho *m* ohl-yoo eye

ombro *m* ohmbroo shoulder

onda *f* ohnda wave

onde? ohnd where?

 onde é? ohndeh where is it?

 onde está? ohnd shta where is it?

 onde vai? vī where are you going?

 de onde? dohnd where from?

 de onde é? dohnd-eh where are you from?

ontem ohntayng yesterday

 ontem à noite noh-it last night

 ontem de manhã di man-yang yesterday morning

onze ohnz eleven

operação *f* opirasowng operation

operador turístico *m* opiradohr tooreeshtikoo tour operator

oposto opohshto opposite

optimista otimeeshta optimistic

óptimo otimoo super

 óptimo! great!, good!, excellent!

o que oo kay what

  o que é isso? oo k-yeh **ee**soo what's this?

ora essa! ora **eh**sa don't be stupid!

orelha f orayl-ya ear

organizar organizar to organize

orgulhoso orgool-**yoh**zoo proud

orquestra f ork**eh**shtra orchestra

os oosh the; them; you

osso m **oh**soo bone

otorrinolaringologista ear, nose and throat specialist

ou oh or

ou... ou... either... or...

ouriço-do-mar m ohr**ee**soo doo sea urchin

ourivesaria f ohrivezar**ee**-a jeweller's

ouro m **oh**roo gold

ousar ohzar to dare

Outono oht**oh**noo autumn, (US) fall

  no Outono noo in the autumn, in the fall

outra coisa ohtra k**oh**-iza something else

outras localidades ohtraJ lookalid**a**dsh other places

outra vez ohtra vaysh again

outro ohtroo different, another; other

Outubro oht**oo**broo October

ouvir ohv**ee**r to hear

  ao ouvir o sinal... when you hear the tone...

ovelha f ov**ay**l-ya sheep

P

P. square

pá f spade

pacote m pak**o**t carton; pack

padaria f padar**ee**-a bakery

padeiro m pad**ay**roo baker

padrasto m padr**a**shtoo stepfather

padre m padr priest

pagamento m pagam**ay**ntoo payment

pagamento a pronto cash payment

pagar to pay

pagar em dinheiro ayng deen-**yay**roo to pay cash

página f pa.Jina page

páginas amarelas pa.Jinaz amar**eh**lash yellow pages

pai m pī father

painel m pin**eh**l dashboard; panel

país m pa-**ee**sh country; nation; homeland

pais mpl pish parents

paisagem f pīza.Jayng scenery

País de Gales m pa-ee.J di g**a**lish Wales

palácio m palas-yoo palace

palavra f word

palco m palkoo stage

pálido palidoo pale

panela f pan**eh**la pan, saucepan

panfleto m panfl**ay**too leaflet

pano m panoo fabric, cloth

pano de cozinha di koozeen-ya tea towel

pano de loiça loh-isa dishcloth

pantufas *fpl* pantoofash slippers

papá *m* dad

papeira *f* papayra mumps

papéis waste paper

papel *m* papehl paper

papelaria *f* papelaree-a stationer

papel de alumínio daloomeen-yoo aluminium foil

papel de carta di writing paper, notepaper

papel de embrulho daymbrool-yoo wrapping paper

papel higiénico iJ-yehnikoo toilet paper

par *m* pair

um par de... oong par di a couple of...; a pair of...

para into; for; to; towards

para onde? ohnd where to?

para alugar paraloogar for hire; to rent

parabéns! parabayngsh congratulations!; happy birthday!

pára-brisas *m* parabreezash windscreen

pára-choques *m* parashoksh bumper

parafuso *m* parafoozoo screw

paragem *f* paraJayng stop

paragem do autocarro *f* doo owtookarroo bus stop

parapentismo *m* parapaynteeJmoo para-gliding

parar to stop

pare! par stop!

pare com isso! kong eesoo stop it!

parecer paresayr to look like

parede *f* parayd wall

páre, escute e olhe stop, look and listen

parente *m/f* paraynt relative

parque de campismo *m* park di kampeeJmoo campsite; caravan site, (US) trailer park

parque de estacionamento shtas-yonamayntoo car park, parking lot

parque de estacionamento subterrâneo soobterran-yoo underground car park/parking lot

parque para roulotes roolotsh caravan site, (US) trailer park

parque recreativo rekr-yateevoo amusement park

parte *f* part part

em parte nenhuma nin-yooma nowhere

em toda a parte tohda everywhere

parte posterior pooshteriohr back (part)

particular partikoolar private

partida *f* parteeda departure

partido (*m*) parteedoo broken; party (political)

partilhar partil-yar to share

partir parteer to break; to leave

a partir de di from

Páscoa *f* pashkwa Easter

passadeira de peões *f* pasadaira di p-yoyngsh pedestrian crossing,

(US) crosswalk

passado (*m*) pasadoo past

no ano passado noo anoo
last year

semana passada simana
last week

passageira *f* pasaJayra,
passageiro *m* pasaJayroo
passenger

passagem de nível *m* pasaJayng
level crossing, (US) grade
crossing

passagem de peões pedestrian
crossing, (US) crosswalk

passagem subterrânea
underpass

passaporte *m* pasaport passport

passar to pass

o que se passa? oo ki si
what's happening?; what's
wrong?

passar a ferro a fehrroo to iron

pássaro *m* pasaroo bird

passatempo *m* –taympoo hobby

passe (*m*) go, walk, cross now;
weekly or monthly ticket

passeio *m* pasay-oo pavement,
sidewalk; walk

ir a dar um passeio to go for
a walk

pasta *f* pashta briefcase

pasta de dentes di dayntsh
toothpaste

pastelaria *f* pashtilaree-a cake
shop, café selling cakes

pastilha elástica *f* pashteel-ya
elashtika chewing gum

pastilhas de mentol *fpl*

pashteel-yaJ di mints

pastilhas para a garganta
throat pastilles

patinar patinar to skid; to skate

patins de gelo *mpl* pateenJ di
Jayloo ice skates

pátio de recreio *m* pat-yoo di
rikray-oo playground

patrão *m* patrowng boss

pavilhão desportivo sports
pavilion

Pç. square

pé *m* peh foot

a pé on foot

ir a pé to walk

estar de pé di to stand

ao pé de ow … di near

peão *m* p-yowng pedestrian

peça de teatro *f* pehsa di t-yatroo
play

peça sobresselente *f*
sobrisilaynt spare part

pechincha *f* pisheensha bargain

pedaço *m* pidasoo piece

pedir pideer to ask; to order

pedir emprestado aymprishtadoo
to borrow

pedra *f* pehdra stone, rock

pega *f* pehga handle; action of
wrestling with the bull during
a bullfight

pegar pigar to catch

peito *m* paytoo breast; bust; chest

peixaria *f* paysharee-a
fishmonger's

pela pila through the; by the;
about the

pelas pilash through the; by the; about the

  pelas três horas by three o'clock

pele *f* pehl skin; leather; suede; fur

peleiro *m* pilayroo furrier

película aderente *f* pileekoola adiraynt clingfilm

pelo piloo through the; by the; about the

pelos piloosh through the; by the; about the

pen *f* memory stick

pena: é uma pena eh ooma payna it's a pity

  que pena! ki what a pity!

  não vale a pena nowng val-ya there's no point

  tenho muita pena mweengta I'm so sorry

pensão *f* paynsowng guesthouse

pensão completa komplehta full board

pensar paynsar to think

penso *m* paynsoo dressing; Elastoplast, Bandaid

pensos higiénicos *mpl* paynsooz iJ-yehnikoosh sanitary napkins/towels

pente *m* paynt comb

peões *mpl* p-yoyngsh pedestrians

pequeno pikaynoo little, small

pequeno almoço *m* almohsoo breakfast

perceber pirsibayr to understand

percebo pirsayboo I understand, I see

perdão pirdowng sorry

perder pirdayr to lose; to miss

perdido pirdeedoo lost

perdidos e achados lost property, lost and found

perfeito pirfaytoo perfect

perfumaria *f* pirfoomaree-a perfume shop

pergunta *f* pirgoonta question

perguntar pirgoontar to ask

perigo *m* pireegoo danger

perigo de desmoronamento danger of landslides

perigo de incêndio beware of starting fires

perigo de morte extreme danger

perigo, parar danger: stop

perigoso pirigohzoo dangerous

período *m* piree-oodoo period

período escolar shkoolar term

permanente *f* pirmanaynt perm

permitido pirmiteedoo allowed

permitir to allow

perna *f* pehrna leg

  (de) pernas para o ar (di) pehrnash proo ar upside down

persianas *fpl* pirs-yanash blinds

pertencer pirtaynsayr to belong

perto pehrtoo near

  perto daqui dakee nearby, near here

  perto de di next to

perturbar pirtoorbar to disturb

peruca *f* pirooka wig

pesadelo *m* pizadayloo nightmare

pesado pizadoo heavy
pesca f pehshka fishing
pescar pishkar to fish
pesca submarina f soob-mareena underwater fishing
pescoço m pishkohsoo neck
peso m payzoo weight
peso líquido net weight
peso neto net weight
pessoa f pisoh-a person
pessoal m pisoo-al staff, employees
peúga f p-yooga sock
piada f p-yada joke
picada f pikada bite; sting
picada de insecto dinsehtoo insect bite
picado pikadoo stung
picante pikant hot, spicy
picar pikar to sting; to chop finely
picar o bilhete stamp/punch your ticket
pijama m pijama pyjamas
pilha f peel-ya battery
pílula f peeloola pill
pinça f peensa tweezers
pincel m peensehl paintbrush
pintado de fresco wet paint
pintar peentar to paint
pintura f peentoora picture
pior p-yor worse; worst
  o pior the worst
piquenique m pikineek picnic
pires m peersh saucer
piscina f pish-seena swimming pool

piscina coberta koobehrta indoor pool
piscina infantil infanteel children's pool
piso m peezoo floor, storey; surface
piso escorregadio slippery road surface
piso irregular uneven road surface
piso superior soopir-yohr top floor
pista f runway
pistola f pishtola gun
plano (m) planoo plan; flat (adj)
planta f plant
plástico m plashtikoo plastic
plataforma f plataforma platform, (US) track
plateia f platay-a audience; ground floor of auditorium
platinados mpl platinadoosh points
P.M.P. (por mão própria) deliver by hand
pneu m pnay-oo tyre
pneu sobresselente soobrisilaynt spare tyre
pó m paw dust; powder
pobre pobr poor
pode pod you can/he/she can
  pode (você)...? vosay can you...?
  pode-se...? podsi is it OK to...?
  pode dar-me...? pod darmi can I have a...?, may I have...?

poder poodayr to be able to
pó de talco m paw di talkoo
  talcum powder
podia...? poodee-a
  could you...?
podre pohdr rotten
põe poyng he/she/it puts; you put
põem poh-ayng you/they put
pões poyngsh you put
polegada f pooligada inch
polegar m pooligar thumb
polícia m poolees-ya police;
  policeman
Polícia de Segurança Pública
  branch of the Portuguese
  police responsible for public
  order
polícia de trânsito traffic
  warden
Polícia Judiciária branch of

the police force responsible for
  investigating crime
poliéster polyester
política f politics
político political
polvo m pohlvoo octopus
pomada f poomada ointment
pomada para calçados
  kalsadoosh shoe polish
pomos pohmoosh we put
pónei m ponay pony
ponho pohn-yoo I put
pontão m pontowng jetty
ponte f pohnt bridge; crown
ponto de encontro meeting
  point
população f poopoolasowng
  population
por poor through; by

por avião by airmail

por noite noh-it per night

pôr pohr to put

porca f porka nut (for bolt)

porção f poorsowng portion

porcaria f poorkaree-a dirt; mess

porcelana f poorsilana china

por cento sayntoo per cent

porco m pohrkoo pig

pôr do sol m pohr doo sunset

por favor poor favohr please

porque poorkay because; why

  porque não? nowng why not?

porreiro! poorrayroo bloody good!

porta f door; gate

porta-bagagens m bagaJayngsh boot, (US) trunk

porta-bagagens na capota, porta-bagagens no tejadilho noo tiJadeel-yoo roof rack

porta-bebés m bebehsh carry-cot

porta de embarque f daymbark gate

portagem toll

porta-moedas m mwehdash purse

porta nº... gate number...

portão m poortowng gate

portão de embarque daymbark gate (at airport)

porteiro m poortayroo doorman, porter

porteiro da noite noh-it night porter

Porto m pohrtoo Oporto

porto m harbour, port

Portugal Telecom National Telecommunications Service

português (m) poortoogaysh Portuguese; Portuguese man

  em português in Portuguese

  os portugueses the Portuguese

portuguesa (f) poortoogayza Portuguese; Portuguese woman

posologia f dose

possível pooseevil possible

posso posoo I can

  posso...? can I...?

  posso ter...? tayr can I have...?

postal m pooshtal postcard

posta-restante f poshta rishtant poste restante, (US) general delivery

poste indicador m posht indikadohr signpost

posterior: parte posterior f pooshtir-yohr back (part)

postigos mpl pooshteegoosh shutters

Posto da Polícia m pohshtoo da poolees-ya police station

posto de enfermagem first-aid post

posto de socorros first-aid centre

pouco pohkoo a little

  um pouco oong a little bit

  um pouco caro karoo a bit expensive

  um pouco disto deeshtoo some of this

pouco vulgar voolgar unusual

poucos pohkoosh few; a few

pouquinho: um pouquinho
oong pohkeen-yo a little bit

pousada *f* pohsada state-owned
hotel, often a historic building

praça *f* prasa square; market

praça de táxis di taxish taxi rank

praça de touros tohroosh bullring

pracista *m* praseeshta taxi-driver

praia *f* prī-a seafront; beach

na praia on the beach

> Travel tip The most popular
> sandy beaches can be found
> on the eastern Algarve, where
> the sea is warmest and
> remains swimmable all year
> round, if you're hardy. The
> west coast faces the Atlantic,
> so beware the heavy under-
> tow and don't swim unless
> there is a red or yellow flag.

prancha à vela *f* pransha vehla
sailboard

prancha de saltos di saltoosh
diving board

prancha de windsurf sailboard

prata *f* prata silver

prateleira *f* pratilayra shelf

praticar pratikar to practise

praticar jogging to go jogging

praticar windsurf to windsurf

prático pratikoo practical

prato *m* pratoo course, dish; plate

**prazer: (muito) prazer em
conhecê-lo/conhecê-la**

(mweengtoo) prazayr aing
koon-yisayloo pleased to meet
you

precipício *m* prisipees-yoo cliff

precisar prisizar to need

preciso de... priseezoo di
I need...

preço *m* praysoo price; charge

pré-comprado bought in
advance

preço de custo cost price

preço por dia poor dee-a
price per day

preço por pessoa pisoh-a
price per person

preço por semana simana
price per week

preços reduzidos reduced prices

preencher pri-aynshayr to fill in

preferir prifireer to prefer

prefiro... prifeeroo I prefer...

prego *m* prehgoo nail (metal); roll
with a thin slice of meat

preguiçoso prigisohzoo lazy

prendas *fpl* prayndash gifts

prender prayndayr to arrest

preocupação *f* pri-ookoo-
pasowng worry

preocupado pri-ookoopadoo
worried

preocupar-se com to worry
about

pré-pagamento choose your
food, drink etc then pay at the
cash desk before being served

preparar priparar to prepare

presente *m* prizaynt present, gift

preservativo m prizirvat**ee**voo condom

presidente m/f prizid**ay**nt president

pressa: estou com pressa shtoh kong pr**eh**sa I'm in a hurry

não há pressa nowng a there's no hurry

pressão f pris**ow**ng tyre pressure

pressão arterial artiri-al blood pressure

presta: não presta nowng pr**eh**shta it's no good

prestável presht**a**vil helpful

preto pr**ay**too black

preto e branco black and white

previsão do tempo f priviz**ow**ng doo t**ay**mpoo weather forecast

prima f pr**ee**ma cousin

Primavera f primav**eh**ra spring

primeira: a primeira vez prim**ay**ra vaysh the first time

primeira à esquerda a-shk**ay**rda first on the left

primeira classe klas first class

primeiro prim**ay**roo first

primeiro andar m first floor, (US) second floor

primeiro ministro m prim**ay**roo min**ee**shtroo prime minister

primeiro piso first floor, (US) second floor

primeiros socorros mpl prim**ay**roosh sook**o**rroosh first aid

primo m pr**ee**moo cousin

princesa f preens**ay**za princess

principal preensipal main

principalmente preensipalm**ay**nt mostly

príncipe m pr**ee**nsipi prince

principiante m/f preensip-**ya**nt beginner

princípio: ao princípio ow preens**ee**p-yoo at first

prioridade f right of way; priority

dar prioridade give way, yield

prisão f priz**ow**ng jail

prisão de ventre di vayntr constipation

privado priv**a**doo private

problema m proobl**ay**ma problem

procissão f proosis**ow**ng candlelit procession held to celebrate feast days and Good Friday

procurar prookoor**a**r to look for; to search

produto m prood**oo**too product

produtos alimentares alimaynt**a**rish foodstuffs

produtos de beleza di bel**ay**za beauty products

produtos de limpeza leemp**ay**za household cleaning materials

professor m proofes**oh**r, **professora** f proofes**oh**ra teacher

programa m proogr**a**ma program(me)

proibida a entrada a... no admittance to...

proibida a entrada a cães no dogs

proibida a entrada a menores de … anos no admittance to those under … years of age

proibida a inversão de marcha no U-turns

proibida a paragem no stopping

proibida a passagem no access

proibido proo-ibeedoo forbidden

proibido… no…

proibido acampar no camping

proibido a pessoas estranhas ao serviço personnel only

proibido estacionar no parking

proibido fazer lume no campfires

proibido fumar no smoking

proibido nadar no swimming

proibido pescar no fishing

proibido tirar fotografias no photography

proibido tomar banho no bathing

proibido ultrapassar no overtaking

prometer proomitayr to promise

pronto prohntoo ready

pronto a vestir ready-to-wear

pronto-socorro *m* prohntoo sookohrroo breakdown service

pronunciar proonoons-yar to pronounce

propósito: de propósito di proopozitoo deliberately

própria: a sua própria soo-a propr-ya, **o seu próprio** oo say-oo propr-yoo his/her/its/your/ their own

propriedade privada private property

proteger prootiJayr to protect

proteger do calor e humidade store away from heat and damp

protestante (*m/f*) prootishtant Protestant

prova: à prova de água dagwa waterproof

provar proovar to try; to try on; to taste

provavelmente proovavilmaynt probably

próxima sessão às … horas next showing at … o'clock

próximo prosimoo near; next

o/a… mais próximo/ próxima miJ the nearest…

próximo de di next to

ps. weight

P.S.P. branch of the Portuguese police

pua *f* poo-a splinter

público (*m*) pooblikoo audience; public

pular poolar to jump

pulga *f* poolga flea

pulmões *mpl* poolmoyngsh lungs

pulseira *f* poolsayra bracelet; watchstrap

pulso *m* poolsoo wrist

pura lã pure wool

pura lã virgem pure new wool

puxar pooshar to pull

puxar (a alavanca) em caso de emergência pull (lever) in case of emergency

puxe pull

Q

Q hot

quais? kwīsh which?; which ones?

qual? kwal which?

qual deles? daylsh which one?

qualidade *f* kwalidad quality

qualquer kwalkehr any

qualquer coisa koh-iza anything

qualquer medicamento deve estar fora do alcance das crianças keep all medicines out of the reach of children

quando? kwandoo when?

quantia *f* kwantee-a amount

quanto? kwantoo how much?

quanto custa? kooshta how much does it cost?

quanto é? kwantweh how much is it?

quantos? kwantoosh how many?

quarenta kwaraynta forty

quarentena *f* kwarayntayna quarantine

quarta-feira *f* kwarta fayra Wednesday

quarta parte *f* part quarter

quarto (*m*) kwartoo bedroom; room; quarter; fourth

quarto andar fourth floor, (US) fifth floor

quarto com duas camas kong doo-ash kamash twin room

quarto de banho das senhoras di ban-yoo dash sin-yorash ladies' toilets, ladies' room

quarto de casal di kazal double room

quarto de hotel dohtehl hotel room

quarto duplo dooploo double room

quarto individual individwal single room

quarto para duas pessoas doo-ash pisoh-ash double room

quarto para uma pessoa ooma single room

quase kwaz almost, nearly

quase nunca noonka hardly ever

quatro kwatroo four

quatrocentas kwatrosayntash, **quatrocentos** kwatrosayntoosh four hundred

que that; than

o que? what?

o que é isso? oo k-yeh eesoo what's that?

que…! what a…!

que bom! ki bong that's nice!

quê? kay what?

quebrar kibrar to break

quebre em caso de emergência break in case of emergency

queda *f* kehda fall

queda de pedras falling stones

queda de rochas falling rocks

queimado kaymado burnt

queimado de sol di sunburnt

queimadura *f* kaymadoora burn

queimadura de sol *f* sunburn

queimar kaymar to burn

queixas complaints

queixo *m* **kay**shoo chin

quem? kayng who?

  de quem? di whose?

  de quem é isto? eh **ee**shtoo whose is this?

  quem é? kayng**eh** who is it?

  quem fala? who's calling?

quente kaynt warm; hot

quer...? kehr would you like...?, do you want...?

querer kir**ay**r to want

queria kir**ee**-a I want; I'd like

  queria...? could I have...?

quero keh**roo** I want

  não quero I don't want (to)

  não quero nada I don't want anything

quieto k-**yeh**too still

quilo *m* keeloo kilo

quilometragem ilimitada kilomitra**J**ayng ilimit**a**da unlimited mileage

quilómetro *m* kil**o**mitroo kilometre

quinhentas keen-**yay**ntash, **quinhentos** keen-**yay**ntoosh five hundred

quinta *f* keenta farm

quinta-feira *f* keenta f**ay**ra Thursday

quinto keentoo fifth

quinze keenz fifteen

quinzena *f* keenz**ay**na fortnight

quiosque *m* k-yoshk kiosk

quiosque de jornais di Joorn**ī**sh newspaper kiosk

R

R. street

rabo *m* tail; backside, behind

radiador *m* rad-yad**oh**r radiator

Radiodifusão Portuguesa Portuguese Radio

radiografia *f* rad-yoograf**ee**-a X-ray

Radiotelevisão Portuguesa Portuguese Television

rainha *f* ra-**een**-ya queen

raio *m* rī-oo ray, beam; spoke

raio X *m* ra-yoo sheesh X-ray

rapariga *f* rapar**ee**ga girl

rapaz *m* rap**a**sh boy

Rápido *m* rapid**oo** express (train)

rápido fast, quick

raqueta *f* rak**eh**ta racket

raqueta de ténis tennis racket

raro raroo rare, uncommon

ratazana *f* rataz**a**na rat

rato *m* ratoo mouse

razão *f* raz**ow**ng reason

  tinhas razão teen-ya**J** raz**ow**ng you were right

razoável razw**a**vil reasonable

r/c ground floor, (US) first floor

R.D.P. Portuguese Radio

realmente r-yalm**ay**nt really

reaver r-yav**ay**r to get back

rebentado ribent**a**doo burst

reboque *m* rib**o**k trailer (for carrying tent etc)

rebuçado *m* riboos**a**doo sweet, candy

recado *m* rikadoo message

deixar um recado dayshar oong to leave a message

receber risibayr to receive

receita *f* risayta recipe; prescription

recepção *f* risehsowng reception

recepcionista *m/f* risehs-yooneeeshta receptionist

recibo *m* riseeboo receipt

reclamação *f* riklamasowng complaint

reclamação de bagagens di bagaJayngsh baggage claim

reclamações complaints

reclamar riklamar to complain

recomendar rikoomayndar to recommend

reconhecer rikoon-yisayr to recognize

rede *f* rayd net; hammock

redondo ridohndoo round

reembolsar ri-aymboolsar to refund

reembolso *m* ri-aymbohlsoo refund

refeição *f* rifaysowng meal

reformada (*f*) rifoormada pensioner; retired

reformado (*m*) rifoormadoo pensioner; retired

reformado de terceira idade *m* senior citizen

refugo *m* rifoogoo rubbish

reg. registered

região *f* riJ-yowng region; area

da região local

Regional local train, usually stopping at most stations

registado riJishtadoo registered

registos registered mail

reg.to. regulation

regulamento *m* regulation

rei *m* ray king

Reino Unido *m* raynooneedoo United Kingdom

relâmpago *m* rilampagoo lightning

religião *f* riliJ-yowng religion

relógio *m* riloJ-yoo clock; watch, wristwatch

relógio de pulso de poolsoo watch, wristwatch

relojoaria *f* rilooJwaree-a watchmaker's shop

relva *f* rehlva grass

relvado *m* relvadoo lawn

rem. sender

remar to row

remédio *m* rimehd-yoo medicine

remetente *m/f* sender

renda *f* raynda lace

reparar riparar to fix, to repair

repele-insectos *m* ripehl insehtoosh insect repellent

repele-mosquitos *m* moosh-keetoosh mosquito repellent

repelente de insectos eléctrico *m* ripilaynt dinsehtoosh elehtrikoo electric mosquito killer

repetir ripiteer to repeat

repousar ripohzar to rest

repouso *m* ripohzoo rest

representante *m/f* riprizayntant agent

repugnante ripoognant revolting

rés de chão *m* rehJ doo showng ground floor, (US) first floor

reserva *f* rizehrva reservation

reserva de lugares di loogarish seat reservation

reservado rizirvadoo reserved

reservar rizirvar to book, to reserve

reservas reservations

residencial *m* rizidayns-yal bed and breakfast hotel

respirar rishpirar to breathe

responder rishpondayr to answer

responsável rishponsavil responsible

resposta *f* rishposhta answer

ressaca *f* risaka hangover

restaurante *m* rishtowrant restaurant

resto *m* rehshtoo rest, remainder

retalho *m* rital-yoo oddment

retirado ritiradoo secluded

retrato *m* ritratoo portrait

retretes *fpl* ritrehtsh toilets, rest rooms

retrosaria *f* ritroozaree-a haberdasher

reumatismo *m* rheumatism

reunião *f* r-yoon-yowng meeting

revisor *m* rivizohr ticket inspector

revista *f* riveeshta magazine

ribeiro *m* ribayroo stream

rico reekoo rich

ridículo rideekooloo ridiculous

rímel *m* reemil mascara

rinque de patinagem *m* reenk di patinaJayng ice rink

rins *mpl* reengsh kidneys

rio *m* ree-oo river

rir reer to laugh

R.N. National bus/coach service

rocha *f* rosha rock

rochedo *m* rooshaydoo cliff

roda *f* roda wheel

rodada *f* roodada round

Rodoviária Nacional National bus/coach service

rolha *f* rohl-ya cork

romance *m* roomans novel

roncar ronkar to snore

rosa *f* roza rose

rótulo *m* rotooloo label

rotunda *f* rootoonda roundabout

roubado rohbadoo robbed

roubar rohbar to steal

roubo *m* rohboo burglary; theft; rip-off

roulotte *f* roolot caravan, (US) trailer

roupa *f* rohpa clothes

roupa de cama di kama bed linen

roupa de homens dohmayngsh menswear

roupa de senhoras sin-yorash ladies' wear

roupa interior intir-yohr underwear

roupão *m* rohpowng dressing gown

roupa para lavar laundry, washing

roxo rohshoo purple

R.T.P. Portuguese Television

rua *f* roo-a road; street

  rua! get out of here!

rua principal preensipal main road

rua secundária sikoondar-ya side street

rua sem saída cul-de-sac, dead end

rubéola *f* roobeh-ola German measles

ruínas *fpl* rweenash ruins

ruivo roo-ivoo red-headed

S

S ladies' toilets, ladies' room

S. saint

S/ without

sábado sabadoo Saturday

saber sabayr to know; to be able to

sabia sabee-a I knew

  não sabia nowng I didn't know

sabonete *m* saboonayt soap

sabor *m* sabohr taste; flavour

saboroso saboorohzoo tasty, delicious

sacana! bastard!

saca-rolhas *m* sakarrohl-yash corkscrew

saco *m* sakoo bag

saco de compras di kohmprash shopping bag

saco de dormir doormeer sleeping bag

saco (de) plástico plashtikoo plastic bag

sacos de lixo *mpl* sakoosh bin liners

saia *f* sī-ya skirt

saia! get out!

saída *f* sa-eeda departure; exit

saída de emergência demirJayns-ya emergency exit

saio sī-oo I get off; I go out; I leave

sair sa-eer to get off, to get out; to go out; to leave

sais de banho *mpl* sīJ di ban-yoo bath salts

saiu sa-**ee**-oo he/she is out; he/
  she has gone out
sala f lounge
sala de chá tea room
sala de convívio di konv**ee**v-yoo
  lounge
sala de embarque daymbark
  departure lounge
sala de espera dishp**eh**ra
  lounge, departure lounge
sala de estar disht**a**r living room
sala de jantar di Jantar dining
  room
salão de beleza m sal**ow**ng di
  bel**ay**za beauty salon
salão de cabeleireiro di
  kabilayr**ay**roo hairdressing salon
saldos mpl sald**oo**sh sale
salgado salg**a**doo savoury; salty
salto m s**a**ltoo heel (of shoe)
sandálias fpl sand**a**l-yash sandals
sangrar to bleed
sangue m sang blood
santinho! sant**ee**n-yoo bless you!
são sowng healthy; they are;
  you are
sapataria f sapatar**ee**-a shoe shop
sapateira f sapat**ay**ra crab
sapateiro m sapat**ay**roo shoe
  repairer's
sapateiro rápido r**a**pidoo heel bar
sapatos mpl sapat**oo**sh shoes
sapatos de treino di tr**ay**noo
  trainers
sarampo m saramp**oo** measles
sardinhada f sardin-y**a**da party
  where grilled sardines are eaten

S.A.R.L. (Sociedade Anónima
  de Responsabilidade
  Limitada) limited company
satisfeito satisf**ay**too satisfied, full
saudável sowd**a**vil healthy
saúde sa-**oo**d health
  saúde! cheers!
  à sua saúde! s**oo**-a your
  health!
se si if; yourself; himself; herself;
  themselves; yourselves; itself;
  oneself
secador de cabelo m sikad**oh**r
  di kab**ay**loo hairdryer
secador de roupa di r**oh**pa
  spin-dryer
secar sik**a**r to dry
secar com secador (de mão)
  kong sikad**oh**r (di mowng)
  to blow-dry
secção f sehks**ow**ng section;
  department
secção de crianças di kry-
  ansash children's department
secção de perdidos e
  achados di pird**ee**dooz
  ee-ash**a**doosh lost property
  office, lost and found
seco s**ay**koo dry
secreto sikr**eh**too secret
século m s**eh**kooloo century
seda f s**ay**da silk
sede: ter sede tayr sayd to be
  thirsty
se faz favor si fash fav**oh**r please;
  excuse me
seguida: em seguida ayng
  sig**ee**da straight away

seguinte sigeengt following; next

  dia seguinte *m* the day after

seguir sigeer to follow

seguir pela direita pila dirayta keep to your right

seguir pela esquerda pilashkayrda keep to your left

segunda classe sigoonda klas second class

segunda-feira *f* sigoonda fayra Monday

segunda mão: em segunda mão sigoonda mowng second-hand

segundo (*m*) sigoondoo second

segundo andar *m* second floor, (US) third floor

segurar sigoorar to hold

seguro (*m*) sigooroo insurance; safe; sure

seguro de viagem di v-yaJayng travel insurance

sei say I know

seis saysh six

seiscentas sayshsayntash, **seiscentos** sayshsayntoosh six hundred

sela *f* sehla saddle

selo *m* sayloo stamp

selvagem silvaJayng wild

sem sayng without

semáforos *mpl* simafooroosh traffic lights

semana *f* simana week

  na próxima semana prosima next week

Semana Santa Easter Week

sem chumbo sayng shoomboo leadfree, unleaded

sem conservantes does not contain preservatives

sem corantes does not contain artificial colouring

sem corantes nem conservantes does not contain artificial colouring or preservatives

semelhante simil-yant similar

sem pensão no meals served

sempre saympr always

sempre em frente saymprayng fraynt straight ahead

sem preservativos does not contain preservatives

senha *f* sayn-ya ticket; receipt; password

Senhor sin-yohr Mr

senhor (*m*) sir; gentleman; you

  o senhor oo you

  os senhores oosh sin-yohrish you

  do senhor doo your; yours

  dos senhores doosh sin-yohrish your; yours

Senhora sin-yora Mrs

senhora madam; lady; you

  a senhora you

  as senhoras ash sin-yorash you

  da senhora, das senhoras your; yours

senhoras ladies' toilet, ladies' room

sensato saynsatoo sensible

sensível saynseevil sensitive

sentar-se saynt**ar**si to sit, to sit down

  como se sente? kohmoo si saynt how are you feeling?

  sente-se sayntsi sit down

sentido proibido no entry

sentido único one way

sentimento *m* saytim**ay**ntoo feeling

sentir saynt**eer** to feel

separadamente siparadam**ay**nt separately

separado sipar**a**doo separate; separated

ser sayr to be

será s**i**ra he/she/it/you will be

serão sir**ow**ng you/they will be

serás s**i**rash you will be

serei sir**ay** I will be

seremos sir**ay**moosh we will be

sério sehr-yoo serious

serve-se … das … horas às … horas … served from … o'clock until … o'clock

serviço *m* sirv**ee**soo service

serviço automático direct dialling

serviço de quartos di kw**a**rtoosh room service

serviço de urgências door**jay**ns-yash casualty department

serviço expresso express service

serviço incluído service included

serviço internacional international service

serviço permanente 24-hour service

servir sirv**eer** to serve

sessenta ses**ay**nta sixty

sete seht seven

setecentas setes**ay**ntash, **setecentos** setes**ay**ntoosh seven hundred

Setembro sit**ay**mbroo September

setenta set**ay**nta seventy

setentrional setayntr-yoon**a**l northern

sétimo sehtimoo seventh

seu say-oo, **seus** say-oosh his; her; hers; its; your; yours; their; theirs

sexo *m* s**eh**xoo sex

sexta-feira *f* s**ay**shta f**ay**ra Friday

Sexta-Feira Santa Good Friday

sexto s**ay**shtoo sixth

S.f.f. please

si see you

SIDA *f* s**ee**da AIDS

siga-me s**ee**gami follow me

significar signif**i**kar to mean

silêncio *m* sil**ay**ns-yoo silence

silencioso silayns-y**oh**zoo quiet

sim seeng yes; it is

  sim? really?

  ah sim! seeng well well!

simpático simpat**i**koo friendly

simples s**ee**mplish simple, easy

sinagoga *f* sin**a**goga synagogue

sinal *m* sign; signal; roadsign

sinal de alarme dal**a**rm emergency alarm

sinal de arroba m darohba at sign

sincero sinsehroo sincere

sino m seenoo bell

sintético sintehtikoo synthetic

sinto-me seentoomi I feel

  sinto-me bem bayng I'm OK, I'm fine

sítio m seet-yoo place

  noutro sítio nohtroo somewhere else

SMS m ehs-ehm-ehs text

só saw alone; just; only

sobrancelha f soobransayl-ya eyebrow

sobre sohbr about, concerning; on

sobretudo m soobritoodoo overcoat

sobrinha f soobreen-ya niece

sobrinho m soobreen-yoo nephew

sóbrio sobr-yoo sober

sociedade f soos-yaydad society; company

socorro! sookohrroo help!

sofá m soofa sofa; couch

sofisticado soofishtikadoo sophisticated; upmarket

sogra f mother-in-law

sogro m sohgroo father-in-law

sogros mpl sogroosh in-laws

soirée evening performance

sol m sun

  ao sol ow in the sun

  está (a fazer) sol shta (a fazayr) it's sunny

solteiro (m) sooltayroo single; bachelor

solto sohltoo loose

solução de limpeza f sooloosowng di leempayza cleaning solution

solução para as lentes de contacto paraJ layntsh di kontaktoo soaking solution

soluços mpl sooloosoosh hiccups

sombra f sohmbra shade; shadow

  à sombra in the shade

sombra para os olhos parooz ol-yoosh eye shadow

somente somaynt only; just

somos sohmoosh we are

sonho m sohn-yoo dream

sonífero m sooneefiroo sleeping pill

sono m sohnoo sleep

  estar com sono shtar kong to be sleepy

sopé: no sopé do... noo soopeh doo at the bottom of...

só pode vender-se mediante receita médica available only on prescription

sorrir soorreer to smile

sorriso m soorreezoo smile

sorte f sort luck

sou soh I am

  sou de... di I am from...

soutien m soot-yang bra

sozinha sozeen-ya, **sozinho** sozeen-yoo by myself

Sr. Mr

Sra. Mrs

Sto. saint

sua soo-a his; her; hers; its; your; yours; their; theirs

suar soo-ar to sweat

suas soo-ash his; her; hers; its; your; yours; their; theirs

suave swav delicate; mild

subir soobeer to go up

subitamente soobitamaynt suddenly

sucesso m soosehsoo success

sudeste m soodehsht southeast

sudoeste m soodwehsht southwest

Suécia f swehs-ya Sweden

sueca (f) swehka, **sueco** (m) swehkoo Swedish; Swede

suficiente soofis-yaynt enough

suficientemente soofis-yayntimaynt enough

Suíça f sweesa Switzerland

suíça (f) sweesa, **suíço** (m) sweesoo Swiss

sujidade f sooJidad dirt

sujo sooJoo dirty

sul m sool south

   no sul noo in the south

sul-africana (f) soolafrikana, **sul-africano** (m) soolafrikanoo South African

supermercado m soopermerkadoo supermarket

suplemento m sooplimayntoo supplement, extra charge

supositório m soopoozitor-yoo suppository

surdo soordoo deaf

surpreendente soorpr-yayndaynt surprising

surpresa f soorprayza surprise

T

tabacaria f tabakaree-a tobacconist; tobacco store; tobacco goods; newsagent

tabaco m tabakoo tobacco

taberna m tabehrna pub

tabuleiro m taboolayroo tray

talheres mpl tal-yehrish cutlery

talho m tal-yoo butcher's shop

talvez talvaysh maybe, perhaps

   talvez não nowng perhaps not

tamanho m taman-yoo size

também tambayng also, too, as well

   eu também ay-oo so am I; so do I; me too

tampa f cap, lid

tampa do ralo f doo raloo plug (in sink)

tampões mpl tampoyngsh tampons

tanto tantoo so much

   tanto faz fash it's all the same to me

tão towng so

   tão ... como ... as ... as ...

   tão ... quanto kwantoo as ... as

   tão ... quanto possível pooseevil as ... as possible

tapete m tapayt carpet

tarde f tard afternoon; late

à tarde in the afternoon

esta tarde ehshta this afternoon

da tarde p.m.

três da tarde 3 p.m.

tarifa *f* tareefa charges

tasca *f* tashka small tavern serving food

taxa de serviço *f* tasha di sirveesoo service charge

te ti you; to you; yourself

teatro *m* t-yatroo theatre

tecido *m* tiseedoo cloth, material

tecto *m* tehtoo ceiling

tejadilho *m* tiJadeel-yoo car roof

tel. telephone

teleférico *m* telefehrikoo cable car

telefonar telefoonar to call, to phone

telefone *m* telefohn telephone

telefone de cartão di kartowng cardphone

telefone público pooblikoo payphone

Telefones de Lisboa e Porto S.A. telephone company for Lisbon and Oporto

telefonista *m/f* telefooneeshta operator

telemóvel *m* telemovil mobile phone

televisão *f* televizowng television

telhado *m* til-yadoo roof

tem tayng he/she/it has; you have

tem...? have you got any...?, do you have...?

ele/ela tem de... he/she must...

têm tay-ayng you/they have

temos taymoosh we have

temos que... ki we've got to..., we must...

temperatura *f* taympiratoora temperature

tempestade *f* taympishtad storm

tempo *m* taympoo time; weather

a tempo on time

por quanto tempo? poor kwantoo for how long?

tenda (de campismo) *f* taynda (di kampeeJmoo) tent

tenho tayn-yoo I have; I am; I have to

não tenho nowng I don't have any

tenho de/que... di/ki I must...

ténis *m* tehnish tennis

ténis de mesa di mayza table tennis

tens taynsh you have

tensão *f* taynsowng tension; voltage

tensão arterial alta artir-yal high blood pressure

tentar tayntar to try

tépido tehpidoo lukewarm

ter tayr to have; to hold; to be; to contain; to have to

ter de/que to have to

terça-feira tayrsa fayra Tuesday

ter calor tayr kalohr to be warm

terceiro tirsayroo third

terceiro andar *m* third floor, (US) fourth floor

termas *fpl* tehrmash spa

terminado tirminadoo over; finished

terminal *m* tirminal terminus

terminar tirminar to finish

termo *m* tayrmoo vacuum flask

termómetro *m* tirmohmitroo thermometer

terra *f* tehrra earth

terraço *m* tirrasoo terrace

terrível tirreevil terrible

tesoura *f* tizohra scissors

testa *f* tehshta forehead

testemunha *m/f* tishtimoon-ya witness

teu tay-oo, **teus** tay-oosh your; yours

teve tayv he/she/it/you had

têxteis textiles

ti you

tia *f* tee-a aunt

tigela *f* tiJehla dish, bowl

tijolo *m* tiJohloo brick

tímido teemidoo shy

tinha teen-ya I/he/she/it/you used to have

tinham teen-yowng you/they used to have

tínhamos teen-yamoosh we used to have

tinhas teen-yash you used to have

tinta *f* teenta paint; tint

tinto teentoo red

tinturaria *f* teentooraree-a dry-cleaner

tio *m* tee-oo uncle

típico teepikoo typical

tipo *m* teepoo sort, type, kind

tiragem *f* tiraJayng collection; edition; circulation

tirar to remove

tive teev I had

tivemos tivaymoosh we had

tiveram tivehrowng you/they had

tiveste tivehsht you had

TLP telephone company for Lisbon and Oporto

toalha *f* twal-ya towel

toalha de banho di ban-yoo bath towel

toalha de cara kara flannel

toalha de mesa mayza tablecloth

toalhas higiénicas *fpl* twal-yaz iJ-yehnikash sanitary towels

tocar tookar to touch

toda a gente tohda a Jaynt everyone

todas tohdash all; all of them

   todas as vezes aJ vayzish every time

todo tohdoo all; all of it

   todo o dia/o dia todo oo dee-a all day

todos tohdoosh all; all of them

   todos os dias tohdooz-ooJ dee-ash every day, daily

   para todos suitable for all age groups

toilette *m* twale**h**t toilet, rest room

tolo to**h**loo silly

tomada *f* tooma**d**a socket; plug; power point

tomada para a máquina de barbear makina di barb-y**ar** shaving point

tomar too**m**ar to take

   o que vai tomar? oo ki vī what'll you have?

tomar antes de se deitar to be taken before going to bed

tomar a seguir às refeições to be taken after meals

tomar banho ban-yoo to have a bath

tomar banho de sol to sunbathe

tomar conta de ko**h**nta to look after, to take care of

tomar em jejum take on an empty stomach

tomar … vezes ao dia to be taken … times a day

tome lá to**h**m there you are

tónico *m* to**n**ikoo toner

tonturas: sinto tonturas see**n**too tonto**o**rash I feel dizzy

topo: no topo de… tohpoo di at the top of…

toque (a campainha) ring (the bell)

torcer toors**ay**r to sprain; to twist

tornar-se too**rn**arsi to become

torneira *f* toornay**r**a tap, faucet

tornozelo *m* toornooza**y**loo ankle

torre *f* to**h**rr tower

tosse *f* tos cough

tossir toos**ee**r to cough

totalmente tootalm**ay**nt totally; altogether

touca de banho *f* to**h**ka di ban-yoo bathing cap

tourada *f* toh**r**ada bullfight

Travel tip The great Portuguese bullfight centre is Ribatejo, where the animals are bred. If you want to see a fight, it's best to witness it there, amid the local aficiona-dos, or as part of the festivals in Vila Franca de Xira and Santarém. Fights are also held in the bullrings in Lisbon, Cascais and at Albufeira and Lagos on the Algarve.

---

toureiro *m* tohr**ay**roo bullfighter

touro *m* to**h**roo bull

tóxico to**k**sikoo toxic, poisonous

trabalhar trabal-y**ar** to work

trabalho *m* trabal-yoo work

tradição *f* tradiso**w**ng tradition

tradicional tradis-yo**o**nal traditional

tradução *f* tradooso**w**ng translation

tradutor *m* tradoot**oh**r, **tradutora** *f* tradoot**oh**ra translator

traduzir tradooz**ee**r to translate

tragédia *f* tra**J**e**h**d-ya disaster

trajecto *m* tra**J**e**h**too route

trancar trank**ar** to lock

tranquilo trankw**ee**loo peaceful

transferência *f* transfir**ayns**-ya transfer

trânsito *m* tran**zi**too traffic

trânsito condicionado traffic congestion

trânsito fechado road blocked

trânsito nos dois sentidos two-way traffic

trânsito proibido no thoroughfare, no entry

transmissão *f* tranJmis**ow**ng transmission

traseiro (*m*) traza**yr**oo bottom (of person); back

traumatismo *m* trowmatee**J**moo concussion

travão *m* tra**vow**ng brake

travão de mão di mowng handbrake

travar to brake

travel-cheque *m* shehk traveller's cheque

travessa *f* tra**veh**sa tray

travessia *f* travis**ee**-a crossing

trazer tra**zayr** to bring

trazer de volta di to bring back

três traysh three

trespassa-se premises for sale

treze trayz thirteen

trezentas trizayntash, **trezentos** triza**yn**toosh three hundred

tribunal *m* triboonal court

tricotar trikootar to knit

trinta tr**ee**nta thirty

tripulação *f* tripoolas**ow**ng crew

triste treesht sad

trocar tro**kar** to change (money)

troco *m* tro**hk**oo change (money)

trombose *f* trombo**z** thrombosis

trombose cerebral sirib**ral** stroke

trovão *m* troo**vow**ng thunder

trovoada *f* troov**wa**da thunder

tu too you

tua too-a, **tuas** too-ash your; yours

tubo de escape *m* too**boo** dish**kap** exhaust pipe

tudo too**doo** everything

   é tudo eh that's all

tudo bem! bayng no problem!

   tudo bem? how are you?

tudo incluído all-inclusive

túnel *m* too**nil** tunnel

turismo *m* tooree**J**moo tourist information office

turista *m/f* tooree**sh**ta tourist

U

UE oo eh EU

úlcera *f* oo**l**sira ulcer

último *m* oo**l**timoo last, latest

ultrapassar ooltra**pa**sar to overtake, to pass

um oong, **uma** oo**ma** a, an; one

umas oo**mash** some

uma vez oo**ma** vaysh once

unha *f* oon-ya fingernail

União Europeia *f* ooni-o**w**ng ay-ooroo**pay**-a European Union

unicamente para adultos for adults only

universidade *f* oonivirsi**dad** university

uns oonsh some

urgência f oorJ**a**yns-ya casualty, emergencies

urgente oorJ**a**ynt urgent

usar oozar to use

uso m oozoo use

uso externo for external use only

utensílios de cozinha mpl ootayns**ee**l-yoosh di kooz**ee**n-ya cooking utensils

útil ootil useful

V

vaca f cow

vacina f vas**ee**na vaccine

vacinação f vasinas**ow**ng vaccination

vagão m vag**ow**ng carriage (on train)

vagão restaurante rishtowr**a**nt dining car

vai he/she/it goes; you go

vais vish you go

vale m val valley

vale postal internacional international money order

validação de bilhetes punch your ticket here

válido validoo valid

   válido até... valid until...

valioso val-y**oh**zoo valuable

valor m val**oh**r value

válvula f valvoola valve

vamos vamoosh we go

   vamos! let's go!

vão vowng you/they go

varanda f balcony

varicela f varis**e**hla chickenpox

vários var-yoosh several

vá-se embora! vasi aymb**o**ra go away!

vassoura f vas**oh**ra broom

vazio vaz**ee**-oo empty

vedação f vidas**ow**ng fence

vedado ao trânsito no thoroughfare

vegetariana (f) viJitar-yana, **vegetariano** (m) viJitar-yanoo vegetarian

veículo m vi-**ee**kooloo vehicle

veículos longos long vehicles

veículos pesados heavy vehicles

veio vay-oo he/she/it came, he/she/it has come; you came, you have come

vela f v**e**hla spark plug; sail; candle

velejar viliJar to sail; sailing

velho v**e**hl-yoo old

velocidade f viloosid**a**d speed

velocidade máxima ... km/h maximum speed ... km/h

velocímetro m viloos**ee**mitroo speedometer

vem vayng he/she/it comes; you come

vêm you/they come

venda f v**a**ynda sale

   à venda v**a**ynda for sale

vendedor de jornais di Jorn**ī**sh newsagent, news vendor

vendem-se vayndaynsi for sale

vender vayndayr to sell

vende-se vayndi-si for sale

veneno *m* vinaynoo poison

venenoso vininohzoo poisonous

venho vayn-yoo I come

vens vaynsh you come

vento *m* vayntoo wind

ventoinha *f* vayntween-ya fan (electrical)

ver vayr to look; to have a look; to see

Verão *m* virowng summer

verdade *f* virdad truth

  de verdade? di really?

verdadeiro virdadayroo real; true

verde vayrd green

vergas *fpl* vayrgash wicker goods

verificar virifikar to check

vermelho virmayl-yoo red

verniz de unhas *m* virneeJ doonyash nail varnish

vespa *f* vayshpa wasp

Véspera de Natal *f* vehshpira di Christmas Eve

véspera do dia de Ano Novo vehshpira doo dee-a danoo nohvoo New Year's Eve

vestiário *m* visht-yar-yoo cloakroom, checkroom

vestido *m* vishteedoo dress

vestir vishteer to dress

vestir-se vishteersi to get dressed

veterinário *m* vitirinar-yoo vet

vez *f* vaysh time

  a próxima vez prosima next time

a última vez ooltima last time

esta vez ehshta this time

às vezes aJ vayzish sometimes

em vez ayng instead

em vez de... di instead of...

via (*f*) vee-a via; lane

via aérea: por via aérea by airmail

viagem *f* v-yaJayng journey

viagem de negócios di nigos-yoosh business trip

via intravenosa intravenously

viajar v-yaJar to travel

via oral to be taken orally

via rápida dual carriageway, divided highway

via rectal per rectum

via superfície surface mail

vida *f* veeda life

videogravador *m* veed-yoogravadohr video recorder

vidraria *f* vidraree-a glazier's

vidro *m* veedroo glass

viela *f* v-yehla lane

viemos v-yaymoosh we came, we have come

vieram v-yehrowng you/they came, you/they have come

vieste v-yehsht you came, you have come

vim veeng I came, I have come

vimos veemoosh we come; we saw

vindima *f* vindeema grape harvest

vindo veendoo come

vinha *f* veen-ya vineyard

vinte veent twenty
vinte e um veenti-oong
  twenty-one
viola f v-yola traditional
  Portuguese guitar
violação f v-yoolasowng rape
vir veer to come
virar veerar to turn; to turn off
vir de carro veer di karroo
  to drive
vire à esquerda/direita
  veer-ya shkayrda/dirayta
  turn left/right
vírgula f veergoola comma;
  decimal point
visita f vizeeta visit
visita guiada vizeeta gee-ada
  tour
visitar vizitar to visit

visor m vizohr viewfinder
vista f veeshta view
visto (m) veeshtoo visa; seen
visto que veeshtoo ki since
viu vee-oo you have seen
viúva f v-yoova widow
viúvo m v-yoovoo widower
vivenda f vivaynda villa
viver vivayr to live
vivo veevoo bright; alive
vizinha f vizeen-ya, **vizinho** m
  vizeen-yoo neighbour
voar v-war to fly
você vosay you
  você primeiro primayroo
  after you
vocês vosaysh you
  de vocês di your; yours

volante *m* voolant steering wheel

com volante à direita kong right-hand drive

volta: por volta de... poor about..., approximately...

voltar to go back, to get back, to come back, to return

voltar a telefonar voltar a telefoonar to ring back

volto já voltoo Ja back in a minute

vomitar voomitar to be sick, to vomit

voo *m* voh-oo flight

voo de ligação di ligasowng connecting flight

voo directo direhtoo direct flight

voo doméstico doomehshtikoo domestic flight

voo fretado fritadoo charter flight

voo regular rigoolar scheduled flight

vou voh I go

voz *f* vosh voice

vulgar voolgar ordinary

X

xadrez *m* shadraysh chess

xarope *m* sharop cough medicine; cordial

Z

zangado zangadoo angry; mad

zona azul *f* zohnazool parking permit zone

zona de banhos swimming area under the surveillance of lifeguards

zona para peões pedestrian precinct

zona perigrosa danger zone

MENU READER

Food

Essential terms

bread o pão powng
butter a manteiga mantayga
cup a chávena shavena
dessert a sobremesa sobrimayza
fish o peixe pay-ish
fork o garfo garfoo
glass o copo kopoo
knife a faca
main course o prato principal
  pratoo prinsipal
meat a carne karn
menu a ementa emaynta
pepper a pimenta pimaynta
plate o prato pratoo

salad a salada
salt o sal
set menu a ementa fixa
  emaynta feeksa
soup a sopa sohpa
spoon a colher kool-yehr
starter a entrada ayntrada
table a mesa mayza

another…, please
  outro/outra…, por favor
  ohtroo – poor favohr
excuse me! (to call waiter/
  waitress) se faz favor! si fash
could I have the bill, please?
  pode-me dar a conta, por
  favor? pod-mi – poor favohr

A–Z

abóbora aboboora pumpkin

acepipes asipeepish hors d'œuvres

açorda de alho asohrda dal-yoo
thick soup of bread and garlic

açorda de mariscos di
mareeshkoosh thick soup of
bread and shellfish

açorda de miolos m-yoloosh
thick soup of bread and brains

açúcar asookar sugar

agriões agr-yoyngsh watercress

aipo īpoo celery

alcachofra alkashohfra artichoke

alface alfas lettuce

alheira al-yayra garlic sausage

alho al-yoo garlic

alho francês fransaysh leek

à lista leeshta à la carte

almoço almohsoo lunch

almóndegas almohndigash
meatballs

alperces alpehrsish apricots

amêijoas amayJwash clams

amêijoas à Bulhão Pato
amayJwaza bool-yowng patoo
clams cooked with fresh
coriander, garlic and olive oil

amêijoas na cataplana
amayJwash clams, ham,
sausages, onions, parsley,
chillies and olive oil cooked
slowly in a covered pan

ameixa amaysha plum

ameixas de Elvas dehlvash
dried plums from Elvas

ameixas secas saykas prunes

amêndoas amayndwash
almonds

amendoins amayndweensh
peanuts

à moda de... di....-style

amoras amorash blackberries

ananás ananash pineapple

anchovas anshohvash anchovies

anho à moda do Minho an-yoo
a moda doo meen-yoo
roast lamb served with rice

aniz aneesh aniseed

anona anohna custard apple

ao natural ow natooral plain

ao ponto pohntoo medium-rare

arroz arrohsh rice

arroz árabe arrohz arab
fried rice with nuts and
dried fruit

arroz à valenciana valayns-yana
rice with chicken, pork and
seafood

arroz branco arrohJ brankoo
plain rice

arroz de cabidela di kabidehla
rice cooked in birds' blood

arroz de frango frangoo
rice with chicken

arroz de funcho foonshoo
rice with fennel

arroz de mariscos mareeshkoosh a soupy dish of rice with
mixed seafood

arroz de pato patoo
rice with duck

arroz de polvo pohlvoo
rice with octopus

arroz doce dohs sweet rice dessert

asa aza wing

assado asadoo roasted

atum atoong tuna

atum assado asadoo baked tuna

avelãs avilangsh hazelnuts

aves avish poultry

azeitão azaytowng
full fat soft goat's cheese

azeite azayt olive oil

azeitonas azaytohnash olives

azeitonas com pimentos
kong pimayntoosh olives stuffed
with pimentos

azeitonas recheadas rish-
yadash stuffed olives

bacalhau bakal-yow
dried salted cod

bacalhau à Brás brash dried
cod with egg and potatoes

bacalhau à Gomes de Sá
gohmsh di dried cod fried with
onions, boiled eggs, potatoes
and black olives

bacalhau assado asadoo
roast dried cod

bacalhau à Zé do Pipo
zeh doo peepoo
dried cod with egg sauce

bacalhau com natas kong
natash dried cod with cream

bacalhau dourado dohradoo
dried cod baked in the oven

bacalhau grelhado gril-yadoo
grilled dried cod

bacalhau na brasa braza
barbecued dried cod

> **Travel tip** The typical
> Portuguese fish dish is dried,
> salted cod (*bacalhau*). It's
> virtually the national dish,
> and there are reputedly 365
> different ways of prepar-
> ing it. The best choices for
> first-timers are fried with
> egg, onions and potatoes
> (*bacalhau á bras*) or baked in
> cream (*bacalhau com natas*).

bacalhau na cataplana dried
cod, onion, tomato, ham,
coriander, prawns and cockles
cooked slowly in a covered pan

banana flambée flambay
flambéed banana

batata assada batatasada
baked potato

batata murro mooroo
small baked potato

batata palha pal-ya French fries

batatas batatash potatoes

batatas cozidas koozeedash
boiled potatoes

batatas fritas freetash
chips, French fries; crisps,
(US) potato chips

batatas salteadas salt-yadash
sautéed potatoes

baunilha bowneel-ya vanilla

bavaroise bavarwaz dessert made
from egg whites and cream

bem passado bayng pasadoo
well-done

berbigão birbeegowng
shellfish similar to mussels

berinjela bireenJehla

aubergine, eggplant

besugos biz**oo**goosh sea bream

beterraba biter**ra**ba beetroot

bifanas beef**a**nash
pork slice in a bread roll

bife beef beef steak

bife à cortador koortad**oh**r
thick tender steak

bife à portuguesa poortoog**ay**za
steak with mustard sauce and
a fried egg

bife de alcatra dalk**a**tra
rump steak

bife de atum dat**oo**ng tuna steak

bife de javali di **ja**val**ee**
wild boar steak

bife de pojadouro pooJad**oh**roo
type of beefsteak

bife de vaca v**a**ka steak

**bife de vaca com ovo a
cavalo** kong **oh**voo a kav**a**loo
steak with an egg on top

bife grelhado gril-y**a**doo
grilled steak

bife tártaro t**a**rtaroo steak tartare

bifes de cebolada beefsh di
sib**oo**l**a**da thin slices of steak
with onions

bifinhos de porco beef**ee**n-yooJ
di p**oh**rkoo small slices of pork

bifinhos na brasa br**a**za
small slices of barbecued beef

bolacha bool**a**sha biscuit, cookie

bola de carne di karn meatball

bolo b**oh**loo cake

bolo de anjo dan**j**oo angel cake

bolo de chocolate shook**oo**lat
chocolate cake

bolo de nozes n**oh**zish
walnut cake

bolo inglês ingl**ay**sh sponge cake
with dried fruit

bolo Rei ray ring-shaped cake
(eaten at Christmas)

bolos e bolachas b**oh**looz ee
bool**a**shash cakes and biscuits/
cookies

bomba de creme b**oh**mba di
kraym cream puff

borrego boorr**ay**goo lamb

brioche br-y**osh** slightly sweet
round bun

broa br**oh**-a maize/corn bread or
rye bread

broas br**oh**-ash small maize/corn
cakes (eaten at Christmas)

cabeça de pescada cozida
kab**ay**sa di pishk**a**da kooz**ee**da
boiled head of hake

cabreiro kabr**ay**roo goat's cheese

cabrito kabr**ee**too kid

cabrito assado as**a**doo roast kid

caça k**a**sa game

cachola frita kash**o**la fr**ee**ta
fried pig's heart and liver

cachorro kash**oh**rroo hot dog

caldeirada kaldayr**a**da fish stew

caldo k**a**ldoo broth

caldo de aves d**a**vish
poultry soup

caldo de carne di karn
meat soup

caldo verde vayrd cabbage soup

camarões kamar**oy**ngsh prawns

canela kane*h*la cinnamon

canja de galinha kan*J*a di galee*n*-ya chicken soup

caracóis karak*oy*sh snails

caranguejo karang*ay*Joo crab

carapau karap*ow* mackerel

carapaus de escabeche karap*ow*J dishkab*eh*sh marinated mackerel

carapaus fritos karap*ow*sh free*too*sh fried mackerel

caril kare*e*l curry

carne karn meat

carne à jardineira Jardin*ay*ra meat and vegetable stew

carne de cabrito di kabre*e*too kid

carne de porco di po*h*rkoo pork

carne de porco com amêijoas kong am*ay*Jwash pork with clams

carne de vaca va*k*a beef

carne de vaca assada roast beef

carne de vaca guisada geez*a*da stewed meat

carne estufada shto*o*fada stewed meat

carneiro karn*ay*roo mutton

carneiro assado as*a*doo roast mutton

carne picada pik*a*da minced meat

carnes karn*i*sh meats

carnes frias free-ash selection of cold meats

caseiro kaz*ay*roo home-made

castanhas kasht*a*n-yash chestnuts

cebola sib*oh*la onion

cenoura sin*oh*ra carrot

cerejas siray*J*ash cherries

chanfana de porco shanf*a*na di po*h*rkoo pork casserole

chantilly shant*i*lee whipped cream

charlottes sharl*o*tsh biscuits/ cookies with fruit and cream

cherne she*h*rn sea bream

chocos sho*h*koosh cuttlefish

chouriço shoore*e*soo spiced sausage

choux shoo cake made with choux pastry

churros sho*o*rrosh long thin fritters

civet de lebre seev*ay* di lehbr jugged hare

cocktail de camarão kokt*eh*l di kamar*ow*ng prawn cocktail

codorniz koodoorne*e*sh quail

codonizes fritas koodoorne*e*zish free*t*ash fried quail

coelho kw*ay*l-yoo rabbit

coelho à caçadora kasad*oh*ra rabbit casserole with rice

coelho de escabeche dishkab*eh*sh marinated rabbit

coelho de fricassé frikas*ay* rabbit fricassee

coelho frito free*too* fried rabbit

coêntros kw*ay*ntroosh coriander

cogumelos kogoom*eh*loosh mushrooms

cogumelos com alho kong al-yoo mushrooms with garlic

comida congelada koomeeda konJilada frozen food

comidas koomeedash meals

compota stewed fruit

compota de laranja di laranJa marmalade

conquilhas konkeel-yash baby clams

consomme konsoomay consommé, clear meat soup

coração koorasowng heart

corações de alcachofra koorasoyngsh dalkashohfra artichoke hearts

corvina koorveena large saltwater fish

costela kooshtehla rib

costeleta kooshtilayta chop

costeletas de carneiro kooshtilaytaJ di karnayroo lamb chops

costeletas de porco di pohrkoo pork chops

costeletas fritas freetash fried chops

costeletas grelhadas grilyadash grilled chops

courgettes com creme no forno koorJehtsh kong kraym noo fohrnoo baked courgettes/zucchini served with cream

courgettes fritas freetash fried courgettes/zucchini

couve kohv cabbage

couve branca com vinagre kong vinagr white cabbage with vinegar

couve-flor kohv flohr cauliflower

couve-flor com molho branco no forno kong mohl-yoo brankoo noo fohrnoo cauliflower in white sauce

couve-flor com natas natash cauliflower with cream

couve roxa rohsha red cabbage

couvert cover charge

couves de bruxelas kohvsh di brooshehlash Brussels sprouts

couves de bruxelas com natas kong natash Brussels sprouts with cream

couves de bruxelas salteadas salt-yadash sautéed Brussels sprouts

couves guisadas com salsichas geezadash kong salseeshash stewed cabbage with sausage

cozido koozeedoo boiled; stewed; poached; cooked (either in a sauce or with olive oil); stew

cozido à portuguesa poortoogayza stew made from chicken, sausage, rice, potatoes and vegetables

creme de cogumelos kraym di kogoomehloosh cream of mushroom soup

creme de mariscos mareeshkoosh cream of shellfish soup

crepe de camarão krehp di kamarowng prawn crêpe

crepe de carne karn meat crêpe

crepe de cogumelos kogoomehloosh mushroom crêpe

crepe de espinafres dishpinafrish spinach crêpe

crepe de legumes ligoomish vegetable crêpe

crepe de pescada pishkada hake crêpe

crepes krehpish crêpes, pancakes

cru/crua kroo/kroo-a raw

damasco damashkoo apricot

dobrada doobrada tripe with chickpeas

doce dohs jam; any sweet dish or dessert

doce de amêndoas damayndwash almond dessert

doce de ovos dovoosh type of egg custard

doces regionais regional desserts

dose doz portion

> **Travel tip** The default size for servings in restaurants is huge. You can usually have a substantial meal by ordering a cheaper half portion (*meia dose*), or a single portion between two. Meals are often listed like this on the menu and it's normal practice; you don't need to be a child.

dose para crianças kr-yansash children's portion

dourada dohrada dory (saltwater fish); browned, golden brown

dourado dohradoo browned, golden brown

éclair de café ayklehr dih kafeh coffee éclair

éclair de chantilly shantilee whipped cream éclair

éclair de chocolate shookoolat
chocolate éclair

eirozes ayrozish eels

ementa emaynta menu

ementa fixa feeksa set menu

ementa turística tooreeshtika
set menu

empada pie

empadão de carne
aympadowng di karn
large meat pie

empadão de peixe paysh
large fish pie

encharcada aynsharkada dessert
made from almonds and eggs

enguias ayngee-ash eels

enguias fritas freetash fried eels

ensopado de... aynsoopadoo
di... stew

ensopado de borrego
boorraygoo lamb stew

ensopado de enguias dayngee-
ash eel stew

entradas ayntradash starters,
appetizers

entrecosto ayntrikohshtoo
entrecôte

entrecosto com amêijoas
kong amayJwash entrecôte
with clams

entrecosto frito freetoo
fried entrecôte

ervas ehrvash herbs

ervilhas irveel-yash peas

ervilhas de manteiga di
mantayga peas in butter

ervilhas reboçadas riboosadash
peas in butter with bacon

escalope ao Madeira shkalop
ow madayra escalope in
Madeira wine

escalope de carneiro di
karnayroo mutton escalope

escalope de porco pohrkoo
pork escalope

escalope panado panadoo
breaded escalope

espadarte shpadart scabbard fish

espaguete à bolonhesa
shpageht a booloon-yayza
spaghetti bolognese

espargos shpargoosh asparagus

esparregado shparrigadoo
stew made from chopped
green vegetables

especiaria shpis-yaree-a spice

espetada de leitão shpitada di
laytowng sucking pig kebab

espetada de rins reensh
kidney kebab

espetada de vitela vitehla
veal kebab

espetada mista meeshta
mixed kebab

espinafre shpinafr spinach

espinafres gratinados
shpinafrish gratinadoosh
spinach with cheese sauce
browned under the grill

espinafres salteados
salt-yadoosh spinach
sautéed in butter

estragão shtragowng tarragon

estufado shtoofadoo stewed

faisão fizowng pheasant

farinha fareen-ya flour

farófias farof-yash cream puff with filling made from egg whites, sugar and cinammon

farturas fartoorash long thin fritters

fatia fatee-a slice

fatias recheadas fatee-ash rish-yadash slices of bread with fried minced meat

favas favash broad beans

febras de porco faybraJ di pohrkoo thin slices of pork

feijão fayJowng beans

feijoada fayJwada bean and meat stew

feijões fayJoyngsh beans

feijões verdes vayrdish French beans

fiambre f-yambr ham

fiambre caramelizado karamileezadoo glazed ham

fígado feegadoo liver

figos feegoosh figs

figos moscatel mooshkatehl moscatel figs

figos secos saykoosh dried figs

filete feeleht fillet

filete de bife com foie gras di beef kong fwa gra beef fillet with foie gras

filhozes feel-yozish sugary buns

folhado de carne fool-yadoo di karn meat in pastry

folhado de salsicha salseesha sausage roll

fondue de carne fondoo di karn meat fondue

fondue de chocolate shookoolat chocolate fondue

fondue de queijo kayJoo cheese fondue

framboesa frambwayza raspberry

frango frangoo chicken

frango assado frangwasadoo roast chicken

frango na púcara pookara chicken casserole with Port and almonds

frango no churrasco noo shoorrashkoo barbecued chicken

frango no espeto nooshpaytoo spit-roasted chicken

frito freetoo fried

frito de... di fritter (usually filled with fruit)

fruta froota fruit

fruta da época ehpooka seasonal fruit

fumado foomadoo smoked

funcho foonshoo fennel

galantine de carne galanteen di karn cold meat roll

galantine de coelho di kwayl-yoo cold rabbit roll

galantine de galinha galeen-ya cold chicken roll

galantine de vegetais viJitIsh cold vegetable roll

galinha galeen-ya chicken

galinha de África dafreeka guinea fowl

galinha de fricassé di frikasay chicken fricassée

gambas gambash prawns

gambas grelhadas gril-yadash grilled prawns

ganso gansoo goose

garoupa garohpa fish similar to bream

gaspacho gaspashoo chilled vegetable soup

gelado Jiladoo ice cream

gelado de baunilha di bowneel-ya vanilla ice cream

gelado de frutas frootash fruit ice cream

geleia Jilay-a preserve

gengibre JaynJeebr ginger

gordura goordoora fat

grão growng chickpeas

grelhado gril-yadoo grilled

groselhas groozehl-yash redcurrants

guisado geezadoo stewed

hamburguer com batatas fritas amboorgir kong batatash freetash hamburger and chips/ French fries

hamburguer com ovo ohvoo hamburger with an egg

hamburguer no pão noo powng hamburger in a roll

hortaliças ortaleesash green vegetables

hortelã ortilang mint

iogurte yoogoort yoghurt

iscas fritas com batatas eeshkash freetash kong batatash dish of fried liver and boiled potatoes

jantar Jantar evening meal, dinner; supper

jardineira Jardinayra mixed vegetables

lagosta lagohshta lobster

lagosta à Americana amirikana lobster with tomato and onions

lagosta thermidor tirmeedohr lobster thermidor

lagostim lagooshteeng saltwater crayfish

lampreia lampray-a lamprey

lampreia à moda do Minho doo meen-yoo marinated lamprey and rice, both cooked in the juices and blood of the lamprey

lampreia de ovos dovoosh dessert made from eggs and sugar in the shape of a lamprey

lanche lansh afternoon tea

laranja laranJa orange

lasanha lasan-ya lasagne

legumes ligoomish vegetables

leitão assado laytowng asadoo roast sucking pig

leitão da Bairrada da birrada sucking pig from Bairrada

leite layt milk

leite creme kraym light custard flavoured with cinammon

limão limowng lemon

língua leengwa tongue

língua de porco di pohrkoo pig's tongue

língua de vaca vaka ox tongue

linguado lingwadoo sole

linguado à meunière moon-yehr sole dipped in flour and fried in butter

linguado frito freetoo fried sole

linguado grelhado gril-yadoo grilled sole

linguado no forno noo fohrnoo baked sole

lista de preços leeshta di praysoosh price list

lombo lohmboo loin

lombo de porco di pohrkoo loin of pork

lombo de vaca vaka sirloin

louro lohroo bay leaf

lulas loolash squid

lulas com natas kong natash stewed squid with cream

lulas fritas freetash fried squid

lulas guisadas geezadash stewed squid

lulas recheadas rish-yadash stuffed squid

maçã masang apple

maçã assada baked apple

macedónia de frutas masidon-ya di frootash fruit cocktail

maionese mi-oonehz mayonnaise

maionese de alho dal-yoo garlic mayonnaise

mal passado pasadoo rare

manjericão manjirikowng basil

manteiga mantayga butter

manteiga de anchova danshohva anchovy butter

manteiga queimada kaymada butter sauce for fish

margarina margareena margarine

marinada marinade

mariscos mareeshkoosh shellfish

marmelada marmilada quince jam

marmelos marmehloosh quinces

marmelos assados marmehlooz asadoosh roast quinces

massa pasta

massa de fartos di fartoosh choux pastry

meia desfeita may-a dishfayta boiled dried cod, potatoes, chickpeas and olive oil

meia dose doz half portion

mel mehl honey

melancia milansee-a watermelon

melão milowng melon

melão com presunto kong prizoontoo melon with ham

meloa com vinho do Porto/ Madeira miloh-a kong veen-yoo doo pohrtoo/madayra small melon with Port or Madeira poured over it

melocotão milookootowng peach

merenda miraynda tea; snack

merengue mirang meringue

mexilhões mishil-yoyngsh mussels

migas à Alentejana meegaz a alayntijana thick bread soup

mil folhas meel fohl-yash millefeuille, custard slice, (US) napoleon

miolos m-yoloosh brains

miolos com ovos kong ovoosh brains with eggs

míscaros meeshkaroosh mushrooms

moleja moolayja soup made from pig's blood

molho mohl-yoo sauce

molho à Espanhola shpan-yola spicy onion and garlic sauce

molho ao Madeira ow madayra Madeira wine sauce

molho bearnaise bayrnehz béarnaise sauce

molho béchamel bayshamehl béchamel sauce, white sauce

molho branco brankoo white sauce

molho holandês olandaysh hollandaise sauce

molho mornay cheese sauce

molho mousseline moosileen hollandaise sauce with cream

molho tártaro tartaroo tartare sauce

molho veloutée vilootay white sauce made from cream and egg yolks

morangos moorangoosh strawberries

morangos com chantilly kong shantilee strawberries and whipped cream

morcela moorsehla black pudding, blood sausage

mostarda mooshtarda mustard

mousse de chocolate moos di shookoolat chocolate mousse

mousse de fiambre f-yambr ham mousse

mousse de leite condensado layt kondaynsadoo mousse made from condensed milk

na brasa braza charcoal-grilled

napolitanas napoolitanash long flat biscuits/cookies

natas natash cream

natas batidas bateedash whipped cream

nectarina nektareena nectarine

nêsperas nayshpirash loquats (yellow fruit similar to a plum)

no churrasco noo shoorrashkoo barbecued

no espeto nooshpaytoo spit-roasted

no forno foh-rno baked

nozes nozish walnuts

noz moscada noj mooshkada nutmeg

óleo ol-yoo oil

omeleta omilayta omelette

omeleta com ervas kong ehrvash vegetable omelette

omeleta de cogumelos di kogoomehloosh mushroom omelette

omeleta de fiambre f-yambr ham omelette

omeleta de queijo kayjoo cheese omelette

omelete omilayt omelette

orelha de porco de vinaigrette orayl-ya di pohrkoo di vinagreht pig's ear in vinaigrette dressing

ostras ohshtrash oysters

ovo ohvoo egg

ovo com maionese kong mi-oonehz egg mayonnaise

ovo cozido koozeedoo hard-boiled egg

ovo em geleia ayng jilay-a egg in aspic

ovo escalfado shkalfadoo poached egg

ovo estrelado shtriladoo fried egg

ovo quente kaynt soft-boiled egg

ovos mexidos misheedoosh scrambled eggs

ovos mexidos com tomate kong toomat scrambled eggs with tomato

ovos verdes vayrdish eggs stuffed with a mixture of egg yolks, mayonnaise and parsley

palha de ovos pal-ya dovoosh egg pastries

panqueca pankehka pancake

pão powng bread

pão branco brankoo white bread

pão de centeio di sayntay-oo rye bread

pão de ló de Alfazeirão law dalfazay-rowng sponge cake

pão de ló de Ovar dohvar sponge cake

pão de milho meel-yoo corn bread

pão integral intigral wholemeal bread

pão torrado toorradoo toasted bread

pargo pargoo sea bream

pargo assado pargwasadoo roast bream

pargo cozido koozeedoo bream cooked in a sauce or with olive oil

parrilhada pareel-yada grilled fish

passas pasash raisins

pastéis pashteh-ish pastries

pastéis de bacalhau di bakal-yow dried cod fishcakes

pastéis de carne karn puff-pastry patties filled with meat

pastéis de Chaves shavish thin dainty puff-pastry patties filled with meat

pastéis de nata custard tarts

pastéis de Tentúgal tayntoogal
filo-pastry patties with an
egg yolk and sugar filling,
sprinkled with sugar

pastel pashtehl cake; pie

pastelinhos de bacalhau
pashtileen-yoosh di bakal-yow
fishcakes made from dried cod

pataniscas pataneeshkash
dried cod fritters

pataniscas de miolos
di m-yoloosh brain fritters

paté de aves patay davish
pâté made from chicken,
duck or goose liver

paté de coelho di kwayl-yoo
rabbit pâté

paté de fígado feegadoo liver pâté

paté de galinha galeen-ya
chicken pâté

paté de lebre lehbr hare pâté

pato patoo duck

pato assado asadoo roast duck

pato com laranja kong laranJa
duck à l'orange

peixe paysh fish

peixe espada shpada swordfish

peixe espada de escabeche
dishkabehsh marinated
swordfish

peixinhos da horta paysheen-
yoosh da orta French bean fritters

pepino pipeenoo cucumber

pequeno almoço pikaynoo
almohsoo breakfast

pequeno almoço continental
kontinayntal continental
breakfast

pêra payra pear

pêra abacate abakat avocado

pêra bela helena behlaylayna
pear in chocolate sauce

percebes pirsehbish shellfish
similar to barnacles

perdiz pirdeesh partridge

perdizes de escabeche
pirdeeziJ dishkabehsh
marinated partridge

perdizes fritas pirdeezish freetash
fried partridge

perdizes na púcara pirdeeziJ na
pookara partridge casserole

perna pehrna leg

perna de carneiro assada
di karnayroo roast leg of lamb

**perna de carneiro
entremeada** ayntrim-yada
stuffed leg of lamb

perninhas de rã pirneen-yash
di rang frogs' legs

peru piroo turkey

peru assado asadoo roast turkey

peru de fricassé di frikasay
turkey fricassée

peru recheado rish-yadoo
stuffed turkey

pescada pishkada hake

pescada cozida koozeeda
hake cooked in a sauce or
with olive oil

pescadinhas de rabo na boca
pishkadeen-yash di raboo na
bohka fried whiting served with
their tails in their mouths

pêssego paysigoo peach

pêssego careca karehka
nectarine

petiscos piteeshkoosh savouries

picante pikant hot, spicy

pimenta pimaynta pepper

pimenta preta prayta
black pepper

pimentos pimayntoosh
peppers, capsicums

piperate peepirat pepper stew

piri-piri peeree-peeree seasoning
made from chillies and
olive oil

polvo pohlvoo octopus

porção poorsowng portion

porco pohrkoo pork

porco à alentejana alayntijana
pork cooked with clams

prato pratoo dish; course

prato do dia doo dee-a
today's special

prato especial da casa
shpis-yal da kaza speciality of
the house

prato principal prinsipal
main course

prego prehgoo thin slice of steak
in a bread roll

prego no fiambre noo f-yambr
steak sandwich with sliced ham

prego no pão noo powng
steak sandwich

prego no prato pratoo steak,
usually served with a fried egg

presunto prizoontoo ham

pudim de ovos poodeeng
dovoosh egg pudding

pudim flan flang crème caramel

pudim molotov molotof
crème caramel with egg whites

puré de batata pooray di
mashed potatoes

puré de castanhas kashtan-yash
chestnut purée

p.v. (preço variado) praysoo var-
yadoo price varies

queijadas de Sintra kayJadaJ di
seentra small tarts with a filling
made from milk, eggs, sugar
and vanilla

queijo kayJoo cheese

queijo curado kooradoo dried
matured hard white cheese

queijo da Ilha eel-ya strong
cheese from the Azores
flavoured with pepper

queijo da Serra sehrra goat's
cheese from Serra da Estrela

queijo de cabra di goat's cheese

queijo de ovelha dovayl-ya
sheep's cheese

queijo de Palmela palmehla
small white mild dried cheese

queijo de Serpa sehrpa small
strong dried goat's cheese

queijo fresco frayshkoo
medium-firm mild cheese

queijos kayJoosh cheeses

rabanadas rabanadash bread
dipped in beaten egg and fried,
then sprinkled with sugar and
cinammon

raia rī-a skate

refeição rifaysowng meal

refeição ligeira liJayra
snack, light meal

remoulade rimoolad dressing
with mustard and herbs

requeijão rikayJowng curd cheese

rillete ree-eht potted pork meat

rins reensh kidneys

rins ao Madeira reenz ow
madayra kidneys cooked in
Madeira wine

rissóis riso-ysh deep-fried meat
patties

rissol risol deep-fried meat patty

rissol de camarão di kamarowng
prawn rissole

robalo roobaloo rock bass

rojões rooJoyngsh cubes of pork

rolo de carne rohloo di karn
meat loaf

rosmaninho rooJmaneen-yoo
rosemary

sabayon saba-yohng
dessert made from egg yolks
and white wine

sal salt

salada salad

salada de agriões dagr-yoyngsh
watercress salad

salada de alface dalfas
green salad

salada de atum datoong
tuna salad

salada de chicória di shikor-ya
chicory salad

salada de frutas frootash
fruit salad

salada de lagosta lagohshta
lobster salad

salada de ovas dovash
fish roe salad

salada de tomate di toomat
tomato salad

salada mista meeshta
mixed salad

salada russa roosa
Russian salad, salad of diced
vegetables in mayonnaise

salgado salgadoo savoury, salty

salmão salmowng salmon

salmão fumado foomadoo
smoked salmon

salmonete salmoonayt red mullet

salmonetes grelhados salmoon**aytsh** gril-ya**doosh** grilled red mullet

salsa parsley

salsicha sal**see**sha sausage

salsichas de cocktail sal**see**shaJ di kok**tehl** cocktail sausages

salsichas de peru pi**roo** turkey sausages

salsichas de porco po**hr**koo pork sausages

salteado salt-ya**doo** sautéed

sandes sandish sandwich

sandes de fiambre di f-yambr ham sandwich

sandes de lombo lo**h**mboo steak sandwich

sandes de paio pī-oo sausage sandwich

sandes de presunto prizoontoo ham sandwich

sandes de queijo kayJoo cheese sandwich

sandes mista meeshta mixed sandwich, usually ham and cheese

santola spider crab

santola gratinada gratin**a**da spider crab with cheese sauce browned under the grill

sapateira sapat**ay**ra spider crab

sarda mackerel

sardinha sard**een**-ya sardine

sardinhas assadas sard**een**-yaz asadash roast sardines

selecção de queijos silehs**owng** di **kay**Joosh selection of cheeses

sobremesas sobrim**ay**zash desserts

solha so**hl**-ya flounder

solha assada no forno noo fo**hr**noo baked flounder

solha frita fr**ee**ta fried flounder

solha recheada rish-y**a**da stuffed flounder

sonho so**h**n-yoo type of doughnut

sopa so**h**pa soup

sopa à alentejana alayntiJana bread soup with a poached egg on top

sopa de agriões dagr-y**oy**ngsh watercress soup

sopa de alho francês dal-yoo frans**ay**sh leek soup

sopa de camarão kamar**ow**ng prawn soup

sopa de caranguejo karang**ay**Joo crab soup

sopa de cebola gratinada sib**oh**la French onion soup with melted cheese on top

sopa de cogumelos kogoom**eh**loosh mushroom soup

sopa de espargos dishp**a**rgoosh asparagus soup

sopa de feijão verde fayJ**ow**ng vayrd green bean soup

sopa de grão gr**ow**ng chickpea soup

sopa de lagosta lag**oh**shta lobster soup

sopa de legumes lig**oo**mish vegetable soup

sopa de mariscos mar**ee**shkoosh shellfish soup

sopa de ostras dohshtrash
oyster soup

sopa de panela di panehla
egg-based dessert

sopa de pão e coentros
powng ee kwayntroosh
bread and coriander soup

sopa de pedra pehdra
thick vegetable soup

sopa de peixe paysh
fish soup

sopa de rabo de boi raboo di
boy oxtail soup

sopa de tartaruga tartarooga
turtle soup

sopa do dia doo dee-a soup of
the day

sopa dourada dohrada egg-
based dessert

sopa e cozido sohpi koozeedoo
meat stew

sopa juliana
sohpa Jool-yana
vegetable soup

sopas sohpash soups

soufflé de camarão
sooflay di kamarowng
prawn soufflé

soufflé de chocolate
shookoolat
chocolate soufflé

soufflé de cogumelos
kogoomehloosh mushroom
soufflé

soufflé de espinafres
dishpinafrish spinach soufflé

soufflé de peixe paysh
fish soufflé

soufflé de queijo kayJoo
cheese soufflé

soufflé gelado Jiladoo
ice-cream soufflé

tarte de amêndoas tart
damayndwash almond tart

tarte de cogumelos di
kogoomehloosh mushroom
quiche

tarte de limão limowng
lemon tart

tarte de maçã masang
apple tart

taxa de serviço tasha di
sirveesoo service charge

tempero da salada
taympayroo da salada
salad dressing

tomar toomar fresh soft
goat's cheese

tomate toomat tomato

tomates recheados
toomatish rish-yadoosh
stuffed tomatoes

tomilho toomeel-yoo thyme

toranja tooranJa grapefruit

torrada toorrada toast

torresmos toorrayJmoosh
small fried rashers of bacon

torta tart

torta de maçã masang
apple pie

torta de nozes di nozish
walnut tart

tortilha toorteel-ya Spanish-style
omelette with potato

tosta toshta toasted sandwich

tosta mista mee*shta* toasted ham and cheese sandwich

toucinho do céu too*seen*-yoo doo *seh*-oo kind of dessert made from eggs, sugar and almonds

tripas tree*pash* tripe

tripas à moda do Porto tree*paza moda* doo *pohr*too tripe with beans and vegetables

trufas de chocolate troofaJ di shookoo*lat* chocolate truffles

truta troota trout

truta assada no forno noo *fohr*noo baked trout

truta cozida koo*zee*da trout cooked in a sauce or with olive oil

truta frita free*ta* fried trout

uvas *oo*vash grapes

uvas brancas *oo*vaJ *brank*ash green grapes

uvas moscatel mooshka*tehl* muscatel grapes

uvas pretas *oo*vaJ *pray*tash black grapes

veado assado v-*ya*doo asa*doo* roast venison

vieiras recheadas v-*yay*rash rish-*ya*dash scallops filled with seafood

vinagre vin*agr* vinegar

vinagre de estragão dishtra*gown*g tarragon vinegar

vitela vi*teh*la veal

Drink

Essential terms

beer a cerveja sirvayJa

bottle a garrafa

brandy o brandy

coffee o café kafeh

  a cup of... uma chávena de...
ooma shavena di

gin o gin Jeeng

  gin and tonic um gin-tónico
oong Jeeng tonikoo

glass o copo kopoo

  a glass of... um copo de...
oong kopoo di

milk o leite layt

mineral water a água mineral agwa

orange juice o sumo de laranja
soomoo di laranJa

port o vinho do Porto veen-yoo
doo pohrtoo

red wine o vinho tinto teentoo

rosé rosé roozay

soda (water) a soda

soft drink a bebida não alcoólica
bibeeda nowng alko-oleeka

sugar o açúcar asookar

tea o chá sha

tonic (water) a água tónica agwa

vodka o vodka

water a água agwa

whisky o whisky weeshkee

white wine o vinho branco
brankoo

wine o vinho veen-yoo

wine list a lista dos vinhos
leeshta dooJ veen-yoosh

another..., please outro/outra...,
por favor ohtroo – poor favoh

A–Z

açúcar asookar sugar

água mineral agwa mineral mineral water

aguardente agwardaynt clear spirit/brandy (literally: 'firewater'), distilled from wine or grape skins

aguardente de figo feegoo fig brandy

aguardente de pêra di payra brandy with a pear or pears in the bottle

aguardentes bagaceiras agwardayntish bagasayrash clear spirit/brandy distilled from grape skins

aguardentes velhas vehl-yash matured brandies

aguardentes velhas ou preparadas vehl-yaz oh preparadash brandies matured in oak

álcool alko-ol alcohol

amêndoa amarga amayndwa amarga bitter almond liqueur

aperitivo apiriteevoo aperitif

bagaço bagasoo clear spirit/ brandy (literally: 'firewater'), distilled from grape skins

Bairrada bīrrada region producing fruity red wines

batido de leite bateedoo di layt milkshake

bebida bibeeda drink

bica beeka small black espresso-type coffee

branco brankoo white

bruto brootoo extra-dry

Bual boo-al medium-sweet Madeira wine

Bucelas boosehlash crisp dry white wine from the Estremadura area

cacau kakow cocoa

café kafeh small black espresso-type coffee

café com leite kong layt white coffee, coffee with milk

café com pingo peengoo espresso with brandy

café duplo dooploo two espressos in the same cup

café glacé glasay iced coffee

café instantâneo inshtantan-yoo instant coffee

caneca kanehka half-litre

capilé kapileh drink made from water, sugar and syrup

carapinhada de café karapeen-yada di kafeh coffee drink with crushed ice

carapinhada de chocolate shookoolat chocolate drink with crushed ice

carapinhada de groselha groozehl-ya redcurrant drink with crushed ice

carapinhada de morango moorangoo strawberry drink with crushed ice

carioca kar-yoka small weak black coffee

cerveja sirvayJa beer

cerveja branca branka lager

cerveja de pressão di prisowng draught beer

cerveja preta prayta bitter, dark beer

chá sha tea

chá com leite kong layt tea with milk

chá com limão limowng lemon tea

chá com mel mehl tea with honey

chá de limão di limowng infusion of hot water with a lemon rind

chá de lucialima loos-yaleema herb tea

chá de mentol mint tea

chá de tília teel-ya linden blossom tea

champanhe shampan-yi champagne

chocolate glacé shookoolat glasay iced chocolate

chocolate quente kaynt hot chocolate

cidra seedra cider

cimbalino simbaleenoo small espresso

clarete klarayt claret

Colares koolarish table wine from the Colares region

com gás kong gash carbonated

com gelo Jayloo with ice, on the rocks

conhaque koon-yak cognac, brandy

Constantino konshtanteenoo Portuguese brandy

cubo de gelo kooboo di Jayloo ice cube

Dão downg red table wine from the Dão region

descafeinado dishkafaynadoo decaffeinated

doce dohs sweet (usually very sweet)

espumante shpoomant sparkling

espumantes naturais shpoomantish natoorīsh sparkling wine made by the champagne method

expresso shprehsoo espresso

figo feegoo fig brandy

galão galowng large weak milky coffee, served in a tall glass

garoto garohtoo small coffee with milk

garrafa bottle

garrafeira garrafayra aged red wine set aside by the producer in years of exceptional quality

gasoso gazohzoo fizzy

gelo Jayloo ice

ginja JeenJa, **ginjinha** JeenJeen-ya brandy with sugar and cherries added

imperial eempir-yal regular glass size for drinking beer (about ¼ litre)

italiana ital-yana half a very strong espresso

jarro Jarroo jug

Lagoa lagoh-a table wine from the Algarve

leite layt milk

licor likohr liqueur; sweet flavoured spirit

Licor Beirão bayrowng cognac with herbs

licor de medronho di midrohn-yoo berry liqueur

licor de ovo dohvoo advocaat

licor de pêras di payrash pear liqueur

licor de whisky weeshkee whisky liqueur

limonada limoonada fresh lemon juice with water and sugar

lista de preços leeshta di praysoosh price list

lista dos vinhos dooJ veen-yoosh wine list

Macieira masi-ayra Portuguese brandy

Madeira madayra wine-producing region; sweet and dry fortified wines

maduro madooroo mature

Malvasia malvasee-a Malmsey wine, a sweet heavy Madeira wine

Mateus Rosé matay-oosh roozay sweet rosé wine

mazagrin mazagrang iced coffee with lemon

meia de leite may-a di layt large white coffee

meia garrafa half-bottle

meio seco may-oo saykoo medium-dry (usually fairly sweet)

morena moorayna mixture of lager and bitter

moscatel mooshkatehl muscatel wine

não alcoólico nowng alko-oleekoo non-alcoholic

pingo peengoo small coffee with milk

ponche pohnsh punch

pré-pagamento pay in advance

região demarcada wine-producing region subject to official controls

Reguengos rigayngoosh table wine from Alentejo

reserva rizehrva aged wine set aside by the producer in years of exceptional quality

Sagres sagrish popular brand of lager

Sagres Europa sagrīz ay-ooropa brand of lager

Sagres Preta prayta dark beer resembling British brown ale

saquinhos de chá sakeen-yooJ di sha teabags

seco saykoo dry

selo de garantia seal of guarantee

sem gás sayng gash still

sem gelo Jayloo without ice

Sercial sirsee-al the driest variety of Madeira wine

sirva gelado served chilled

sirva-se à temperatura ambiente serve at room temperature

sirva-se fresco serve cool

sumo de laranja soomoo di laranJa orange juice

sumo de lima leema lime juice

sumo de limão limowng lemon juice

sumo de maçã masang apple juice

sumo de tomate toomat tomato juice

Sumol soomol fizzy fruit juice

Super Bock brand of lager

tarifas de consumo price list

Tavel tavehl rosé wine

tinto teentoo red

Tri Naranjus treenaranJoosh brand name for a range of fruit drinks

Valpaços valpasoosh table wine from Trás-os-Montes

velha vehl-ya old, mature

velhíssima vehl-yeesima very old (spirits)

Verdelho virdayl-yoo a medium-dry Madeira wine

vermute vermoot vermouth

vinho veen-yoo wine

vinho branco brankoo white wine

vinho da casa kaza house wine

vinho da Madeira madayra Madeira wine

> **Travel tip** Portuguese wine lists don't just distinguish between red, white and rosé, but also between *verde* ('green', meaning young, acidic and slightly sparkling) and *maduro* ('mature', meaning the wines you're probably accustomed to). You'll find a decent selection from around the country in even the most basic of restaurants, and often in half-bottles too.

vinho de aperitivo dapiriteevoo
aperitif
vinho de mesa di mayza
table wine
vinho de Xerêz shiraysh sherry
vinho do Porto doo pohrtoo
port
vinho espumante shpoomant
sparkling wine
vinho moscatel mooshkatehl
muscatel wine
vinho rosé roozay rosé wine
vinho tinto teentoo red wine
vinho verde vayrd young, slightly
sparkling white, red, or rosé
wine produced in the Minho

whisky de malte weeshkee di
malt malt whisky

xarope sharop cordial,
concentrated juice
xarope de groselha di groozehl-
ya redcurrant cordial
xarope de morango moorangoo
strawberry cordial

Picture credits

All maps and photos © Rough Guides, unless otherwise stated.

Photography by: Natascha Sturny (pp.6, 16, 21, 36, 39, 44, 48, 77, 88, 119, 130, 183, 191, 202, 213, 234, 253), Ian Aitken (pp.5, 66, 108, 139, 156, 165, 174, 222, 243, 260), Matthew Hancock (pp.28, 56, 99, 147, 150, 236, 248), Eddie Gerald (p.257), Linda Whitwam (pp.238). Front cover image: © Picture Contact/Alamy
Back cover image: © Ian Aitken

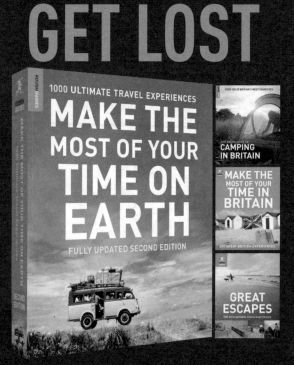